YEAVERING
People, Power & Place

YEAVERING
People, Power & Place

Edited by
Paul Frodsham & Colm O'Brien

This volume is respectfully dedicated to the memory of
Brian Hope-Taylor (1923-2001)

First published in 2005 by Tempus Publishing

Reprinted in 2009 by
The History Press
The Mill, Brimscombe Port,
Stroud, Gloucestershire, GL5 2QG
www.thehistorypress.co.uk

© Paul Frodsham & Colm O'Brien, 2005

The right of Paul Frodsham & Colm O'Brien to be
identified as the Authors of this work has been asserted in
accordance with the Copyrights, Designs and Patents Act 1988.

All rights reserved. No part of this book may be reprinted
or reproduced or utilised in any form or by any electronic,
mechanical or other means, now known or hereafter invented,
including photocopying and recording, or in any information
storage or retrieval system, without the permission in writing
from the Publishers.

British Library Cataloguing in Publication Data.
A catalogue record for this book is available from the British Library.

ISBN 978 0 7524 3344 8

Typesetting and origination by
Tempus Publishing Limited
Printed in Great Britain

CONTENTS

List of contributors 7
Foreword 9
Acknowledgements 12

PART I SETTING THE SCENE
1. 'The stronghold of its own native past'
   Some thoughts on the past in the past at Yeavering
   Paul Frodsham 13
2. Yeavering and air photography: discovery and interpretation
   Tim Gates 65

PART II PREHISTORIC YEAVERING
3. Yeavering in its Stone Age landscape
   Clive Waddington 84
4. Yeavering Bell hillfort
   Alastair Oswald and Trevor Pearson 98

PART III EARLY MEDIEVAL YEAVERING
5. Early medieval burial at Yeavering: a retrospective
   Sam Lucy 127
6. The Great Enclosure
   Colm O'Brien 145
7. The social use of space at *Gefrin*
   Carolyn Ware 153

8. *Ad Gefrin* and Scotland: the implications of the Yeavering excavations
    for the north
    Stephen T. Driscoll   161
9. Anglian Yeavering: a continental perspective
    P.S. Barnwell   174
10. An historical context for Hope-Taylor's *Yeavering*
    Ian Wood   185

PART IV AFTER *AD GEFRIN*

11. *Gefrin*: organisation, abandonment, aftermath
    Colm O' Brien   189
12. *Ad Gefrin* today and tomorrow
    Roger Miket   193

PART V 'AN UNLOCKING OF WORD-HOARDS.'
       REFLECTIONS ON BRIAN HOPE-TAYLOR   201

13. My friendship with Brian Hope-Taylor
    Forbes Taylor   202
14. Yeavering revisited
    Philip Rahtz   208
15. Brian Hope-Taylor: a personal reminiscence
    Rosemary Cramp   212
16. Brian Hope-Taylor: a personal reflection on his life and his archive
    Diana Murray   214
17. *A Process of Discovery*.
    Exhibiting the work of Brian Hope-Taylor
    Laura M. Sole   224

Appendix   235
Notes   237
Bibliography   240
Index   253

LIST OF CONTRIBUTORS

P.S. Barnwell
English Heritage, York

Rosemary Cramp
Department of Archaeology, University of Durham

Stephen T. Driscoll
Department of Archaeology, University of Glasgow

Paul Frodsham
Oracle Heritage Services, Weardale

Tim Gates
Flying Past Ltd, York

Sam Lucy
Department of Archaeology, University of Cambridge

Roger Miket
The Gefrin Trust, Wooler

Diana Murray
Royal Commission on the Ancient and Historical Monuments of Scotland, Edinburgh

Colm O' Brien
Centre for Lifelong Learning, University of Sunderland

Alastair Oswald
English Heritage, York

Trevor Pearson
English Heritage, York

Philip Rahtz
Harome, North Yorkshire

Laura M. Sole
Bede's World, Jarrow

Forbes Taylor
Beccles, Suffolk

Clive Waddington
Archaeological Research Services Ltd, Bakewell

Carolyn Ware
The North of England Open Air Museum, Beamish

Ian Wood
School of History, University of Leeds

FOREWORD

With the twenty-fifth anniversary approaching of the publication of Brian Hope-Taylor's monograph *Yeavering: an Anglo-British centre of early Northumbria* (2002 or 2004, depending on whether you count from 1977, the stated date of publication, or 1979 when the book was actually released for sale), it seemed opportune to look again at Yeavering and to take stock of our present state of knowledge. Accordingly, Laura Sole and the editors of this volume arranged a conference: *Yeavering: context, continuity, kingship* which was held in 2003 at Bede's World and, on a memorably bright early spring day, at Yeavering itself.

A feature of the conference was an after-dinner session given over to reflection on Brian Hope-Taylor. His contribution to archaeology, and particularly to archaeological draughtsmanship, was acknowledged in an exhibition, *A Process of Discovery*, curated by Laura Sole and opened on the eve of the conference by Forbes Taylor who had directed the programmes for Anglia Television which Hope-Taylor presented in the 1960s and 1970s.

This book is not limited to the site of the cropmarks on the terrace above the River Glen which was the principal focus of Hope-Taylor's study, but pays attention also to Yeavering Bell, the great twin-peaked hill which rises 1000ft above this, and to the wider landscape beyond. The first four chapters demonstrate the complex nature of human activity at Yeavering, reaching back into early prehistoric times; then the focus is on aspects of the site as excavated by Hope-Taylor and themes which relate to history, kingship and cult practice in the early medieval era. The final section includes personal reflections on Brian Hope-Taylor and a chapter drawing on the exhibition.

For Yeavering, its excavator has become personally associated with the site in a way which is unusual, and perhaps even unique, in British archaeology. In the widely read Penguin book, *The Anglo-Saxons*, Professor James Campbell saw fit to approach Yeavering through its excavator: 'his was the infinitely difficult and subtle task of discovering the remains of numerous timber buildings from the faint traces they had left in the ground. His success was brilliant.' This is the excavator as hero and it is not the way in which archaeological evidence is usually introduced. But, somehow, in the case of Yeavering, this is how it is. And the text, *Yeavering: an Anglo-British centre of early Northumbria*, has over the years come to attain a monumental status in its own right which encompasses site, excavation, text and excavator through the way in which the author has written himself into the narrative structure: it is a heroic work.

Consequently, there has been a tendency to take the work on its own terms of reference and, with some notable exceptions, few have attempted in published literature to develop fundamental critiques or to pose other interpretative models. Rosemary Cramp perceived very early a problem with this text when she reviewed the volume in 1980, commenting that 'no doubt, in the future this work will find its correct chronological position in the history of British archaeology, but in 1979 the position is ambiguous'. Chronological ambiguities are all too clear: the publication date is given as 1977, after 1975 had been set on the title page and over-printed; the author's preface is dated 1969; and the text refers to no literature later than 1965, and this only in a footnote. It has taken time, as Professor Cramp suggested it would, to place this study; but it is easier now than it was in 1979 to understand that Hope-Taylor's *Yeavering*, and particularly its long and difficult final chapter, has to be read as a text conceived in about 1960.

But time has moved on and in the ensuing quarter-century since publication new approaches and new knowledge have been developed in history and archaeology which can be brought to bear on Yeavering: ideas on the cultural dimension of landscape and the embedding of meaning in place; of monumentality and the time dimension of landscape; of meanings of places and structures; of places of leadership and kingship; understandings of ethnicity in early medieval Europe and, following this, new readings of the archaeology of burial; in Britain generally, a hugely developed knowledge of settlement, burial, ceremonial and environmental archaeology of all periods; and within the proximity of Yeavering, systematic air and field survey projects and, not least, a renewed interest in Bamburgh. There are many new standpoints for looking again at Yeavering and for reassessing the knowledge that we have from previous studies, which began not just with Brian Hope-Taylor in 1953 but – where to define the start – with George Tate in the 1860s; with William Camden in 1600; with the Venerable Bede in 731?

There is no single view nor new orthodoxy on Yeavering to emerge from these pages, and thus no neat summary from the editors. It is time to open up Yeavering again for discussion and especially to explore the implications of the long chronology of the site and its surrounds, reaching deep into prehistoric times: the time for new synthesis will come later. This volume does not cover all aspects of Yeavering in detail; the omissions speak of topics where fresh thinking is needed: how, for instance, are we to understand this traditional place of political leadership, 40 miles north of Hadrian's frontier, during the Roman era?

We began this venture convinced of two points: that we still have much to learn about Yeavering and that Yeavering still has much to contribute to the archaeology of Britain. We make no apologies for expressing the opinion that it is now time for archaeologists and colleagues in cognate disciplines again to take to the field at Yeavering; to frame new research questions; to question, test and extend the scope of investigations beyond those of previous investigators. Already we see the beginnings of such work in the Northumberland National Park Authority's *Discovering our Hillfort Heritage* project and in the studies of topography and environment of Clive Waddington and his collaborators. Circumstances are propitious for new work. The Northumberland National Park Authority has secured access and management agreements for the hill lands and the cropmark site is now, through a far-sighted and generous gesture on the part of Roger Miket, in the care of a trust dedicated to archaeological and conservation interests.

The final words in this volume come from Brian Hope-Taylor himself, in the form of a letter. This is a valuable part of the Yeavering archive, but it is more than just that. It is a poignant document which shows him, near the end of his life, still thinking about the site and still open to the idea of new investigations. The chapters in this volume are a contribution to the process of review and rethinking. If they stimulate new research and new insights they will represent a fitting tribute to the memory of Brian Hope-Taylor.

C.F. O'B; P.F.
Tynemouth and Hexham
July 2005

ACKNOWLEDGEMENTS

The editors are grateful to colleagues at Bede's World and the Northumberland National Park Authority who helped to organise the 2003 Yeavering conference. In addition to all the contributors, we would particularly like to thank Richard Morris, Rob Young and Iain Hedley for their help with the planning and presentation of the conference. For help with various aspects of the preparation of this book we are grateful to Tom Chadwin, Sally Foster, James Graham-Campbell, Catherine Hills and Roxanna Waterson.

PART I SETTING THE SCENE

1

'THE STRONGHOLD OF ITS OWN NATIVE PAST' SOME THOUGHTS ON THE PAST IN THE PAST AT YEAVERING

Paul Frodsham

> Few places in Northumberland have attracted more attention than Yeavering Bell ... Its old written history, beginning with the Venerable Bede, and its older unwritten history, as seen in its great stone walls, its hut circles and mounds have given rise to much speculation among antiquaries. Every tourist too and pleasure-seeker, who rambles along the Borders, must climb to its summit, pore over its mysterious monuments and enjoy the extensive and rich view it commands. (George Tate 1863, 431)

INTRODUCTION

The above quotation from George Tate (*1*) is taken from his splendid paper on Yeavering, published nearly a century and a half ago, which should have provided the basis for much subsequent archaeological fieldwork here. However, Brian Hope-Taylor's magnificent 10-year excavation project (1953-62) centred on the Anglian palace site, and Anthony Harding's investigation of the Yeavering henge as part of his Milfield Basin project in the 1970s, represent the only recorded excavations here since Tate concluded his investigations. More recently, two surveys have been undertaken by the Royal Commission for the Historical Monuments of England (RCHME) in association with the Northumberland National Park Authority. The first of these was completed in November 1986 and produced a small-scale survey of the hillfort within its landscape setting (RCHME 1986). The second was a detailed survey of the hillfort undertaken by Keith Blood and Trevor Pearson in the summer of 1998 (see chapter 4).

1 George Tate (1805-1871) worked at Yeavering a century before Brian Hope-Taylor. Reproduced from an original in the possession of Roger Miket

These surveys, and more recent fieldwork projects in the surrounding Cheviot Hills (e.g. work completed by the National Park Authority's *Discovering our Hillfort Heritage* project: Frodsham 1999b) and in the Milfield Basin (Waddington 1999), have served to reinforce the apparent significance of Yeavering during prehistory. This account will argue that the key factor ultimately underlying the significance of the place is the towering presence of Yeavering Bell, but the wider landscape context was also a critical factor which must not be overlooked. Yeavering lies on the boundary between upland and lowland, on the first lowland east–west route north of the Cheviots (*2*).

At Yeavering, the inclination to focus on the Anglian 'palace', while acknowledging that its location was influenced by the presence of the Iron Age hillfort and a couple of Bronze Age burial monuments, has tended to detract from the study of the wider landscape. My purpose in this introductory chapter is to consider questions of continuity within the Yeavering landscape, and in so doing to attempt to demonstrate the critical importance of 'the past in the past' from the earliest times. I certainly have no desire to question the importance of *Ad Gefrin*, but we must remember that it represents less than 1 per cent of the human story at Yeavering since the end of the Ice Age (about a century in more than 10,000 years), and to try to understand it without reference to earlier times would be futile. In examining various aspects of Yeavering's past, I will also make,

'THE STRONGHOLD OF ITS OWN NATIVE PAST'

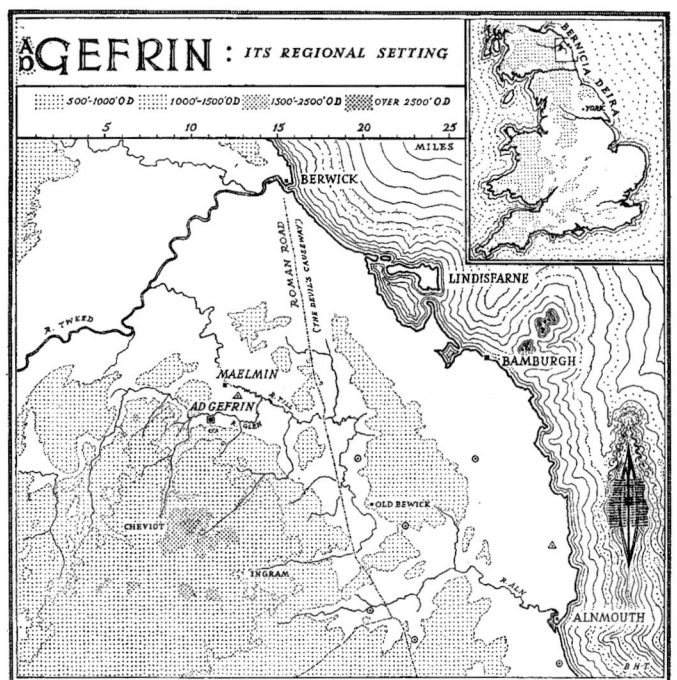

2 Yeavering location map, drawn by Brian Hope-Taylor. *Hope-Taylor 1977, figure 1.* © *Crown copyright – reproduced by permission of English Heritage*

in passing, a few suggestions for further investigation which could perhaps be worked up into a project design for a new campaign of fieldwork using modern techniques unavailable to George Tate or Brian Hope-Taylor.

LIVING IN THE YEAVERING LANDSCAPE

The real value of Yeavering to the archaeologist lies in the quality of the local archaeological landscape as a whole, rather than in its collection of individual 'sites'. But what exactly do we mean by 'landscape'? In the past archaeologists may have defined the landscape as the 'backdrop against which archaeological remains are plotted', but today 'the most prominent notions of landscape emphasise its socio-symbolic dimensions: landscape is an entity that exists by virtue of its being perceived, experienced, and contextualised by people' (Knapp and Ashmore 1999, 1). Many recent accounts (e.g. those in Ashmore and Knapp 1999; Hirsch and O' Hanlon 1995) have stressed the intimate relationships between non-western societies and the landscape, often highlighting an element of 'sacredness' which seems to apply to elements of the landscape, if not to the land as a whole, in such societies (Carmichael *et al.* 1994). It is also important to realise that in ancient times elements of the landscape, including natural features and man-made structures, would have been of both practical and ritual significance at the same time. Actions, too, such as agricultural work or house building, would have been imbued with symbolic significance so that activities we might refer to today as either 'ritual' or 'domestic' were inextricably linked. This important point has recently been stressed by Richard Bradley (2005, 120):

> The modern distinction between the sacred and the profane is meaningless here, and so is any attempt to divide the archaeological record on the same lines. In prehistory ritual gave domestic life its force, and domestic life in turn provided a frame of reference for public events. Ritual and domestic life were not two halves of a single phenomenon, to be picked apart by the archaeologist. Instead they formed two layers that seem to have been precisely superimposed.

It can be difficult for the western mind to fully appreciate alternative attitudes towards the land, even when they are explained in depth by, for example, an Australian Aborigine or a native American. It might be thought a hopeless task, therefore, to seek to explain the possible significance of the Yeavering landscape to its former inhabitants. However, recent developments in phenomenological archaeology have much potential to help us appreciate how people in the past may have experienced and understood their world. A phenomenological approach seeks to place processes of human perception (based ultimately on our five senses) at the centre of research, in preference to 'scientific' approaches which might seek to explain the archaeology of a place like Yeavering through the analysis of distribution maps of apparently contemporary sites and finds. The leading practitioner in the application of phenomenology to prehistoric archaeology over recent years has been Christopher Tilley (e.g. 1994, 2004). According to Tilley (2005, 203):

> It is quite clear that simply measuring and quantifying aspects of a thing tell us very little about it. As a form of representation of that thing these measurements are a very poor substitute for the rich sensuous qualities that we know to be characteristic of actual human experience and dwelling in the world. It is these, through elaborate and precise description, from the point of view of a human subject, that a phenomenologist attempts to capture and re-present.

Clearly, at a place like Yeavering, there is much potential to merge traditional approaches to archaeological data-gathering with a phenomenological perspective to try and understand how people may have thought about aspects of themselves and their landscape through time. In attempting any such analysis, we must appreciate that people in the past had their own historic environments, and that evidence of earlier times must always have been of interest and significance to them. As Richard Bradley (2002, 53) tells us:

> ...prehistoric lives would always have been conducted according to an awareness of history, even if it could not be measured in the terms that we use today. That awareness would have extended from the origins and use of artefacts acquired in daily life, through the built fabric that ancient people inherited, to the wider landscapes in which they lived. The past was constantly caught up in the present, for this was where so many different time scales intersected.

Although Bradley is discussing prehistoric societies, his argument is equally relevant to all societies at Yeavering from the Stone Age through until early medieval times. As we shall see, 'the past in the past' is a key concept in seeking to account for developments through time at this very special place.

A BRIEF INTRODUCTION TO THE ARCHAEOLOGY OF YEAVERING

When I talk of Yeavering I am referring to an area than includes both the Bell with its hillfort and the much smaller 'whaleback hill' immediately to the north on which the Anglian 'palace' *Ad Gefrin*, was situated (*3; colour plate 1*). I would suggest that the Bell, by nature of its unusual form and impressive location at the very edge of the Cheviot massif (*colour plate 2*), must have been a place of special significance to people from the earliest times. Tate (1863, 431) tells us that 'There is a beauty in its shape – a cone truncated at the top, and separated by valleys and deep ravines, from the other hills with which it is connected.' We perhaps catch a glimpse of its potential importance to Palaeolithic or Mesolithic people by considering attitudes of native American or Australian aboriginal people to their landscapes. In Australia,

> ...where every major topographical feature was endowed with mythological significance, it was not part of Aboriginal culture to build monuments such as megalithic tombs or pyramids....Natural landmarks are the centres of religion and ceremony. The places where Aboriginal people gather for the great ceremonies are not marked by formal structures – the land is their cathedral. (Flood 1983, 240)

Brian Hope-Taylor (1977, 6) may have been thinking along such lines when he wrote that Yeavering Bell 'is the key feature of the landscape. Its bulk, position and characteristic shape make it an instantly recognizable landmark from far off. At close range it dominates the site of the ancient township and establishes those

3 Aerial view looking north over Yeavering Bell towards *Ad Gefrin*. Several of the fort's 125 recorded house platforms are visible here, as is the ditched enclosure encircling the Bell's eastern summit. The 'old palace' can be seen just beneath the cottages towards the top-left corner. The site of *Ad Gefrin*, the Anglian palace complex, is to the north-east of these cottages, in the field immediately north of the road, where the old quarry which once threatened the destruction of the site is clearly visible. The henge is in the field to the east of the cottages, with the 'Battle Stone' in the next field to the east. Agricultural terraces are visible in the foreground, and the earthworks of two undated enclosures (probably settlements of late Iron Age/Roman date) can be seen towards the base of the Bell's northern face. The River Glen winds its way eastwards across the top of the photograph. © *Tim Gates*

qualities of character and atmosphere which, though partially indefinable, are yet not wholly irrelevant to studies such as this.'

While they certainly are partially indefinable, these 'qualities of character and atmosphere' do occur repeatedly at particular types of place, perhaps most notably in association with massive landscape features that can make us, as human beings, feel very small. 'Places such as sacred mountains associated with light and air that lie up and above always tend to be privileged culturally and emotionally....

Natural and cultural things of significant height...most usually impress and we find them awe inspiring as they relate to the physicality of our bodies' (Tilley 2004, 6). It is precisely this awe-inspiring aspect of Yeavering Bell, that must also have been appreciated by prehistoric people, that I believe ultimately underlies the archaeology of the place.

Flints provide evidence that the Yeavering whaleback was occupied (although not necessarily of any special status in comparison to other contemporary settlement sites) during the Mesolithic, and Gill Ferrell (1990) has summarised the ceramic evidence for activity here from the early Neolithic onwards. It is also possible that structures of Mesolithic or Neolithic date could lie concealed amongst the multitude of undated post-holes recorded by Hope-Taylor. A small henge monument, one of several in the Milfield Basin, was constructed here during the late Neolithic/early Bronze Age, apparently in association with a nearby standing stone (*colour plate 3*). These henges may somehow have formed an integrated network aligned on the north face of Yeavering Bell (Waddington, this volume), reinforcing the suggestions that the Bell was of ceremonial importance by this time, but we do not really know how these sites were used or for how long they remained in use.

The Stone Age and Iron Age at Yeavering are considered in some detail in chapters 3 and 4 of this volume, but as no background to the Bronze Age is included elsewhere, we will provide a brief overview here. Archaeologists have recognised serious problems with the 'three-age' system for nearly as long as the system has been in place. Nearly a century and a half ago, George Tate (1863, 444) noted that 'Fascinated with the simplicity of the Scandinavian classification of stone, bronze and iron ages, many of our antiquaries with more zeal than success have applied it to British antiquities'. However, this is not the place to attempt the deconstruction of the Bronze Age, which we will accept for now as a convenient label covering the period from about 2400 BC, when beakers and bronzeworking were first introduced into Northumberland, through until about 700 BC when ironworking was introduced into the area.

Today, the Bronze Age is perhaps best regarded as essentially a period of transition from the monument dominated landscape of the Neolithic to the agricultural landscape of the Iron Age, rather than as a coherent period with its own distinctive identity. Whether or not it should be retained as a useful concept in Cheviot prehistory is open to question, but there can be little doubt that the 70 or so generations of people who lived through the times we now refer to as the Bronze Age brought about major changes to the Yeavering landscape. Unbeknown to these Bronze Age people, these changes would have profound effects on developments here many centuries later, during what we refer to today as early medieval times.

Palaeoenvironmental research suggests communities expanded into upland areas in the Cheviots during the early Bronze Age (Young 2004). It may well be that occupation of such upland areas was largely seasonal throughout the Neolithic, but in about 2000 BC the first permanently occupied villages of roundhouses appeared in the hills. One such site has been excavated at Houseledge, just 2km south-east of Yeavering Bell (Burgess 1984; 1995). Half a dozen timber roundhouses clustered together here in association with a field system of clearance cairns, terraces and field walls. Although no radiocarbon dates were obtained for Houseledge, its excavator considers that the first houses here were probably standing by the early second millennium BC and that the settlement may well have been occupied continuously for several centuries.

Many other sites of broadly similar form await investigation in the Cheviots, including a group of at least eight circular buildings at Yeavering, just 500m south of the hillfort. Much of the area still awaits detailed archaeological survey, but it certainly seems that many square kilometres of upland in the vicinity of Yeavering were cleared of woodland and used for a combination of pasture and cultivation during the Bronze Age. Broadly similar settlements and mixed farming regimes to those in the uplands probably also existed on the lowlands, north of Yeavering, during the Bronze Age. Many of the 'ring-ditches' recorded as cropmarks in north Northumberland may prove to be the remnants of such settlements, as was the case at Lookout Plantation (10km north of Yeavering) where a single excavated roundhouse was shown to have been occupied during the mid-second millennium BC (Monaghan 1994).

Having briefly considered the effect our Bronze Age ancestors had on the landscape while they were alive, we must now consider some monuments associated with their death. Such monuments were not, of course, solely for the dead: they were constructed by, and must have exercised constant influence over, the living. There are several such monuments in the Yeavering area. The mutilated remains of a cairn survive on top of Yeavering Bell's eastern summit (see chapter 4). This implies that this summit of the Bell, at least, was of some ritual importance in the early Bronze Age, but we cannot say whether or not it was of special significance in relation to other cairn sites in the vicinity. Several such cairns were investigated by George Tate in the mid-nineteenth century. These include Worm Law, adjacent to a large standing stone 1km north-east of the hillfort, and three examples on Swint Law (4). About a 1km south of Yeavering Bell, at a location which today commands a splendid view of the hillfort, a large cairn once stood adjacent to Tom Tallon's Crag. Tate records that this was 'the largest in the district', measuring 240ft in circumference. Tate also noted that half of this cairn provided sufficient stone to build more than 1000 yards of the adjacent fieldwall to a height of 5ft and a breadth of 2ft 2in. The cairn contained

'THE STRONGHOLD OF ITS OWN NATIVE PAST'

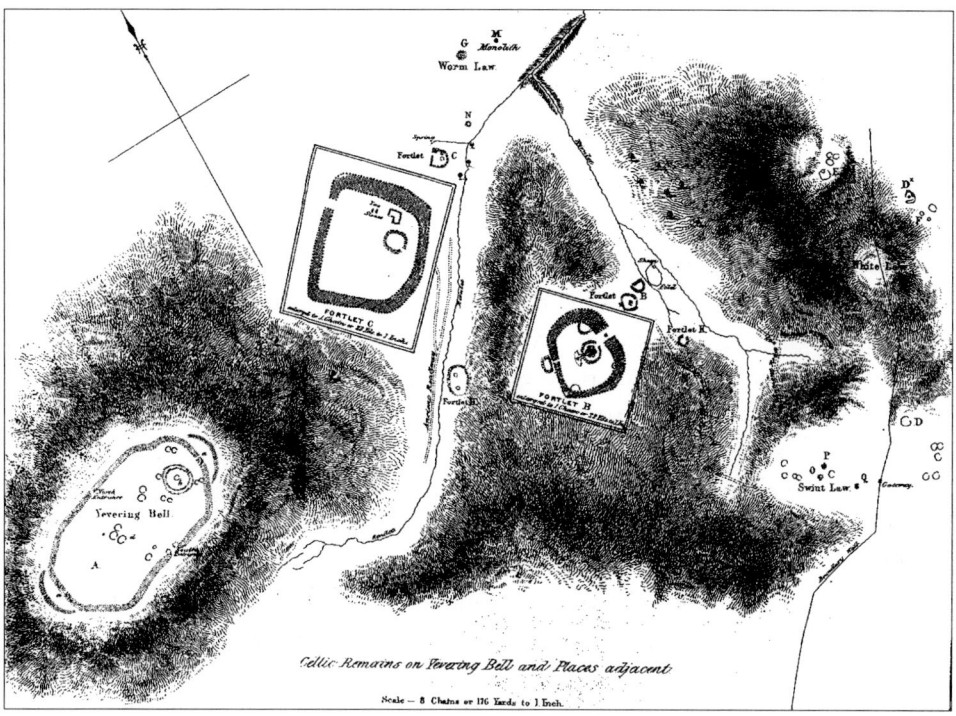

4 Plan of George Tate's excavations at Yeavering, drawn by William Wightman of Wooler. *Reproduced from Tate 1862, plate XV*

a cist but no finds of interest were recorded from it, although MacLauchlan (1867a) does record that 'there were a few bones towards the middle of the cairn, and towards the bottom there was a very disagreeable smell'. MacLauchlan also records the investigation of a cist on lower ground 365m west of *Ad Gefrin*, in a field known as Sandy Knowe, but this was apparently entirely devoid of finds. Many other cairns of various sizes are known in the hills to the south of the Bell, and while a proportion of these could be the results of field clearance, there can be little doubt that several of them are primarily sepulchral in origin. It may well be that most cairns were initially constructed for the burial of important individuals, perhaps the founders of the new upland settlements discussed above, and then became foci for many more burials over subsequent generations. In addition to all these cairns on higher ground, the two 'ring-ditches' and the Bronze Age cemetery excavated by Hope-Taylor on the *Ad Gefrin* site are very important in their own right, as well as being of crucial importance to later developments here: these are considered later in this chapter.

In summary, we must record that the influence of 'Bronze Age' people on the general appearance of the Yeavering landscape was immense, arguably of greater magnitude than that of any people before or since. Over a few centuries, probably beginning in about 2000 BC, they transformed a largely wooded environment in the hills around Yeavering into an essentially open landscape, dotted with small settlements of timber roundhouses within extensive field systems. Many burial cairns stood adjacent to these settlements. For some reason, during the earlier first millennium BC people began constructing defended settlements of wooden roundhouses behind timber palisades. These palisaded sites eventually gave way to the hillforts, of which several fine examples exist in the vicinity of Yeavering. The fort on Yeavering Bell itself, however, is a far from typical such example (*colour plates 4-6*). As Al Oswald and Trevor Pearson demonstrate in chapter 4 of this volume, it is altogether different from all the others in terms of scale and probably also in chronology. Rather than being an 'Iron Age' hillfort, it may well have originally been constructed by late Bronze Age people, perhaps as long ago as 1000 BC.

During the later Iron Age and/or Roman period, parts of the lower slopes of the Bell and surrounding hills became littered with enclosed settlements of stone-built roundhouses and associated field systems (*colour plate 7*). Tate, who excavated at several of these sites (*4*), classifies them as 'fortified dwellings' or 'fortlets', consisting of houses within stone-walled enclosures, and settlements of unenclosed roundhouses. He notes, due to different types of artefact being found at different levels, that some sites appear to have undergone more than one phase of occupation. However, the detailed chronology of these sites remains unclear. Finds included pottery, burnt wood, flints (which could be residual from earlier times, but might suggest that the use of flint continued into the Iron Age), a quernstone, an iron implement that may have been a spearhead, and a colourful glass and enamel armlet which 'doubtless adorned the arm of some Ancient British beauty' (Tate 1863, 438-443, 447) (*5*). Tate observed that some of the pottery from these settlements is of the same type as some from the hillfort, and concluded that 'all the Forts, fortified dwellings and hut circles examined, appear to me to be pretty nearly of the same age and to be the work of one people or race' (Tate 1863, 446). However, as we have already noted, the chronology of the hillfort is far from clear, so the detailed dating and phasing of the surrounding settlements must await further fieldwork.

The 'fortified dwellings' around the Bell must have been architecturally very impressive. It is quite possible that some of them could have been occupied continuously from the late Iron Age through into post-Roman times, perhaps functioning as elite residences between the heydays of the hillfort and *Ad Gefrin*. Most people during this period may have lived in the numerous unenclosed roundhouses, which were once even more common in the vicinity of Yeavering than the many surviving examples might suggest. Tate (1863, 441) notes that on Swint Law 'and in the high valley between White law and Gleedscleugh,

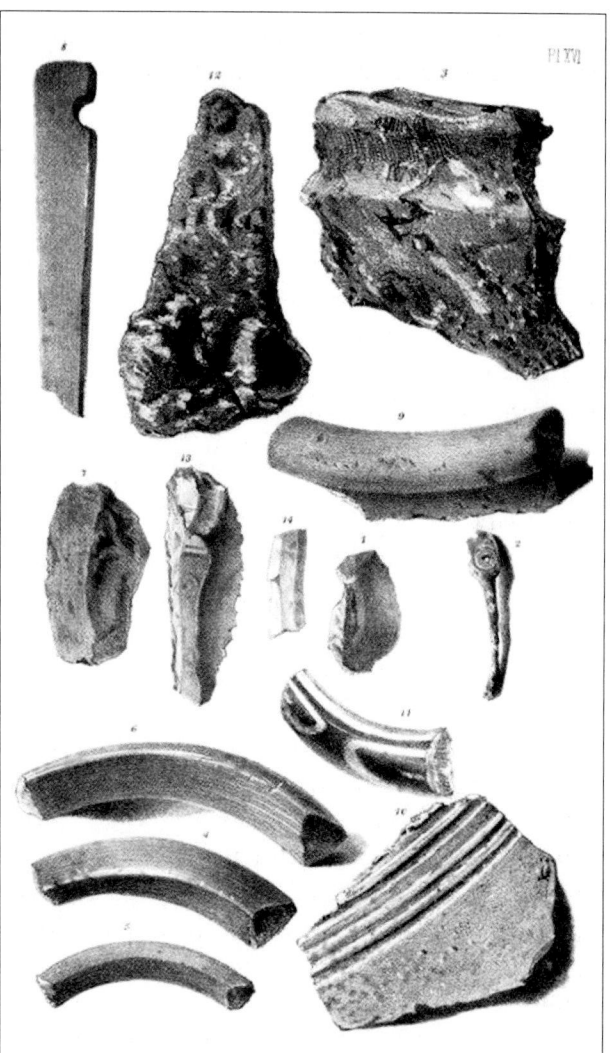

5 Some of George Tate's finds from his investigations at Yeavering, described by him as: 1, flint knife; 2, part of a copper fibula; 3, pottery; 4, 5 & 6, oak rings; 7, flint javelin head; 8, stone relic; 9, pottery with rounded rim; 10, ornamented pottery; 11, glass armlet; 12, iron weapon; 13, flint saw. (Item 14 is from a different site). Items 1-6 are from the hillfort, 7-10 from 'fortlets' near Yeavering, 11 & 12 from the Swint Law hut circles; 13 from the Worm Law barrow. *Reproduced from Tate 1862, plate XVI*

numbers of hut circles could be traced a few years ago, some in groups, others isolated, and many of them with their walls standing above the ground; but when the boundary fence between the Akeld and Yevering estates was built in 1859, all the camps and dwellings near this boundary were pillaged of their stones.' This serves to remind us that the ruins to be seen in today's landscape represent but a fraction of what once existed: unless there was a reason for a structure to be retained, or an area was largely abandoned or difficult to access, then potentially useful building stone would normally be recycled.

Although the issue of Iron Age burial in the Cheviots is rarely discussed, two cremations of apparent Romano-British date were recovered from the whaleback, and it is possible that many of the other (apparently unaccompanied) cremations recorded from the *Ad Gefrin* excavations may post-date the Bronze Age. Hope-Taylor (1977, 337) states that 'it is greatly to be doubted whether the whole history of the Yeavering cremation-cemetery is completely or evenly represented by those remains that happen to have survived recognizably', and it is just possible that the old Bronze Age cemetery continued to attract cremations, albeit perhaps intermittently, throughout Iron Age and Roman times. No other cemetery covering this period is known in Northumberland, and possible alternative ways in which the dead may have been disposed of are considered later in this chapter. However, Yeavering is unique in many ways, and if such cemeteries exist anywhere then we might reasonably expect one to be here. Hopefully, further fieldwork will be able to cast some light on this important question.

In terms of currently available information, the fifth and sixth centuries at Yeavering remain very much a 'Dark Age', but by the early seventh century, the 'palace' complex (which some authorities prefer, perhaps more correctly, to term a 'villa' or 'estate centre') stood proudly on the whaleback, in the shadow of the Bell (*colour plates 8-13*). Its most striking structures (all of which saw phases of modification or rebuilding) were a great hall, a unique 'theatre' and the 'Great Enclosure' (all of which are discussed in part III of this volume). It provided short-term accommodation for the king, who would probably have stayed here once or twice a year, no doubt hunting in the hills during the daytime and feasting in the great hall long into the nights. The king and his retinue would have moved around the kingdom staying at a number of different such settlements each year. However, *Ad Gefrin* seems to have been of particular importance, and apparently became the centre of Bishop Paulinus' mission in Bernicia. Bede tells us that Paulinus came to *Ad Gefrin* to preach the Christian faith in the presence of King Edwin, and that he baptised the local people in the adjacent River Glen:

> So great is said to have been the fervour of the faith of the Northumbrians and their longing for the washing of salvation, that once when Paulinus came to the king and queen in their royal palace at Yeavering, he spent thirty-six days there occupied in the task of catechizing and baptizing. During these days, from morning till evening, he did nothing else but instruct the crowds who flocked to him from every village and district in the teaching of Christ. When they had received instruction he washed them in the waters of regeneration in the River Glen, which was close at hand (Colgrave and Mynors 1969, 189).

(This event is usually assumed to have taken place in 627, though in fact Bede is unclear as to the exact date and it could conceivably have occurred at any time between Edwin's conversion in 627 and his death in 633.)

Ad Gefrin was clearly an important place within the kingdom of Bernicia throughout most of the seventh century. Hope-Taylor (1977, chapter 6) interprets the results of his excavations in the light of what is known of the history of Bernicia, linking particular phases to the reigns of Aethelfrith, Edwin and Oswald. In his account, the two occasions on which *Ad Gefrin* was destroyed by fire are linked with the ravaging of Northumberland by Penda and Cadwallon in 632-33, and with Penda's 'burning and pillaging of the district' in the early 650s. After the second of these sackings, the township was rebuilt on an altogether less extravagant scale, and Bede tells us that it was eventually abandoned in favour of an alternative site at *Maelmin* (present-day Milfield), where cropmarks no less spectacular than those of *Ad Gefrin* still await the intervention of the archaeologist's trowel. Hope-Taylor dates the abandonment of *Ad Gefrin* to about 685, noting that 'the actual moment of its final abandonment cannot be determined' but that it probably followed a 'lengthy process of devolution.'

Although the visible remains of the great hillfort and various other prehistoric structures survived in the hills throughout medieval times, nothing survived for long on the site of *Ad Gefrin* to identify it as anything other than an ordinary patch of ground. Occasional surviving references from the late thirteenth century onwards (Vickers 1922, 241-3) suggest that the area was unremarkable agricultural land throughout the medieval and post-medieval periods. During the excavation of the henge, some 'thirteenth or fourteenth century pottery of local Tweeddale types, was recovered from residual contexts and the plough-soil' (Tinniswood and Harding 1991, 103). This is most likely to have found its way here along with domestic waste spread on the fields, suggesting that this was arable land during the prosperous thirteenth century. There was apparently a small medieval hamlet or village in the area now known as 'Old Yeavering', between *Ad Gefrin* and the Bell, where the ruined structure somewhat confusingly known as the 'Old Palace' (*colour plate 14*), probably originally a late sixteenth-century tower, stands adjacent to two cottages which provide the only currently occupied dwellings in the area. A few shielings litter the hills, and George Tate found glazed pottery which he states could be medieval, though he considers it probably Romano-British, in some of the 'fortified dwellings' he investigated around the Bell (Tate 1863, 447). However, there are no visible remains surviving in the landscape to suggest that the area continued to enjoy any kind of special ceremonial significance during medieval times.

Census returns (listed in Vickers 1922, 241) suggest that in excess of 50 people lived in Yeavering township throughout most of the nineteenth century, although by 1901 the population had dropped to five. One cannot help but wonder what, if anything, all these residents of Yeavering (and, indeed, their medieval predecessors) knew, or thought they knew, of their local history. It was in 1949 that the true location of the palace site was revealed through air photography (see chapter 2), and Brian Hope-Taylor's subsequent excavations have ensured that it will never again be forgotten.

It is the issue of continuity, and in particular the relationship between the prehistoric hillfort and the Anglian Palace, that has most intrigued students of Yeavering. However, the relationship between hillfort and palace, while extremely interesting, is but one element of the story of Yeavering. Gill Ferrell (1990, 41), in a consideration of the prehistoric pottery from Hope-Taylor's excavations, observes that throughout prehistory Yeavering appears to have been 'a dynamic site capable of adapting to change and surviving', and that 'it is the continuity at Yeavering that is significant and any interruptions in this seem to be fairly minor episodes in its long history'. In an important contribution to this debate, Richard Bradley (1987) questions the degree of actual continuity of activity at Yeavering and introduces the idea of the 'creation of continuity', whereby social elites attempt to legitimise their positions through reference to the past. In effect, ancient monuments are appropriated by the elite in order to 'create' direct links with the ancestral past. This system is directly analogous to the creation of fictitious genealogies whereby individuals trace their origins back to a prestigious and perhaps mythical past. Bradley is surely correct in stressing the 'strategic use of monuments surviving from the distant past and their incorporation in a different cultural landscape'. Indeed, I would argue with some confidence that this process has been going on at Yeavering, to varying degrees, throughout much of the past five millennia, with Yeavering Bell itself playing a role no less important than any artificially constructed ancient monument.

AN UNMISTAKEABLE THREAD OF CONTINUITY?
THE POWER OF THE PAST AT YEAVERING

So what can we offer to this debate about the past in the past at Yeavering? I think it highly likely that Bradley's 'creation of continuity' went hand in hand with a large degree of actual continuity of occupation and activity here. Hope-Taylor (1977, 280) implies as much when he states that the creation of *Ad Gefrin* is possibly to be seen as 'an act of revival prompted by thoughts of political expediency and exploitation; but even so there is an unmistakeable thread of continuity back into the local past.' While periods of abandonment could have contributed to the power of the place, enabling the incorporation of more 'made up' elements into the 'continuity' that was created when one or more old sites were later reoccupied, it is not necessary to have periods of abandonment in order to create a fictitious continuity. Yeavering is a complex landscape and various elements of it were selectively abandoned or appropriated, no doubt linked with social memory maintained and reinforced by communal activity and oral tradition, at various points in its history. Let us now analyse, in no particular order, a number of themes that might repay more detailed study and which it is hoped to develop further in due course.

A FORM OF TOTEMISM?
THE ORIGIN AND SURVIVAL OF THE NAME 'YEAVERING'

We will begin by briefly considering the continuity implicit in the retention of the old British name '*Gefrin*', which, it is relevant to note (given the present-day name), should correctly be pronounced 'Yefrin'. (Note: throughout this chapter *Gefrin* is assumed to have been the British name for the hill (and hillfort) we now call Yeavering Bell, the name *Ad Gefrin* is used specifically for the palace site, and the modern place name 'Yeavering' is used when referring to the general area including both hillfort and palace sites.

George Tate, writing in the middle of the nineteenth century, was unable to explain the origins of the name. He noted that 'Antiquaries of a past generation threw by their speculations a mysterious sacredness over Yevering Bell' (Tate 1863, 434), noting past references to sun temples, fire-worship, Druid altars and Academies of the Druids. Support for these old suggestions was provided by the place-name 'evidence': Yeavering Bell had been translated via a rather tenuous route into 'Bel-ad-gebrin' or 'Mount of the Sun'. Tate himself acknowledged that 'these etymologies are forced and exceedingly improbable', before concluding that 'of the old name Ad-gefrin, I can offer no probable explanation.' It is a shame that Tate was unable to establish the origin of the name, as he would doubtless have provided some interesting discussion of it. It is now generally accepted that '*Gefrin*' translates as 'Hill of the Goats' (Ekwall 1977, 544), and '*Ad Gefrin*' (as Bede refers to the Anglian palace site) as 'at the Hill of the Goats'.

It is an interesting coincidence that Yeavering Bell is one of the few places in Northumberland that still supports a herd of wild goats (*6*), but we should avoid reading too much into this, as these goats are apparently descended from a herd introduced in the nineteenth century rather than from any prehistoric goats that may once have lived here. Regardless of this, it seems inconceivable that a site as important as Yeavering would be named after a few goats that happened to live on the hill, and it is surely more likely that the choice of name was linked in some way with Celtic mythology: could the goat even have been a totemic beast for the local population? The goat is rarely considered as a major mythological player in comparison to, for example, the horse, bull, stag or boar, but it does occur regularly, often in very important roles. Pan is well known

6 A friendly wild goat joins a meeting of the *Gefrin Trust* trustees at Yeavering, May 2005. Photograph: Chris Burgess

to students of classical mythology, and in Scandinavia Thor's chariot is drawn across the sky by two goats (Ellis Davidson 1969, 67). In Celtic mythology the goat appears to represent fertility; 'the horns reflect both virility and aggression' (Green 1992, 106).

Having already written the above paragraph, and wondering whether I was being somewhat over-fanciful, I was pleased to note that Hope-Taylor (1977, 260) had been thinking along similar lines while working at Yeavering:

> More probably ... what is represented here is a form of totemism involving zoomorphic emblems. The known self-identification of certain Celtic tribes with animals ... provides some warrant for this conjecture; and, viewed in that speculative light, the implications of the place-name *Gefrin* and its remarkable survival appear possibly to transcend mere reference to original natural fauna.

This continuity of nomenclature does not, of course, imply any continuity in the type of activity going on here, but does suggests that the site was continually of such importance that its old name was retained through the ages: thus, for example, the Anglian palace, which could have been given a new name when it was founded, retained the ancient Celtic label. It may or may not be significant in this context that Hope-Taylor found a goat's skull (1977, 69) and a 'ceremonial staff' decorated with what may have been a goat motif (1977, 200-203) in what was apparently one of the most significant Anglian period burials at *Ad Gefrin*. Perhaps the symbolic significance of the goat to the later prehistoric inhabitants of Yeavering was so great that it survived undimmed throughout the Roman interlude, being retained in some way into post-Roman times, long after the fort on the 'hill of the goats' had been abandoned.

Several variations of the name are recorded in medieval and post-medieval documents. Tate (1863, 433) lists *Gevera*, *Geteryne* and *Yevern Villa*. Hope-Taylor (1977, 359) notes that '*Yevering* is the form used on Dacre's map of 1584' and 'Speed's map of 1608 gives *Yeverin*', while 'it was apparently the adoption of *Yeavering* by the Ordnance Survey that brought about the gradual abandonment of the more ancient spellings.' Even when people (such as George Tate) no longer understood its meaning, the name still remained stubbornly in place. Yeavering has been 'the hill of the goats' for longer (and possibly much longer) than two millennia. It will always be so.

A SUITABLE AREA FOR METAL-WORKING ACTIVITY? A POSSIBLE 'AFTERLIFE' FOR THE YEAVERING HENGE

The henge at Yeavering was partially excavated by Anthony Harding in 1976 as part of a wide-ranging investigation into the henges of the Milfield Plain. Harding concluded that these sites were interlinked in some way, with the different orientations of the henge entrances 'connected with the desire to view different parts of the horizon from each one' (Harding 1981, 132). In particular, the eastern entrance of the Yeavering henge was aligned towards the distinctive profile of Ros Castle, and the Milfield North henge (*7*) was aligned on Yeavering Bell (see also chapter 3). These alignments may well relate to places that were imbued with spiritual significance long before the construction of the henges, and the recovery of Mesolithic and early Neolithic material from the site of *Ad Gefrin* suggests that this particular place may have been integrated within such a network of special places from a very early period.

Like several other Neolithic monuments, in Northumberland and elsewhere, the Yeavering henge was apparently reused in early medieval times. It was not, however, used as a cemetery. Instead it seems to have become a focus for metalworking within the Anglian palace complex (Tinniswood and Harding 1991). A large number of shallow pits were discovered within and adjacent to the henge (*8*). Most of these were of uncertain date or purpose, but a few contained evidence for early medieval industrial activity in the form of crucible fragments, pieces of slag and fired clay. Analysis of the 13 crucible fragments recovered from the excavation demonstrated the working of copper-alloys,

7 A modern reconstruction of the Milfield North henge at the *Maelmin* archaeology trail, Milfield. The reconstruction is based closely on the results of Anthony Harding's excavation of the original site. The Yeavering henge was of similar proportions, although no evidence for timber posts was recovered from its excavation. *Photograph: Paul Frodsham*

probably bronze and possibly brass. These finds do not actually prove that the henge itself was used for metalworking, as 'the finds may all be residual material from a nearby working area' (Tinniswood and Harding 1991, 107). Perhaps adjacent buildings which show up on air photographs represent an 'industrial area', removed from the main focus of *Ad Gefrin* but still an essential element of the complex: further excavation should be able to resolve this suggestion one way or the other.

There is no suggestion of long-term continuity here, as there is nothing to suggest that the henge functioned in any way throughout later prehistoric and Roman times. Indeed, the henge ditches seem to have become gradually infilled, and the banks largely flattened, by Anglian times, and it is possible that subsequent activity may have been located here by coincidence. The excavators conclude that 'the only reliable conclusion that can be reached from existing evidence is that Anglo-Saxon exploitation of the site involved its use as a suitable area for long-term but probably sporadic metal-working activity…of at least copper-alloys; and that this activity should be linked with the probably intermittent royal presence at the adjacent settlement site' (Tinniswood and Harding 1991, 108). Although the field evidence is admittedly flimsy, it must surely be possible that metalworkers

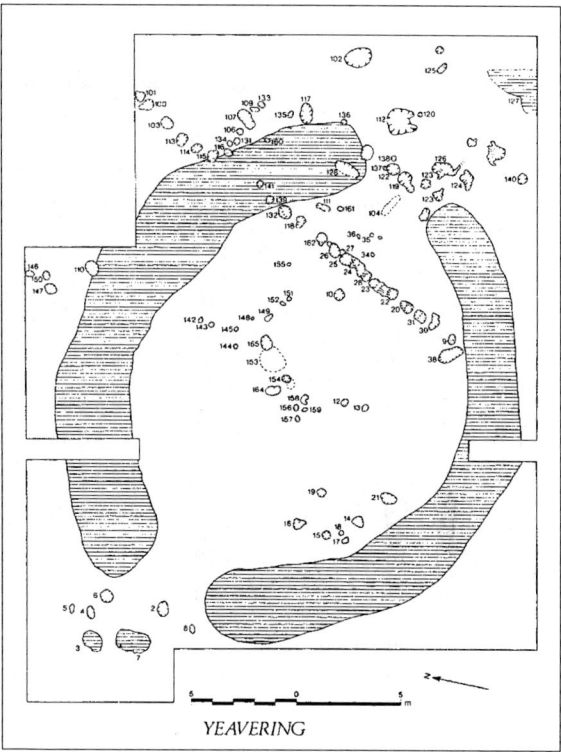

8 Plan of the Yeavering henge and later features. The henge ditches and other known prehistoric features are cross-hatched (3 & 127 are earlier Neolithic pits, one of which was radiocarbon dated to 3950-3350 BC, perhaps 1500 years before the construction of the henge; 7 is a grave, thought to be contemporary with the henge). Most of the other features are strictly undated, and of unknown purpose, but some contained evidence for Anglian metalworking. *Reproduced from Tinniswood & Harding 1991, figure 3*

(and indeed other high status craftworkers) could have been attracted to the site of the mysterious ancient henge (conceivably with its surrounding bank much denuded but still clearly visible) as a powerful site on which to produce exotic material for a royal patron. Richard Hingley has recently considered the symbolic associations of metalworking in Iron Age Britain, noting that 'many ethnographic and historical accounts suggest that ironworking was considered a mystical process during which rocks were converted into powerful cultural artefacts' (Hingley 1997, 9). He suggests that associations may have existed between the process of ironworking and the agricultural cycle, and between the life-cycles of iron objects and of people. Although Hingley is specifically concerned with Iron Age ironworking, early Irish historical sources record the special status accorded to the smith in later times, and it would seem reasonable to assume that such status would also have been enjoyed by the craftsmen responsible for the production of metal objects at a royal palace site such as *Ad Gefrin*. Where better to engage in the magical processes of metalworking than on the site of the ancient temple of the ancestors, especially when the site is to the south-east of the main settlement focus in a relative position which Hingley suggests may have been of ritual significance to ironworking at many Iron Age sites?

THE ANCIENT ERECT STONE CALLED THE GREY STONE.
A BRIEF HISTORY OF THE BATTLE STONE

Writing of Yeavering in the latter half of the eighteenth century, John Wallis (1769, 481) tells us that:

> At this village the Scots, after a long engagement, were defeated on St. Mary Magdalen's day...1415, by Sir Robert Humfranvil, captain of Roxbrough-Castle; the Earl of Westmorland then lord warden of the marches. Above sixty Scotchmen were slain, and one hundred and sixty taken prisoners. A thousand of them were pursued upwards of twelve miles. On the south side of the village, midway between the hill and the road from Kirk Newton to Wooler, is an unwrought column of whinstone erected in memory of it, of a vast magnitude; in height fourteen feet, and four inches; in diameter at the base as many; and towards the middle, eleven feet, and seven inches.

It is not known how Wallis acquired his detailed but rather inexact measurements: although visually impressive, the stone actually stands to a height of only about 2m (*colour plate 3*). In 1867, Henry MacLauchlan referred to the stone as 'the ancient erect stone called the Grey Stone' and correctly surmises that it must have stood here for a long time prior to the battle of 1415. Nevertheless, the stone continues to be known locally as 'the Battle Stone'.

The stone had toppled some time before 1925, when it was re-erected and set in concrete. Its original position cannot, therefore, be known with certainty, although it probably does stand on or immediately adjacent to its original site. While it may appear to stand in isolation, Anthony Harding (1981, 115) notes that it 'lies in a direct line with the henge entrances...so may well have been correctly re-positioned'. Given this alignment (which extends to the profile of Ros Castle on the distant horizon), it is reasonable to suppose that the stone's original purpose related in some way to the functions of the henge, although the exact details of this arrangement remain obscure.

Throughout Europe, many megalithic monuments were treated by the Christian Church in one of two ways: they were either transformed into 'good sites' (e.g. by carving crosses into them, or building churches adjacent to them) or became associated with the devil or paganism and were in many cases destroyed (Holtorf 1997). In this context it is interesting to note that the standing stone at Yeavering, despite the area's Christian heritage, has no apparent links with the church, although it was at one time linked in local legend with Druids.

Between 1846 and 1859, Michael Aislabie Denham wrote many intriguing articles about the folklore of Northumberland. These articles were subsequently edited by James Hardy and published in 1895 as *The Denham Tracts*. Amongst discussion of several standing stones and cairns, Denham notes that:

> The standing stone at Yevering in Glendale is a large column of porphyry planted upright in a field at the northern base of the hill called Yevering Bell. It is usually spoken of as indicating a battle, but is in reality prehistoric, there being another, now prostrate, among the old forts and tumuli on the eastern end of the lower slope of that hill. By the common people it is called the 'Druid's Lapfu'. A female Druid's apron string broke there, and the stone dropped out and remained in its present position. Another account is that one of the Druids, who are represented like the Pechs or Picts to have had very long arms, pitched it from the top of the Bell, and it sunk into the soil where it fell. (Hardy 1895, 216)

Bizarrely, local legends accounting for cairns and standing stones as having fallen out of aprons are linked with a number of Neolithic and early Bronze Age sites throughout Britain. Indeed, Tate (1863, 445) notes that the now-destroyed burial cairn to the south of Yeavering Bell known as Tom Tallon's grave was also once known as 'the auld wife's apron fu' o' stanes'. Such names must be ancient, though their origins are lost in time: Tate suggests that 'such traditions and phrases...probably have their origin in the belief in witchcraft supposed to have been exercised by old women'. Today, the stone is thought by local folklore (reinforced by Ordnance Survey maps) to have been erected in honour of the Battle of Geteryne, as described Wallis. At what point was this ancient standing stone (which seems originally to have been erected in Neolithic times, and which presumably stood throughout the life of the Anglian palace) ascribed its new identity? What, we may wonder, did King Edwin, or Paulinus, make of it several centuries before the occurrence of the battle it is now said to commemorate? The history of this stone certainly accords with Holtorf's (1997, 80) observation that 'megaliths, together with the landscapes as part of which they were received, have continuously been reconstructed, cognitively'.

On the subject of battles it is also worth noting that the area around Yeavering witnessed several confrontations of varying intensity throughout Anglo-Saxon and medieval times, and a number of other local standing stones are also thought to commemorate battles. Indeed, our hazy knowledge of these ancient battles adds still further to the enigmatic power of the place, whether or not we choose to believe the local legend that the British King Arthur won one of his most heroic victories right here in Glendale (Nennius *Historia Brittonum*: 56).

AN IMMENSELY LONG CONTINUITY? THE *AD GEFRIN* CEMETERIES

A discussion of ritual and religion at Yeavering could easily fill a volume of this size on its own. Here we will restrict ourselves to a few observations relating to burial practice through the ages. By way of introduction, it is worth recalling Richard Bradley's warnings relating to time and apparent continuity of ritual in the archaeological record. Bradley (1987, 3) notes that 'ritual time' is often divorced from 'everyday time', and that consequently it is difficult to discuss ritual continuity in the same terms as continuity of land use or domestic settlement. He also notes that 'proponents of ritual continuity are forced to make imaginative leaps across impossibly long periods of prehistoric time ... in order to support a model which is difficult to sustain as archaeological theory' (1987, 15). Bradley interprets the juxtaposition of prehistoric and early medieval monuments as attempts by a social elite to legitimise their position through reference to the past, rather than as evidence for any actual continuity in ritual practice. Undoubtedly there has been an element of this at Yeavering, but it is legitimate to ask to what extent such 'creation of continuity' may, on occasions, have gone hand in hand with some degree of actual continuity of occupation, activity, or even perhaps belief.

The number and diversity of human burials at Yeavering are astonishing. Ranging in date from the apparent Neolithic burial adjacent to the henge (Harding 1981, 122) to the final stages of *Ad Gefrin*'s existence in the late seventh century AD, these burials provide an enthralling resource for the archaeologist to play with (see also chapter 5). They include 'text book' examples such as Bronze Age cremations, and unique cases such as the inhumation with goat skull at the threshold to the Anglian great hall. Attempts to categorise these burials into standard forms inevitably result in confusion: some are prehistoric and others historic, some are cremations while most are inhumations, most are 'native' while a few may be 'Germanic', and many are pagan while others are apparently Christian. Monuments associated with these burials include round barrows, a pagan temple containing numerous ox skulls which Hope-Taylor (1977, 278) suggests may have been re-consecrated as a Christian site by Paulinus, large timber (presumably decorated) upright posts, and what was apparently a Christian church within a fenced graveyard.

Most of the recorded burials at Yeavering fall essentially into two general categories: 'Bronze Age' cremations and early medieval inhumations, the two being conveniently separated by a period of unknown duration during Iron Age/Roman times when, according to Hope-Taylor, a field system existed on the whaleback. Here I must stress one of the most important developments in our understanding of the Yeavering sequence since Hope-Taylor's publication.

This is Tim Gates' crucial observation that the putative Iron Age field system at Yeavering never existed: the ditches found by Hope-Taylor are now recognised as natural periglacial frost cracks (see chapter 2). This has major implications for the chronology of various phases of *Ad Gefrin*, but for now we will only consider its impact on the burial record. The field system had been interpreted as representing a break in sanctity of the whaleback hill, and a few cremations (including two with glass beads of Romano-British date) were thought to have been placed within the ditched field boundaries. However, this argument has now been completely turned on its head: the fact that the area was *not* ploughed or used for settlement suggests that it may indeed have been of special importance through the Iron Age and Romano-British periods. And, after all, what sort of ceremonial monuments would one expect to find on a sacred site of this period?: precisely what is found at Yeavering – nothing. The presence of cremation burials of this date, which are very rare in Northumberland, further suggests that the place was special. In addition, many unaccompanied cremations, originally deposited in shallow pits, may date from Iron Age/Roman times: it is indeed a unfortunate that 'the large sum of money required for radiocarbon dating of all the unurned deposits' (or even a sample of them) was not available, and that the loss of the samples made subsequent dating impossible (Hope-Taylor 1977, 337). If cremations were added to the whaleback, however intermittently, throughout Iron Age and Roman times, then this would have massive implications for questions of ritual continuity at Yeavering. We must hope that future investigations will recover further samples that will enable this issue to be adequately addressed.

In order to inform the subsequent discussion, we must now consider Hope-Taylor's excavation of the Bronze Age monuments and burials on the whaleback in some detail. As we will see, these monuments were to be critical to much later developments at the site. There are two monuments to consider: the 'Western Ring-ditch' with associated cremation cemetery, and the 'Eastern Ring-ditch'. (The henge [see chapter 3] is probably a century or two older than these, and is usually considered to be 'late Neolithic' rather than 'early Bronze Age' in date. It did not attract burials during the Bronze Age or later times, so is not considered further in this section, although its use must presumably have overlapped to some extent with that of the two ring-ditches.)

Towards the western edge of the whaleback hill, in Hope-Taylor's 'area D', was the Western Ring-ditch which became the focus for a cremation cemetery. The exact original form of this monument is uncertain. Hope-Taylor believes it to have incorporated a stone circle: this is a fair interpretation of the excavated evidence, but no stones were recovered and we cannot be certain that any stood here. Regardless of the monument's exact form, Hope-Taylor considered it to be of particular importance to subsequent events at Yeavering, noting that

The whole history of the Western Ring-ditch is hardly to be explained save in terms of institutional continuity. For centuries the focal point for both urned and unurned cremation-burials, its significance survived even the last and greatest change in funerary fashion, and ultimately it became the formal centre for the site's first inhumation-burials. (1977, 336)

No less than 35 separate cremation burials are catalogued and described in Appendix III of Hope-Taylor's report, in addition to which he notes that 'there was a remarkable scatter of cremated and pounded bone throughout the bottom level of the modern topsoil, and in all the fillings of later foundation-trenches, especially in the south-west quarter of the site (as Ian Richmond characteristically remarked, "like the bits of nut in a well-mixed Christmas pudding").' It appears that a large number of cremations had been scattered by the plough, and that the cemetery was much more extensive than the individually excavated cremations alone would suggest.

Perhaps surprisingly, given the apparent evidence for the special nature of Yeavering during late Neolithic times, only three or four sherds of beakers were recovered from Hope-Taylor's excavations and none were found during Harding's excavation of the Yeavering henge (Harding 1981). Of the sherds that were recovered, all were from within and around the Western Ring-ditch, evidence which Hope-Taylor (1977, 354) used to support his view that 'it appears all the more likely that the Western Ring-ditch has first claim to be regarded as Yeavering's most significantly ancient monument.' (We must remember that he was unaware of the existence of the henge.) Beakers are usually thought to have been introduced as prestigious vessels at the very beginning of the Bronze Age, but here at Yeavering they appear to play an insignificant role alongside other forms of later Neolithic pottery. A fine beaker was found in the nineteenth century at Akeld, just 3km east of Yeavering, but relatively few beakers have been recovered from the Milfield area in comparison to other regions of Northumberland (Tait 1965). This is initially surprising, given the clear importance of Yeavering and the Milfield Basin in late Neolithic times, but perhaps it was this very importance that somehow fed a conservative approach that did not welcome the beakers and other innovations that came with them. If the relative lack of beakers is surprising, then the complete absence of food vessels, commonly found with early Bronze Age burials throughout Northumberland, is even more baffling. Gill Ferrell (1990) notes this lack of food vessels at Yeavering, but neither she nor anyone else (so far as I am aware) has provided a convincing explanation of it.

The finds from the cemetery are considered in detail by Hope Taylor (1977), and have subsequently been reconsidered by Gill Ferrell (1990), so will not be detailed here, other than to note in passing one particularly interesting example

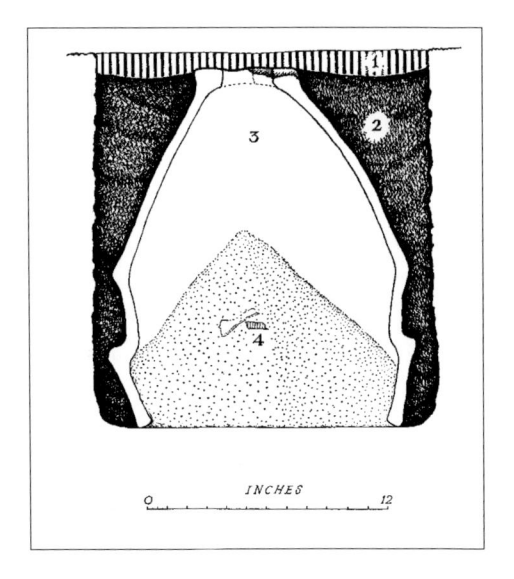

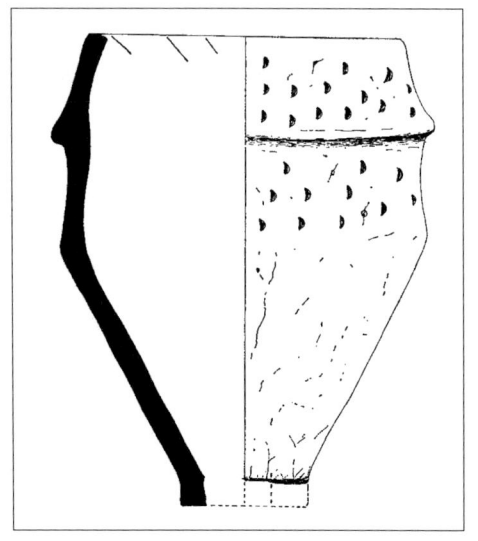

9 Left: Diagrammatic cross-section of cremation-burial 19 (1, clay sealing-layer; 2, black soil, densely packed, with much charcoal; 3, air-space; 4, cone of cremated bones, showing stratification of sherd detached from inside of urn's base, in relation to exceptionally large fragment of bone – Hope-Taylor suggests that this sherd was detached as the adjacent large fragment of bone was forced through the hole in the base). *Right:* The collared urn from cremation burial no. 19. (Hope Taylor 1977, figures 116 & 117. © *Crown copyright – reproduced by permission of English Heritage*

(9) described by Hope-Taylor (1977, 343) as 'in several ways, Yeavering's most remarkable cremation-burial.' After meticulous excavation, Hope-Taylor was able to demonstrate that the inverted urn, with a small hole in its base, was placed in a pit in the ground before the cremation was poured into the pot through the hole. It has recently been suggested that such inverted urns, containing cremations, were intended as symbolic representations for the dead of the roundhouses of the living (Bradley 1998, 151). Whether true or not, this appears to be but one of several different traditions employed within the Yeavering cemetery. Despite its relative anonymity in comparison to Neolithic, Iron Age and early medieval Yeavering, this cemetery is actually a very important site in its own right, and is certainly a key element of the Yeavering story.

Two hundred metres east of the Western Ring-ditch, Hope-Taylor excavated his 'Eastern Ring-ditch', which he interpreted, not unreasonably, as a round barrow, although no burial survived within it. There is very little that we can say with any degree of certainty about this structure, other than that it seems to have played a key role in subsequent developments.

We now move forward through time to the seventh century AD, to consider the influence that Bronze Age monuments may have had on early medieval burial and ceremonial activity at the 'palace' site of *Ad Gefrin*. The *Beowulf* poem as we know it may well be of rather later date than *Ad Gefrin*, but similar stories must surely have been told here. The key point to this discussion is the importance which the *Beowulf* poet clearly applies to ancient monuments such as Bronze Age burial mounds: the dragon slaid by Beowulf, after dealing the hero a mortal wound, guarded its treasure within 'the steep vaults of a stone-roofed barrow where he guarded a hoard'. The theatre for Beowulf's last great battle was an ancient burial mound, and his foe was a dragon that guarded a hoard of ancient treasure.

We noted above the presence of the Western Ring-ditch, of presumed early Bronze Age date: this became a focus for ritual activity in the Anglian period. A number of posts were erected towards the centre of the ring-ditch, and inhumation burials seem initially to have been aligned with these (*40*). At some stage, a timber fence, square in plan, was erected around the site, forming a structure which Hope-Taylor refers to as a mortuary enclosure or shrine. Although its exact dating remains uncertain, this structure was clearly an important and early element of the early medieval complex. It, in turn, provided a focus for *Ad Gefrin*'s 'western cemetery' and associated buildings including what Hope-Taylor believes to have been a heathen temple, later adapted for Christian worship. The fact that early medieval burials and this temple were carefully located by reference to the ancient ring-ditch surely demonstrates beyond reasonable doubt that people in the fifth or sixth century must have regarded the old ring-ditch as of very great importance. Thus, the Western Ring-ditch seems to have provided the focus for ceremonial activity during *Ad Gefrin*'s earlier phases, perhaps even through until after the initial introduction of Christianity. Only much later in the sequence, apparently after the death of Edwin and a temporary reversion to pagan ways, were burials focused towards the opposite end of the complex. These later burials seem also to have owed their location to the presence of an already ancient feature: Hope-Taylor's Eastern Ring-ditch.

The Eastern Ring-ditch was taken into the bounds of the Great Enclosure, which according to Hope-Taylor was probably constructed 'within the period AD 300-500'. A large post was apparently erected at the centre of this barrow at about the same time. When *Ad Gefrin*'s first great hall was constructed, probably in about AD 600, it seems to have been carefully aligned upon the post standing within this ancient burial mound. Hope-Taylor presents a persuasive argument for the careful alignment of *Ad Gefrin*'s buildings upon early Bronze Age structures (*colour plate 10*). The extent to which early medieval architects may have concerned themselves with all of this detail must remain open to some doubt, but the presence of these Bronze Age structures was clearly of major significance to the location and design of the *Ad Gefrin* complex. Late in the sequence at *Ad Gefrin*, after the Great Enclosure had been destroyed by fire, a building interpreted by Hope-Taylor as a Christian church within a fenced graveyard was constructed. The northern fence of this graveyard seems to have incorporated the post standing within the Eastern Ring-ditch.

Hope-Taylor (1977, 249) notes that 'there is here the possibly startling suggestion of an immensely long continuity in local 'ritual' observance – of a thread running unbroken (if at times weakened) from the Bronze Age to the Anglo-Saxon Age.' As has already been discussed, such 'continuity' may or may not have been strictly speaking 'continuous', but there can be no doubt that Yeavering was deemed to be of special importance during Anglian times, and that this importance was rooted to a large degree in the importance it had enjoyed during early Bronze Age times, perhaps two and a half millennia earlier.

Christopher Scull has suggested that the earliest inhumations in the ring-ditch cemetery may relate to an early (mid-sixth century) Anglian village on the site, and that the adjacent 'temple' and its cemetery replaced this as *Ad Gefrin* grew in importance. Whether true or not, the sequence here is in marked contrast to that at the Eastern Ring-ditch, which was not apparently reused as a focus for burial until much later in the life of *Ad Gefrin*, but which seems to have played a significant role in the location of the Great Enclosure, the great hall, and eventually the church. It would appear that ancient monuments were being selectively used in different ways throughout later prehistory and into post-Roman times at Yeavering. In short, whatever the detail, there can be no doubt that the legacy of Bronze Age people had considerable influence over the activities of people at Yeavering during Anglian times: 'the past in the past' is undeniably a key concept when seeking to account for the development of *Ad Gefrin*.

It would be interesting to analyse the burial record, and in particular the changing early medieval attitude to prehistoric monuments at Yeavering, in the light of Sarah Semple's (1998, 118) observation that the prehistoric burial mound may 'have been perceived in the early Anglo-Saxon period as the home of spirits, ancestors or gods and was a focus of pagan spiritual activity', while the specific *fear* of barrows (encapsulated within texts such as *Beowulf*) may have developed only following the adoption of Christianity. However, regardless of our ability to recognise trends and isolate specific events in the record, it can surely be stated with some certainty that the site of *Ad Gefrin*, largely as a result of its own history, acted as a powerful magnet for burials and ritual activity over an immensely long period of time. This makes it all the more puzzling that it should have been so completely abandoned by the Christian Church – a quandary to which we will return.

Stephen Driscoll (1998 and this volume) has examined the development of royal centres in early medieval Scotland and Ireland, noting that the location of many such centres exploited already ancient monuments for political advantage and suggesting that 'Northumbria, the northernmost Anglo-Saxon kingdom appears to follow the Celtic pattern' (Driscoll 1998, 143). The ancient monuments 'with their associated lore can be seen as the building blocks of the royal centres, analogous to the fragments of myth and legend which were drawn upon in the contemporary construction of the Celtic literary corpus' (Driscoll 1998, 144). Driscoll goes on to suggest that the value of ancient monuments at this time was linked to a large extent to the development of a linear concept of time, adopted along with literacy and Christianity rather later here than had been the case in those areas of Britain that had been firmly within the bounds of the Roman Empire. This is an interesting idea, but the situation is somewhat complicated at *Ad Gefrin* by the numerous pagan burials and the apparent Germanic influence which owe nothing to either literacy or Christianity. We should also bear in mind that the appropriation of ancient monuments apparently had a considerable history at Yeavering long before the invention of Christianity, as it did at many of the Irish and Scottish sites cited by Driscoll. The initial advent of Christianity may not have been very different from the dawn of many other 'new ages' that must have been witnessed by the ancient monuments here over the centuries, but, as will soon be suggested, the eventual acceptance of Christianity may have played a key role in the abandonment of *Ad Gefrin*.

Throughout England, early medieval burials were added to all sorts of ancient monuments, ranging from Neolithic henges to Roman bathhouses (Williams 1998), so on the face of it the reuse of Bronze Age burial sites at *Ad Gefrin* need not be regarded as anything particularly special. However, the burial sequence here is unique, and is certainly worthy of further study. In his discussion of the Scottish evidence, Stephen Driscoll believes that the use of prehistoric sites for early medieval burials 'can be seen as an attempt to establish a physical relationship between recently dead kin and an ancestral past, thereby establishing a claim of descent' (1998, 155). This is a sound argument which undoubtedly holds true at a number of sites, but at *Ad Gefrin* we do not have a single demonstrably 'Anglian' burial that might have been seeking to claim ownership in this way. Rather, what we appear to have is a sequence of largely undated 'native' burials with no need to 'invent' such links with the local past. Driscoll further observes that 'In situating royal activities at these sites a sense of political ownership and historical legitimacy was claimed, which sought to develop exclusive access to positions of authority and secure popular support' (1998, 155). This, I have no doubt, was a fundamental issue behind the location of *Ad Gefrin*, although the question of the extent to which any new authority was imposed from afar over the surrounding natives remains open to debate. Perhaps the key issue here relates to the desire of people to align themselves with those in power: if the Yeavering cemetery was a prestigious site associated with the aristocracy, whether in Bronze Age or early medieval times, then this is where most people would hope to end up, whether out of allegiance primarily to the aristocracy or to society in general. Clearly, much interpretive work remains to be done with regard to the Yeavering cemeteries, and the dead laid to rest therein may yet have much to tell us.

Finally in this section, I would like to consider a potentially crucial role which Christiantity may have played in the story of Yeavering. When Paulinus invited local people to join the new faith, they may well have opted to do so primarily out of expediency, rather than out of any great loyalty to, or fear of, the new god. In Hope-Taylor's account, the earliest recognisably Christian structure at *Ad Gefrin* is the remodelled 'heathen temple', clearly rooted in the pagan past, where elements of pagan practice may have become superficially Christianised. It then seems that a reversion to the paganism occurred after Edwin's death, before Christianity took a more permanent grip of society under Oswald. However, it would appear that even Oswald's church at Yeavering had to be grounded in the pagan past, its location apparently having been influenced by the ancient Eastern Ring-ditch. It certainly seems as though Christianity, in its earliest phases, relied upon the appropriation of already ancient but apparently still very significant monuments, which, in turn, must have owed their location, at least in part, to the towering presence of the adjacent Bell.

After the second great fire, *Ad Gefrin* was rebuilt in a far less grand form, but still with a church. From this point, 'the township's vigour and importance dwindle, and at last it is left to die on its feet' (Hope-Taylor 1977, 169). Bede tells us that the functions of *Ad Gefrin* were transferred to *Maelmin*, but this would surely not have been possible in former times when the power was invested in the very place where the ancestors had lived and were buried. Perhaps it was the introduction of Christianity, which at first sought to gain authority over established pagan sacred places, which eventually brought about the circumstances under which it became possible for *Ad Gefrin* to be abandoned. Churches for Christian worship, focused on a god 'up there', could be built anywhere, and powerful places such as Yeavering, rooted in the pagan past, could be abandoned and forgotten. Kings now ruled as God's representatives on earth, rather than as individuals reliant upon ancestors for the legitimisation of their authority. There was no longer a need for Yeavering.

FOR THE HOLDING OF GREAT ASSEMBLIES? TOWARDS AN ALTERNATIVE INTERPRETATION OF THE YEAVERING BELL HILLFORT

Yeavering Bell is by far the largest hillfort in the Northumberland Cheviots (*colour plates 4 & 5*), and clearly played a different role to the dozens of smaller forts which litter the hills on both sides of the Anglo-Scottish border. Attention has recently been focused on the Yeavering Bell fort through the Northumberland National

Park Authority's three-year, £1 million *Discovering our Hillfort Heritage* project (Frodsham 1999b). This Heritage Lottery Fund and European Union funded initiative completed much research, survey, conservation and interpretation work relating to hillforts and prehistoric landscapes throughout the Cheviots. The recent RCHME survey by Keith Blood and Trevor Pearson (Pearson 1998; chapter 4, this volume) was undertaken as part of the *Discovering our Hillfort Heritage* project.

Yeavering Bell rises dramatically from Glendale, forming a dramatic link between the low-lying Milfield Plain and the rugged uplands of the Cheviots. As has already been noted, it must have been of some significance to people in the area long before the hillfort ramparts were constructed (see also chapter 3). If we accept the case for the communal, and presumably sacred, importance of the Bell, we cannot help but wonder about the circumstances which led to the construction of the hillfort ramparts around its summit. Ramparts which, incidentally, were originally built of bright pink andesite, quarried from within the hill itself.

The recent RCHME survey (*35*), showing for the first time the relative location, size, form and orientation of 125 visible hut platforms on the site, provides an opportunity for endless speculation into the origin, use, and eventual abandonment, of the fort. It is quite possible that the fort was occupied seasonally by people who spent the winter months in less exposed locations. It may even be that the fort was only fully occupied at specific times when the local population gathered together for seasonal ceremonies. Such an interpretation would see the hillfort very much as a communal ceremonial monument rather than simply as a functional, defensive settlement. Regardless of its exact function, there must be a substantial amount of symbolism built into its structure, both in relation to its form and in terms of its landscape setting (e.g. the dramatic form of Hedgehope Hill to the south of the fort's main entrance, and the contrast in views from the fort over the flat, fertile Milfield Plain to the north and into the dramatic heart of the Cheviot Hills to the south). Hopefully, it will soon be possible to combine such speculation with further excavation within the fort, enabling us to establish its chronology and gain more detail about its occupants. Basic issues, such as variations between houses and the extent to which individual structures were maintained or rebuilt, cannot be adequately addressed without such a campaign of excavation (which could perhaps begin with the re-excavation and detailed recording of the trenches dug by Tate and Hope-Taylor).

The artist's reconstruction of Yeavering Bell (*10*) is based on the RCHME survey. It does not include the large ditched enclosure around the Bell's eastern summit, as the survey concluded that this is later than the hut platforms which surround it, and therefore by implication was not present during the phase represented by the reconstruction. In the past this had been interpreted as a pre-

10 Reconstruction of the Yeavering Bell hillfort based on the 1998 RCHME survey. © Eric Dale

fort palisade, something it clearly is not. It may belong in a Dark Age context, perhaps linked in some way with the palace site which it overlooks. Brian Hope-Taylor briefly discussed his investigation of this feature in a letter to the writer dated October 1999 (see Appendix). In this he states that:

> within the palisade, small interstitial patches of reddened clay (flecked with charcoal) appeared possibly to be survivals from a more extensive deposit....I suspected, on insufficient evidence, the possibility of a very large hearth – or even a beacon site – at the centre of the palisade enclosure, and certainly regarded the palisade-enclosure as a very late (if not final) feature of the Bell's structural history.

A century earlier George Tate (1863, 436) had discovered charred wood here, and noted that stones in the area had been reduced to a 'calx' by fire. Almost another century earlier, William Hutchinson (1778, 247) 'after removing the turf and soil for a little depth...found the stones reduced to a sort of calx, and everywhere retained a strong impression of fire'. Tate noted that it was here, 'according to popular fancies, that Druidical rites were performed', and suggested that the clear evidence for fire was the result of cremation rituals. On balance, Hope-Taylor's suggestion that the enclosure, on the highest part of the Bell, was used as a beacon at some unknown point in its history is perhaps the more likely: it is tempting to speculate that this might have been during the lifetime of *Ad Gefrin*, but this cannot be resolved without further fieldwork.

Figure 10 shows the outer enclosures to the east and west of the fort as robbed out ruins, something that might seem odd to anyone familiar with the conventional view that these were cattle enclosures of crucial importance to the functioning of the fort. In fact, casual observation in advance of the RCHME survey suggested that these ramparts belonged to an earlier phase of activity on the hill, and that the fort had been remodelled at some point: a suggestion reinforced by the survey (RCHME 1998, 26). Unfortunately, the dating of this remodelling remains open to conjecture, as indeed does the dating of the entire fort sequence. Recent work in Scotland (Rideout, Owen and Halpin, 1992) suggests that a defended settlement was already present on Eildon Hill North (which, as *colour plate 6* demonstrates, is visible from Yeavering Bell) by the late Bronze Age, and that the site may have been abandoned during much of the Iron Age before being reoccupied in Roman times. A similar pattern of occupation and abandonment has been suggested for Traprain Law and may also apply at Hownam Law, a massively impressive site with some 200 house platforms contained within a single rampart, just 15km south-west of Yeavering. The large enclosures on Yeavering Bell, Traprain Law, Eildon North and Hownam Law all occupy the summits of particularly striking hills that may well have been of great spiritual significance long before anyone thought of constructing ramparts around their summits. Further afield, the same observation can be applied to other large enclosures such as Carrock Fell (Cumbria), Ingleborough (Yorkshire) and Mam Tor (Derbyshire), all of which may prove to have origins back in the Bronze Age. Clearly, the use of the blanket term 'hillfort' masks great variety in size and probable function amongst this class of monument. Most so-called hillforts probably did function primarily as settlements during the later Iron Age, but it does seem that some of our large forts, such as Yeavering, may differ from the majority in terms of function, form and chronology.

A further issue relating to the hillfort is that of the possible relationship between its occupants and the Roman military. Although we claim to know much about the Roman occupation, we remain unable to discuss in any detail the impact of Rome throughout the Cheviots. Hope-Taylor observes that during Roman times 'there is no reason to suppose that the old stronghold still served as a major, defensible centre' (1977, 9) and also suggests that the fort's 'presently exceptionally ruinous condition might be witness to Roman slighting late in the first century' (1977, 267). However, we have no basis on which to attempt to draw links between Yeavering and the Romans, and do not even know whether the fort was occupied on the occasions that Roman troops pushed northwards into Scotland. Any occupation of the fort during Roman times may well have been subject to the

11 Aerial view of Brian Hope-Taylor's excavations in progress within the hillfort, taken by J.K.S. St Joseph on 16 July 1958. *Cambridge University Collection: Crown copyright*

approval of the Roman authorities, and an effective working relationship between Rome and the native aristocracy would, of course, have been of mutual value to both. Clearly, the hillfort could have served a defensive purpose if required, but its form may have owed more to the perceived prestige of its occupants (or at least some of them) than to the need to provide a defensive barrier for its resident population, or that of the surrounding area, to hide behind.

The abandonment of the hillfort is another issue demanding further attention. Hope-Taylor's investigations within the fort (*11, 34*) recovered 'some scraps of samian ware and two late-Roman coins' which he interprets as evidence of 'no more than desultory, small-scale use or occupation of its interior during the second, third and fourth centuries' (Hope-Taylor 1977, 267). Whether or not these finds represent any form of permanent settlement cannot be known for sure, but it is significant that activity of some kind was occurring within the fort during the Roman period, and future investigations may demonstrate that this was on a greater scale than is suggested by excavations to date. Regardless of what went on here during Roman times, it is hard to argue with Hope-Taylor's contention (1977, 267) that 'during or soon after the Roman Iron Age, some part of the function earlier associated with the oppidum had been transferred to the lowland site which emerges historically in the seventh century bearing its name.' The nature of this transfer, and the possible roles played at the time by Tate's 'fortified dwellings' and the *Ad Gefrin* Great Enclosure (see below), are key issues yet to be resolved in the story of Yeavering.

The extensive use of timber for the construction and maintenance of so many houses within the fort, as well as for fuel and other uses, suggests that abundant mature woodland was available in the vicinity of Yeavering throughout the fort's occupation. Several centuries later, further vast quantities of mature timber were available for the construction (and when necessary the rebuilding) of the Anglian palace complex. The construction of both the fort and the palace complex must have had major impacts on the local landscape, and the past exploitation and management of woodland within this landscape could make a fascinating fieldwork project for a palaeobotanist. Clearly, as with everything else at Yeavering, the hillfort should not be studied in either spatial or chronological isolation.

Whatever the hillfort's exact functions (which may well have changed through time), the monument was constructed at great expense on top of what was apparently already a 'sacred mountain'. It served to reinforce and possibly augment the long-established social significance of the place – significance which would eventually give rise to *Ad Gefrin*. I do not believe that the Yeavering Bell hillfort was built simply as a defensive 'fort', but as a great communal monument that could, admittedly, serve a defensive purpose if required but which functioned primarily as a regular ceremonial gathering place for communities dispersed throughout the surrounding area. Such an interpretation of the fort has potential implications regarding the function of *Ad Gefrin*. Hope-Taylor (1977, 169) sees *Ad Gefrin* as a place:

> for the holding of great assemblies [based on] the largest and oldest of Yeavering's wooden structures: the Great Enclosure, which was the primary nucleus around which the township grew. In the beginning the enclosure stood alone for a long period, and the likelihood of its having originally been brought into existence to safeguard communal gatherings and musterings of herds, rather than as a military post, is greatly increased by the pattern of later events.

Perhaps *Ad Gefrin*'s 'ancient institutional function' actually reflected very closely that of the old hillfort, where seasonal gatherings may have been taking place for some 1500 years prior to the construction of the Great Enclosure. It is even possible that such gatherings were taking place on the Bell at still earlier times. Tate (1863, 438) recovered 'a round jasper ball, artificially rounded, 3 inches in circumference and resembling a large marble' from his excavation of a house platform near the centre of the hillfort. This may be a small example of a Neolithic stone ball, suggestive of some sort of ceremonial activity on top of the Bell perhaps as long ago as 3000 BC, although it is also possible that the object could have been found elsewhere and brought to the hillfort during the Iron Age. The presence of what would appear from Tate's account to be flint debitage (waste flakes indicative of on-site flint knapping) further suggests Neolithic or early Bronze Age activity on the Bell. Perhaps seasonal gatherings were already taking place here way back into the Stone Age, providing a long-established context for the origins of both the hillfort and *Ad Gefrin*.

A PAST DISPLACED?
BURIAL AND RITUAL IN THE IRON AGE LANDSCAPE

Several so-called 'Romano-British' settlements and field systems are scattered around the flanks of Yeavering Bell (*4, 12, 13; colour plate 7*). As already noted, their chronology is poorly understood, but they must date in general from Iron Age/Roman times, from which we have little evidence of funerary or ceremonial monuments. Some cremations may have been added to the Bronze Age cemetery around the Western Ring-ditch, but it seems likely that most bodies were disposed of in some way that leaves no archaeological trace, perhaps cremated and scattered in sacred places. Can we identify any such places at Yeavering? One candidate could be the River Glen, the ancient name of which can be translated as the 'clean', 'beautiful' or 'holy' river (Ekwall 1977). There are also other possibilities around Yeavering that are well known to the archaeologist but rarely considered in discussions of Iron Age or Roman-British 'ritual'. The great hillfort itself is perhaps the most obvious example. The Bell, crowned by its probably already ancient hillfort ramparts, would have towered above those working in the surrounding fields during late Iron Age and Roman times. Elsewhere in this volume, Oswald and Pearson make the intriguing observation that the Roman coins from Hope-Taylor's excavations within the hillfort are precisely the kind of thing one might expect to find on a 'sacred site', deposited here as ritual offerings to the gods. It is certainly not impossible that the dead were cremated and their ashes scattered to the wind from the top of the old sacred mountain.

Left: 12 Aerial view of late prehistoric settlements and field systems south-east of Yeavering Bell. © *Tim Gates*

Below: 13 The 1986 RCHME survey, based largely on air photography. Some of the remains of settlements and field systems shown here date back to the Bronze Age, but most are of Iron Age/Roman date. © *Crown copyright – reproduced by permission of English Heritage*

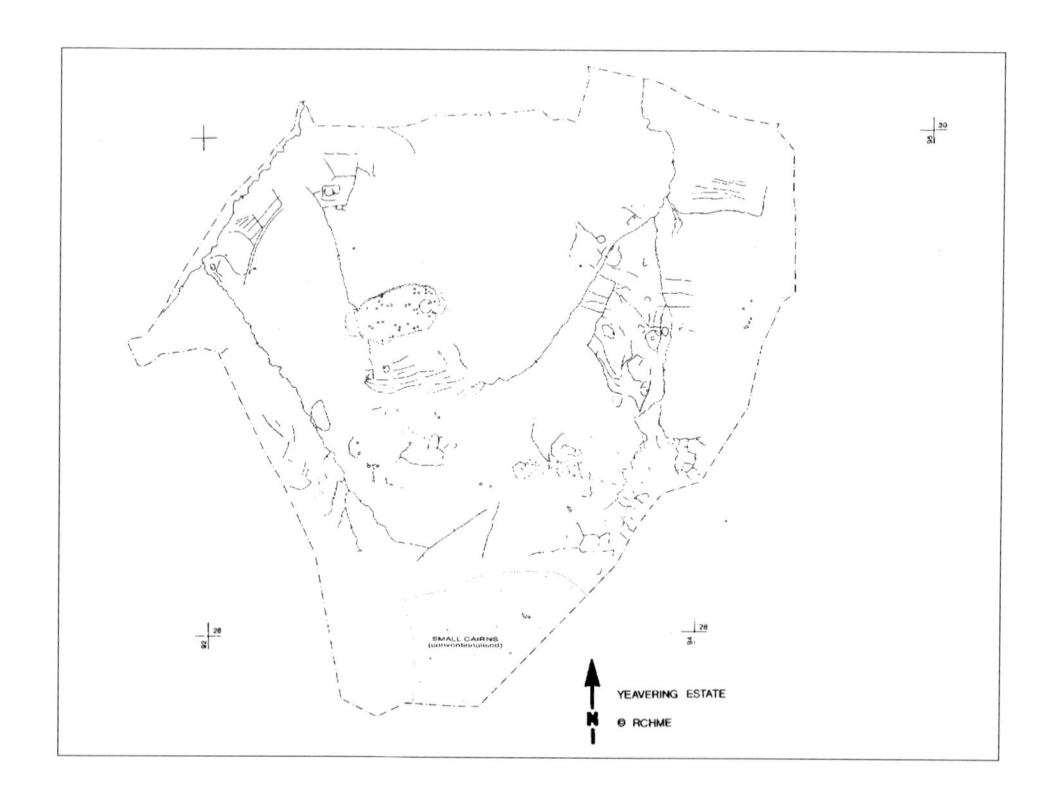

A further intriguing suggestion regarding the disposal of the dead in later prehistory comes from Tate's excavations of burial cairns at Yeavering. He excavated several such cairns, but failed to find the characteristic early Bronze Age pottery normally found in such monuments. At the Worm Law barrow, he notes that 'immediately above the Cist and among the covering earth and stones, flints, potsherds, iron slag, and fragments of bone were discovered…. The pottery is of the same coarse thick kind as was found on the summit of the Bell' (Tate 1863, 444). Could it be that Iron Age people were still using the old cairns as foci for ritual activity, possibly associated with funeral ceremonies? Some of the cairns recorded by Tate, such as those on Swint Law (4) lie very close to settlement sites of Iron Age/Roman date, and these may have retained great significance throughout the life of the settlements even if they no longer functioned as actual burial sites. It would be interesting to undertake some detailed fieldwork to investigate the possible relationships between cairns and field systems surrounding Yeavering Bell. It may be that the fields and settlements were carefully laid out around older cairns, with the cairns being deliberately retained rather than dismantled as convenient quarries for building stone. Alternatively, although work elsewhere might suggest it unlikely, we cannot deny the possibility that some of the cairns Tate investigated were actually of Iron Age rather than Bronze Age origin, perhaps representing a continuation of burial practice stretching back many centuries into the local past.

We must also consider the possibility that the fields in later prehistory functioned as communal ritual monuments in their own right, in addition to their practical use for the production of food. Perhaps the agricultural calendar provided a metaphor for human reproduction, with seeds being sown in order to produce plants which in turn provided further seeds which could be stored for sowing the following season. There is certainly much evidence from many societies, widely dispersed in time and space, for links between 'practical' agricultural activity and 'ritual' or religious ceremonies (Bradley 2005) and there is every reason to believe that this would have been the case at Yeavering during later prehistoric times. After all, the fields were effectively the constructs of the ancestors, and had to be maintained and passed on to future generations. Perhaps cremations were deposited within them in ceremonies linking human death and possible rebirth (either on earth or elsewhere) to the ongoing agricultural cycle. If so, then the archaeologist searching for contemporary burial monuments will continue to fail in his quest. Perhaps, one day, we might find burials in field walls to support this suggestion, but whatever the processes by which the Iron Age dead were disposed of at Yeavering, they appear (assuming that the whaleback cemetery and local burial cairns were not in continuous use) to represent a major break with earlier tradition.

John Barrett has argued for just such a break with long established tradition at about this time. While stressing that monuments of earlier periods (e.g. Bronze Age burial mounds) must have still retained considerable significance in the Iron Age, he believes that for Iron Age people 'the mythical past stood apart from the present' (Barrett 1999, 262). He contrasts the 'sacred' landscapes of the Neolithic in which 'social practices reworked ... the presence of a general order which was one of creation and origins but remained vital and ever present' with an Iron Age in which 'the past was displaced ... linked to the present by a trajectory of legitimate inheritance' which grew out of the tradition of single burial practised throughout much of the Bronze Age (Barrett 1999, 263). The Iron Age landscape at Yeavering must surely have incorporated references to older structures and stories, but further speculation is perhaps best avoided until we are able to better establish the chronology of a sample of cairns, fields and settlements within the landscape.

A HAUNTING PRESENCE IN THE MIND.
AD GEFRIN AND *BEOWULF*

The origins of *Ad Gefrin* are far from clear. Brian Hope-Taylor favours the development of a native British settlement of rectangular timber structures, in association with the Great Enclosure, prior to the development of the Anglian palace complex in the later sixth century. In contrast, Roger Miket (1980, 301) argues that 'before Yeavering became a royal centre, it consisted of a settlement of rectangular timber buildings. That they stemmed from good Anglo-Saxon traditions cannot be denied on chronological grounds and it has yet to be convincingly demonstrated that rectangular forms were part of the Northern British native repertoire.' More recently, Christopher Scull, drawing on evidence of excavations elsewhere that was unavailable to Hope-Taylor, agrees with Miket in suggesting that the earliest rectangular buildings are probably those of a modest Anglian agricultural settlement of the mid-sixth century 'which was transformed in the later sixth century by the establishment of the site as a major centre' (Scull 1991, 60). More work is needed to clarify the nature of activity at Yeavering during the fourth, fifth and sixth centuries, but things certainly seem to have changed dramatically during this period. As we have already discussed, coins and pottery from Hope-Taylor's excavations suggest that the old hillfort may still have been occupied in some way during the early fourth century, but by the late sixth century the focus seems to have moved downhill to *Ad Gefrin*.

To what extent was this change imposed by incoming Anglian aristocracy? The evidence would suggest that if it was imposed, then it met with little resistance. Hope-Taylor (1977, 282) notes that the native British:

were so trustworthy that from the start the alien power could set up its halls on open ground in their midst, and were fundamentally contributive to the development of a hybridising culture....The local picture, at this point of the Central Zone of Bernicia, is of a harmonious relationship between the native population and a minute, governing Anglo-Saxon elite, itself susceptible and responsive to formative influences from its British environment. All the evidences would be consistent with the proposition that what is at issue was an English overlordship which, from a very early stage, had been found mutually convenient and congenial.

Thus, Yeavering retained its long-established special status, to which *Ad Gefrin* would further contribute.

It is impossible to consider *Ad Gefrin* without conjuring up some of the graphic yet haunting imagery presented to us in the epic story of *Beowulf*. This was apparently composed in England, perhaps as long ago as the mid-seventh century, although many experts favour a rather later origin in the eighth or ninth century. Seamus Heaney, in a brilliant new translation (Heaney 1999, xii), notes that *Beowulf* 'possesses a mythic potency ... it arrives from somewhere beyond the known bourne of our experience, and having fulfilled its purpose ... it passes once more into the beyond'. He further observes that the 'opening and closing scenes retain a haunting presence in the mind; they are set pieces but they have the life-marking power of certain dreams'. Although *Beowulf* is clearly set in Scandinavia, John Marsden (1992, 209) makes a fascinating comparison between the landscape around *Ad Gefrin* and the 'uncharted territory – wolf-infested hillsides, windy crags and the perilous waterways' surrounding *Heorot*. Marsden notes that 'The lines describing the dark uplands patrolled by Grendel and his mother would correspond to the landscape suggested by the Cheviot range ... to the Old English imagination', and that 'The mead-hall of Heorot lying below the monster-haunted fells must have stood on fields alike to those where once the timber halls of *Ad Gefrin* stood below the former hillfort of the Britons on Yeavering Bell'. In a similar spirit, Hope-Taylor (1977, 373) writes that Hall A4 (which he ascribes to Edwin) 'marks Yeavering's closest approach to a Heorot', and asks 'Did its door-keeper, buried in Grave AX, ward off a Cheviot Grendel?' We will never know whether the story of Beowulf was ever actually told at Yeavering, but similar tales must have been recited here, perhaps recalling great deeds of local warriors on the 'monster-haunted fells' of the Cheviots.

We must be cautious when using scenes from *Beowulf* to interpret the archaeology of Yeavering, but, as Rosemary Cramp (1957, 71) notes in relation to the Yeavering great halls: 'these magnificent buildings, the grandest in the Germanic world before the Viking Age, are worthy to be set beside descriptions of *Heorot* in *Beowulf*? It is not, therefore, unreasonable to seek to breathe life into the excavation plans and conjectural reconstructions of *Ad Gefrin's* most elaborate great hall, apparently constructed during Edwin's reign, by citing the descriptions of activities at *Heorot* offered to us by the *Beowulf* poet:

> ... and we took our places at the banquet table.
> There was singing and excitement: an old reciter,
> a carrier of stories, recalled the early days.
> At times some hero made the timbered harp
> tremble with sweetness, or related true
> and tragic happenings; at times the king
> gave the proper turn to some fantastic tale,
> or a battle-scarred veteran, bowed with age,
> would begin to remember the martial deeds
> of his youth and prime and be overcome
> as the past welled up in his wintry heart.
> (Heaney 1999, 67).

This is not the place to attempt a detailed discussion of the palace complex (*colour plates 8 & 9*), elements of which are considered in some detail in Part III of this volume. However, a few basic points are central to the question of 'the past in the past' at Yeavering. *Ad Gefrin* was constructed at a place which had been a focus for ceremonial activity for thousands of years, although the extent to which this activity may have actually been continuous throughout this period remains unresolved. The palace complex was clearly designed to accommodate elements of the earlier landscape, notably two early Bronze Age burial monuments and possibly (depending on its date) the Great Enclosure. In addition, it is sited literally in the shadow of the Bell with its great hillfort, meaning that the sun hardly shines on the site at all during midwinter (*colour plate 11*). Clearly, the site was located here for reasons which made the lack of light and warmth from the sun during the winter months a relative irrelevance. Was the history in the landscape already of greater significance than practicalities such as the desire for sunlight?

The Great Enclosure, presumably a stock enclosure of considerable functional and ceremonial significance, was considered by Hope-Taylor (1977, 280) as perhaps 'the true key to understanding of the regard anciently shown for this obscure place in the northern Cheviot foothills'. Hope-Taylor regards it as the 'vital link between the "sub-Romano-British" and "Anglo-Saxon" chapters of Yeavering's history', noting that in all its early forms it is 'completely in harmony with the palisade works that are accepted as one of the characteristic features of the pre-Roman, native world' (1977, 268). He suggests that its initial construction occurred during the fourth or fifth century, but that 'the possibility of a still earlier origin is not by any means to be dismissed' (1977, 268). Scull's suggested chronology for Phase I at *Ad Gefrin* does not help to resolve this issue, as 'the structural phases of the Great Enclosure would be free to float independently' (Scull 1991, 58). Leslie Alcock (2003, chapter 15) considers the Great Enclosure to be 'certainly an Anglian development', although he notes that the Angles may have 'derived the structural concept initially from palisades erected by the Britons during the Roman and early post-Roman centuries.' Whatever its origins, the Great Enclosure was continually maintained and modified until Edwin's reign, when it was 'brought to the highest point of dignity and aggrandisement it had ever known' (Hope-Taylor 1977, 280). Clearly, this structure, much of which still survives unexcavated on the site (*23; colour plate 12*), offers vast potential for the refinement of *Ad Gefrin*'s chronology and must feature prominently in any future fieldwork campaign, as indeed must the rarely discussed and, as yet, wholly uninvestigated palisaded enclosure adjacent to the Yeavering henge (discussed by Tim Gates in chapter 2), which may relate to the Great Enclosure both in form and function.

The Great Enclosure's prime function is usually thought to have been as a kraal for cattle brought to the site at particular times of the year, perhaps as some form of taxation to be consumed during the feasting, which no doubt continued throughout each of the king's visits. This suggestion is lent support by David Hinton's (1990, 9) observation that 'the high proportion of young calf bones suggest a profligate disregard for the need to maintain breeding herds' at *Ad Gefrin*. However, it is perhaps equally likely that the Great Enclosure's main purpose related to horses. This is suggested by the discovery of 'enormous quantities of horse-bones' (apparently complete skeletons) found below the enclosure's main entrance during the construction of the adjacent railway in 1885-86 (Hope-Taylor 1977, 13-14). Why should the remains of so many (admittedly undated) horses have been found here? Perhaps Alcock's (1981, 180) suggestion that 'the Bernician Angles inherited from the Britons a major military technique: the use of cavalry' offers an explanation. If horses were used in this way by the Votadini, and subsequently by the Bernicians, then the breeding and training of horses would have been a major, long-term undertaking, presumably incorporating ancient practical and ceremonial traditions, that may have continued largely unaltered throughout later prehistory through into the seventh century. Could not the Great Enclosure be associated with this activity in some way, thus accounting for its origin and subsequent maintenance over such a long period of time?

According to Hope-Taylor's chronology, the Great Enclosure was abandoned after the sacking of *Ad Gefrin* by Penda and Cadwaller in 632-33, but exactly why such a long-established structure was no longer required, and its site partly occupied by a Christian church and cemetery, is open to conjecture. What must be beyond question, however, is that removal of the Great Enclosure must signal a major change in some of *Ad Gefrin*'s functions at this time.

As already noted, King Edwin's great hall at *Ad Gefrin* surely bore comparison with *Heorot*, 'the greatest of hall buildings ... magnificent and agleam with gold' as described by the *Beowulf* poet, and the references to ancient burial mounds within this great epic and other sources provide further evidence of the continuing importance of ancient monuments to the people of the time. This importance of the past is dramatically illustrated by the remains at Yeavering, and it was to this supremely important site, already steeped in history, that Paulinus came, probably in 627, to preach the Christian message and baptise the pagan natives (many of whom may still have resided in the so-called 'Romano-British' villages of roundhouses which litter the adjacent hills) in the nearby River Glen. Today, nearly 14 centuries later, this event is commemorated on the roadside monument at *Ad Gefrin* (*colour plate 13*) which Brian Hope-Taylor apparently helped to design after his plan to have a Henry Moore sculpture commissioned for the field failed to materialise (Rosemary Cramp, pers comm.).

Following the abandonment of *Ad Gefrin*, some of its religious mystique may eventually have been appropriated by the nearby church and village of Kirknewton, although why a later settlement of some kind did not develop on the actual palace site itself remains something of a mystery. Perhaps practical issues, such as a desire for winter sunlight, were of greater relevance to those planning later settlements than they had been to the founders of *Ad Gefrin*.

UNKNOWN TO HISTORY AND BEYOND MEMORY. THE OLD PALACE

Nestling beneath Yeavering Bell's northern face is a dilapidated old cottage labelled on nineteenth-century Ordnance Survey maps as 'King Edwin's Palace' and still known locally as 'The Old Palace' (*14, colour plate 14*). This is indeed an old building, but rather less old than King Edwin. It may have begun life as a form of defensible house or 'pele' in about 1550 (Ryder 1991), although the nearby earthworks which appear to have formed a dam just upstream suggest that it may at one time have functioned as a mill. It is a fascinating old building for a number of reasons. Tate (1863, 433) notes that it was occupied by a shepherd at the time he was writing, and provides the following accurate description and characteristically astute interpretation:

> The walls are five feet in thickness and built of porphyry blocks, but not in regular courses, and seemingly without lime; squared oak posts pass perpendicularly through the middle of the walls, and they supported the roof and helped too to give stability to

'THE STRONGHOLD OF ITS OWN NATIVE PAST'

14 A view of the 'Old Palace', seen from the below the north face of Yeavering Bell, with two wild goats in the foreground. Photograph: Paul Frodsham

> these walls. Old doorways and windows with square headings are traceable; but besides rudeness of structure, there are no characters to carry back this building to the Saxon period. Possibly it may stand on or near the site of the old palace; it probably belongs to mediaeval times, and may have been a rude pele for the protection of the village against the raids which rendered life and property insecure in the border land.

The 'Old Palace' is primarily of relevance to this chapter by virtue of its name. I quote from Hope-Taylor (1977, 14):

> there can be no hesitation in dismissing its local name, or rather nickname, as the lingering result of a belated and fanciful christening, probably performed by a local 18th or 19th century parson who knew his Bede. Doubtless the name was attached to this particular structure because it was the only building in the area whose origin was unknown to history and beyond memory.

This provides a lovely example of a process that must have been going on at Yeavering for millennia, and one cannot help but wonder exactly when, and under what circumstances, the 'Old Palace' label was first attached to the structure.

A tower is shown at Yeavering on Christopher Dacre's 1584 map of the castles and towers of Northumberland (Long 1967), and it seems probable that the ruins

15 Fergus Storey's gravestone in Kirknewton church. *Photograph: Iain Hedley*

of this were eventually incorporated within the 'Old Palace'. As no such structure is recorded on the 1541 Border Survey, it seems that the Yeavering tower (and therefore the 'Old Palace') must date originally from the mid- to late sixteenth century. Hope-Taylor excavated within the Old Palace in 1955, and recovered seventeenth-century pottery from beneath 3ft of later deposits. It is perhaps interesting to note, in this context, an early seventeenth-century grave slab built into the floor of nearby Kirknewton church (*15*). This slab commemorates 'Fergus Storey of Yevering'. We know from documentary sources that the Storey family was effectively in charge of Yeavering at this time, and that Fergus Storey, an agent of the Duke of Northumberland, was arrested after the gunpowder plot of 1605 before eventually being released without charge (Iain Hedley, pers comm.). Could it be that Fergus Storey actually lived in the Old Palace? Whether he did or not, he would presumably have been familiar with the building, and may have been aware of old tales relating to the history of his neighbourhood.

In the early seventeenth century, William Camden (1637, 815) was apparently in no doubt that Yeavering was the site of Bede's *Ad Gefrin*, though he could not possibly have known its exact location. The tower at Yeavering, although only a few decades old, may already have been in a state of disrepair by the time that Camden was writing. Perhaps it was the ruins of the old tower, coupled with a hazy yet persistent communal memory of Yeavering's great past, that first led to the 'Old Palace' label being applied to this spot, a label which was retained as later structures were built out of the ruins of the old tower over subsequent centuries.

In 1769, in *The Natural History and Antiquities of Northumberland*, John Wallis describes Yeavering as 'a mean village', but tells the story of *Ad Gefrin* (quoting Bede) and describes local archaeological sites including the hillfort, which he ascribes to the Danes, and the Battle Stone, which he believed to have been erected after the Battle of Geteryne (1415). A few years later, William Hutchinson, in his scholarly *A View of Northumberland*, introduces Yeavering as 'now a mean village, and little regarded by travellers, though once a place of royal residence' (Hutchinson 1778, 243). In discussing the hillfort, he notes that 'Mr. Wallis's account of this remarkable place, is loose and unsatisfactory.' Hutchinson was clearly intrigued by Yeavering, and even undertook a small excavation on the summit of the Bell. He provides 15 pages of description and wide-ranging speculation about Yeavering before observing that he has 'dwelt too long on this subject, though an interesting one to those who may hereafter visit these places' (1778, 257). Eneas Mackenzie, in his early nineteenth-century *Historical, Topographical, and Descriptive View of the County of Northumberland*, describes Yeavering as 'a small village…formerly a place of considerable consequence', and notes that the Bell 'undoubtedly deserves the attention of the traveller and the research of the antiquarian (Mackenzie 1825, 375-79). The Old Palace presumably stood, either as an occupied dwelling or as a ruin, throughout the period in which Camden, Wallis, Hutchinson and Mackenzie were writing, but none of them sought to manufacture a direct link between it and *Ad Gefrin*. Indeed, none of them even refers to it, either as an old palace or as anything else. Hutchinson, who clearly spent much time exploring the area, stresses that 'there are not the least remains of any considerable structure here, or any thing to denote that a royal palace once existed on the spot.' (Hutchinson 1778, 244). Exactly how 'the Old Palace' obtained its name must, therefore, remain something of a mystery, like so much else at this 'remarkable place'.

CONCLUSION
REMEMBERING, FORGETTING AND REDISCOVERING *GEFRIN*

> Ritually, as politically, the history of Yeavering is meaningless unless the place survived as the stronghold of its own native past: a horse (or a goat?) that could by persuasion be led to new waters, but could not be forced to drink. (Hope-Taylor 1977, 266)

'The tangible past is in constant flux, altering, ageing, renewing, and always interacting with the present' (Lowenthal 1985, 248). Clearly, this has been the case at Yeavering for thousands of years. Christopher Tilley (2004, 12) tells us that:

> Time is the fourth 'hidden' dimension of being or existence, always part of places, landscapes and things....The body carries time into experience of place and landscape. Any moment of lived experience is thus orientated by and towards the past, a fusion of the two. Past and present fold in upon each other. The past influences the present and the present rearticulates the past.

From this, it follows that archaeological monuments cannot simply be placed into chronological boxes and ignored when studying later periods. This is because they would have retained significance long after the circumstances leading to their initial construction and use had passed; a concept which Richard Bradley (1993, chapter 6) eloquently labels 'the afterlife of monuments'. Without doubt, the significance of particular elements of the landscape will have changed considerably through time, but it would appear that Yeavering as a place retained a peculiar degree of importance, albeit perhaps intermittently, over a vast amount of time. Without doubt, many stories would have become intimately associated with the place, and these would have reinforced its importance. Some of these stories may have been rooted in fact, others may have been largely constructs of the imagination, fuelled by a desire to explain what may have happened at Yeavering in the distant past. Simon Schama (1995, 61) has noted that:

> Landscapes are culture before they are nature; constructs of the imagination projected onto wood, water and rock ... but it should also be acknowledged that once a certain idea of landscape, a myth, a vision, establishes itself in an actual place, it has a peculiar way of muddling categories, of making metaphors more real than their referents; of becoming, in fact, part of the scenery.

At Yeavering, these ideas, regardless of their origin, undoubtedly influenced the future. Indeed, much of what is happening here today (landscape management agreements, interpretive and educational material, this book) is firmly rooted in the distant past.

These links between landscapes, myths and visions can be complex, and indeed can underlie and sustain many aspects of society:

> Embedded in the collective memory of a community and in the individual memories of its members are mythical or cosmological concepts, as well as folk memories of burial grounds, meeting places, valleys, mountains, and more, all situated in a specific temporal and historical context. Such concepts or memories are not simply reflections of landscape, but also often the means of organizing, using, and living in the landscape. (Knapp and Ashmore 1999, 14)

Clearly, future studies of the archaeological landscape at places such as Yeavering have much more potential to inform us about the people who lived in and contributed to the history of the landscape than conventional studies of particular sites or periods.

It is important to bear in mind that many of the themes discussed above are by no means unique to Yeavering. It is becoming increasingly obvious from a large number of regional studies that, once a place has gained a particular degree of significance, that significance is often maintained and enhanced through subsequent developments. Such sequences can be seen on a number of different timescales, and in many cases can traced back to 'natural' places which may have been regarded as of special significance since the earliest times: Yeavering Bell is surely one such place. These 'natural' places 'have an archaeology because they acquired a significance in the *minds* of people in the past' (Bradley 2000, 35), but conventional archaeological techniques alone are inadequate when seeking to understand them. Christopher Tilley (204, 220) notes that:

> Since its inception, modern archaeology has been, above all, about artifice: identifying, classifying and recording cultural work and distinguishing between material culture and those forms and materials which are not a product of human agency....It can easily be claimed that recognizing and recording culture, as opposed to nature, provides the conceptual basis for all field archaeology....What we understand to be natural tends to be ignored precisely because it is not culture and is therefore considered to be relatively unimportant in interpretation...but...in thinking about, describing and interpreting cultural landscapes, we need to spend as much time and effort considering 'natural' form as 'cultural' form....Nature and culture are two sides of a coin which cannot be separated, part of a complex system of signification.

It is extremely doubtful that people in the distant past at Yeavering classified elements of their landscape as 'natural' or 'cultural' in the way that we do today. Rather than worrying about isolating, measuring and classifying every element of Yeavering's archaeological landscape, if we hope to approach an understanding of what it might have been like to have lived here in the past then we need to break down some of the barriers imposed by our modern way of thinking.

No one can hope to appreciate the power of Yeavering, or how this power influenced, and was influenced by, the activities of people in the past, by simply reading a book. In order to approach such an appreciation, one must visit the place and experience the landscape as a whole, ideally on many different occasions under different conditions. After this, the 'hard facts' gained from archaeological survey and excavation can be better understood as part of the Yeavering story.

In this story, the landscape can be thought of as a passive stage on which generations of people have performed, and which in turn records aspects of those performances. But it is far more than that. Indeed, a case can be made for considering the landscape, and specific features of it, 'animistically, in an analogous manner to the way in which we like to think about persons, as entities who can and do make a difference' (Tilley 2004, 31). In discussing the reliability of documentary sources relating to *Ad Gefrin*, Hope-Taylor (1977, 284) observes that 'The soil of Yeavering is in effect a palimpsest document, far more contemporaneous with the events it records than are the writings of Bede and the belated Celtic apologetics on which he had to draw.' To an extent this is true: the past can be 'read' from the archaeological record. But the Yeavering landscape is more than a text or discourse reflecting past social identities. It is also an active agent which helped to create, sustain, reproduce and transform such identities. It continues to function in this way today, as local communities seek to develop policies for sustainable economic and social development based on the 'special qualities' of the landscape. Yeavering Bell cast a powerful spell over people who encountered it thousands of years ago, and that spell is still very much in place today.

It certainly seems to be true that 'Memory stresses continuity in the landscape, often through re-use, reinterpretation or restoration, and reconstruction' (Knapp and Ashmore 1999, 14). Why, then, were so many previously important places abandoned? In many ways this is a more difficult issue to address than why an important place should have retained its significance through time. How could such an important site as *Ad Gefrin* be forgotten? No church, no visible monument of any kind: without Bede there would not even have been a memory.

What can we say about the abandonment and 'forgetting' of *Ad Gefrin* and its complex symbolic landscape? Bede informs us that *Ad Gefrin* was abandoned in favour of *Maelmin*, and Hope-Taylor places the abandonment at no later than AD 685. The site may have been gradually forgotten following its abandonment, perhaps disappearing from collective memory within a few generations. The references held within the wider Yeavering landscape could also have been forgotten through a gradual and passive process. However, there may be an alternative explanation. If the juxtaposition of monuments and burials from different times at Yeavering results from the fact that 'a local elite was making a considered effort to strengthen its position through reference to the past', and that 'the selective reconstruction of important monuments was really equivalent to the composition of prestigious but fictitious genealogies' (Bradley 1987, 10), then could the abandonment and forgetting of the site be equivalent to the wiping of an individual from such a genealogy? There are numerous historical references to the erasing of individuals from genealogies, denying them a place within the society to which they once belonged. Could it be that *Ad Gefrin* was removed from collective memory in a similar way? Perhaps it held bad or inappropriate memories which were better completely forgotten than merely suppressed through the building of new structures at this once prestigious location.

I have suggested that Christianity may have been primarily to blame for the abandonment and forgetting of *Ad Gefrin*. I believe that this suggestion equates with the available archaeological and historical data, but it is far from being proven. An alternative is that the forgetting of sites like Yeavering was simply the norm. Several abandoned early medieval settlements are known in Northumberland, and many more have been recorded throughout the whole of Britain. Richard Muir (1982, 21) has noted that 'through the Dark Ages and Roman periods and deeply into the prehistoric era, we find that the great majority of places which once supported a village or a hamlet are now deserted' . The desertion of Dark Age settlements, according to Muir, was the norm rather than the exception, although 'no obvious explanation for their desertion has been found'.

In discussing individual life experiences, David Lowenthal tells us that 'only forgetting enables us to classify and bring chaos into order.... The most vividly remembered scenes and events are often those which were for a time forgotten' (Lowenthal 1985, 205). Lowenthal quotes Roger Shattruck (interpreting Proust): 'If an image or a sensation out of the past is to be truly recognised ... it must be summoned back ... after a period of absence. The original experience must have been forgotten, completely forgotten.... True memory or recognition surges into being out of its opposite: *oubli.*' Are these thoughts of any relevance to society's forgetting, and subsequent rediscovery, of *Ad Gefrin*? It may well have required an element of forgetting to enable the creation of a special place on a number of different occasions at Yeavering. Was it the mystery of what may have happened here over the centuries that gave the place much of its power, enabling people, whether in the Dark Ages or earlier, to put their own interpretations on what may have gone on before? Interpretations which would have been based partly on long-forgotten but conveniently recalled 'facts', and which would have acted as society's 'memory' of its distant past. Today, we can subject the Yeavering landscape to the vigorous scientific techniques of modern archaeology, yet on a personal level our experiences of the place may not be very different from those of our prehistoric or medieval ancestors. Every new archaeological discovery may lead us to think that we are 'remembering' elements of the forgotten past, but in truth that past will remain largely forgotten.

We must accept that we will never be able to tell anything approaching the full story of Yeavering. However, thirteen centuries after the abandonment of *Ad Gefrin*, we probably possess more 'facts' about it than did the people who lived and died in the region during the eighth century, within a few decades of its abandonment. We also possess 'facts' about the prehistory of the region that

16 The popular Yeavering leaflet, incorporating a self-guided trail, produced by the Northumberland National Park Authority as part of its *Discovering our Hillfort Heritage* initiative

residents of *Ad Gefrin* would have found quite extraordinary, although there is still much to learn. Answers to an infinite number of fascinating questions lie concealed within the Yeavering landscape, but these will only become accessible to us if we are prepared to make the effort to begin asking some of the questions. Nearly 150 years have passed since George Tate completed his commendable early attempt at what we would today term 'landscape archaeology' at Yeavering. He dug within the hillfort and also in a number of surrounding monuments in the attempt to understand the fort within its local landscape context, noting that:

> Too much must not be expected from each digging....Sometimes indeed some object of peculiar significance may turn up; but it is more by the accumulation of facts made known by the extensive and systematic application of the pick-axe and spade, that we can hope to arrive at sound general views respecting the military and domestic arrangements, and the habits and character of pre-historic times. (Tate 1863, 433)

'THE STRONGHOLD OF ITS OWN NATIVE PAST'

Tate's observations regarding the use of pick-axe and spade remain as valid today as they were when he made them, and I feel a sense of duty to him and to Brian Hope-Taylor (as well as to future generations) to continue to progress our understanding of Yeavering through the cautious yet vigorous use of the trowel. Tate's investigations were funded by the Duke of Northumberland, and he had no need to spend time drawing up comprehensive project designs or scheduled monument consent applications. Today, a project with similar objectives would require many months of planning, and obtaining the necessary funds would not be easy. Nevertheless, the time is now right to mount a modern-day fieldwork campaign at Yeavering. Such a project would add still further to the 'specialness' of this most special of places.

As David Lowenthal (1985, 412) eloquently informs us, 'The past remains integral to us all, individually and collectively. We must concede the ancients their place.... But their place is not simply back there, in a separate and foreign country; it is assimilated in ourselves, and resurrected into an ever-changing present'. I believe that Yeavering was a special and powerful place, being continuously resurrected into the 'ever-changing present', from the Stone Age through until to the late seventh century AD. In my view, it took the introduction of Christianity to effectively break the spell of *Gefrin*, bringing its long established special status to an end and eventually enabling its abandonment. Today, as Christianity's stranglehold on society continues to weaken, Yeavering is increasingly becoming regarded as a special place once again, this time as an atmospheric tourist attraction (*16; colour plate 15*). Its growing importance is based upon public appreciation of its stunning landscape setting, together with a hazy awareness of things that happened here, or may have happened here, in the past: precisely the same factors, I would suggest, that ultimately underlay the power of this magnificent place throughout much of the past 10,000 years.

ACKNOWLEDGEMENTS

This chapter, extracts of which were presented to the 2003 Yeavering conference, is a much revised (and hopefully improved) version of a paper originally published in *Northern Archaeology* (Frodsham 1999a). Rewriting the paper for this volume, and cross-referencing it to the other chapters without excessive overlap and repetition, has not been straightforward: I hope, nevertheless, that it provides a stimulating introduction to what follows.

I am grateful to many friends and colleagues for discussions about Yeavering over the years. At the risk of omitting some, these people include: Brian Hope-Taylor, Anthony Hill, Roger Miket, Colm O' Brien, Tim Gates, Al Oswald, Trevor

Pearson, Keith Blood, Clive Waddington, Iain Hedley and Deborah Anderson. I would particularly like to thank Roger Miket, Colm O' Brien and Rob Young for their helpful comments on a draft of this chapter. As ever, responsibility for all errors and excessive flights of interpretive fancy must be mine and mine alone.

1 Aerial photograph of Yeavering, looking south over the site of *Ad Gefrin* towards the hillfort. © *Airfotos Ltd*

2 View of Yeavering Bell's distinctive profile seen from the Milfield Plain to the north. © *Paul Frodsham*

3 The Battle Stone. © *Paul Frodsham*

4 Aerial view of Yeavering Bell hillfort from the south, taken in May 1997. © *Tim Gates*

5 Yeavering Bell from the south, with the hillfort rampart clearly visible. © *Graeme Peacock*

6 Looking westwards from inside the Yeavering Bell hillfort: the Eildon Hills are just visible on the far horizon. © *Paul Frodsham*

7 Earthworks of late prehistoric settlements and fields to the south-east of Yeavering Bell. The hillfort rampart can be seen encircling the top of the Bell. © *Albert Weir*

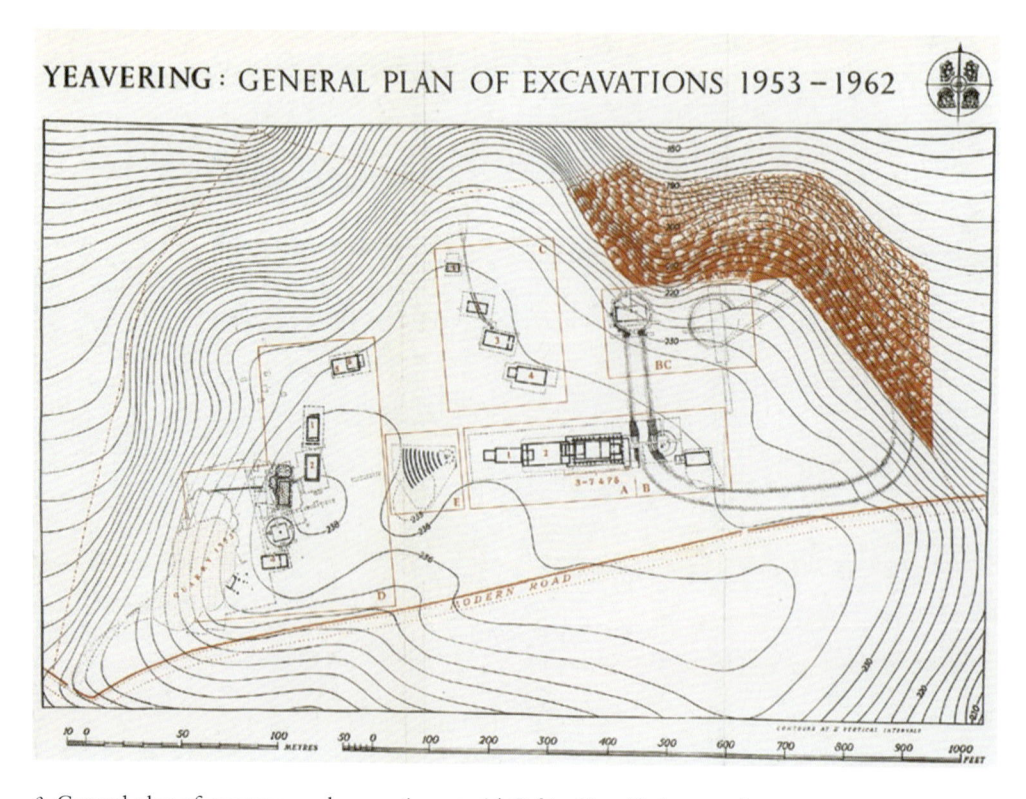

8 General plan of structures and excavations at *Ad Gefrin*. Hope-Taylor 1977, figure 12.
© *Crown copyright – reproduced by permission of English Heritage*

Right: 9 Artist's impression of *Ad Gefrin* by Peter Dunn. © *English Heritage*

Below: 10 Diagram showing possible relationships between prehistoric and early medieval features at *Ad Gefrin*. Note Hope-Taylor's original caption, which eloquently explains what he is trying to depict here. *Hope-Taylor 1977, figure 63.* © *Crown copyright – reproduced by permission of English Heritage*

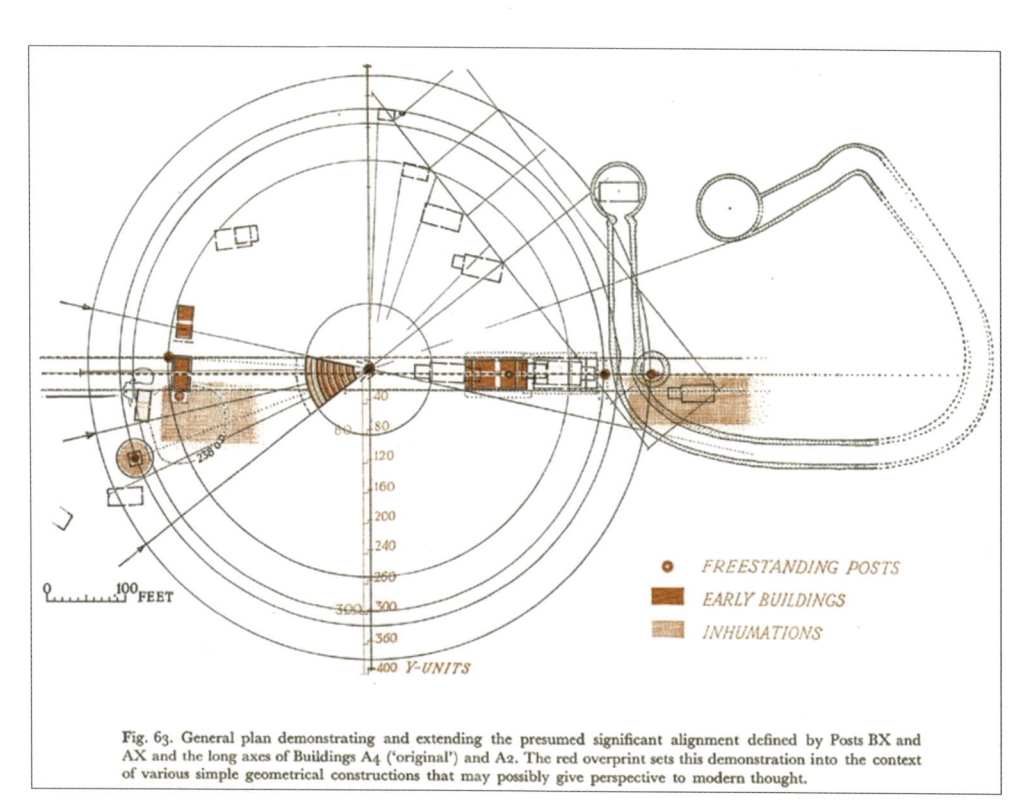

Fig. 63. General plan demonstrating and extending the presumed significant alignment defined by Posts BX and AX and the long axes of Buildings A4 ('original') and A2. The red overprint sets this demonstration into the context of various simple geometrical constructions that may possibly give perspective to modern thought.

11 Early afternoon in December, showing the site of *Ad Gefrin* (in the middle distance) completely within the shadow cast by the Bell, while the northern side of Glendale basks in golden sunshine. © *Paul Frodsham*

12 Aerial view of *Ad Gefrin* taken in July 1994. Various features show up clearly as parch marks, including the henge and the Great Enclosure. © *Tim Gates*

13 The *Gefrin* Monument, which Brian Hope-Taylor helped to design.
© *Paul Frodsham*

14 The south elevation of 'the Old Palace', photographed in 1993. Note the massive masonry in the bottom left-hand corner.
© *Northumberland National Park Authority*

15 Local people visiting Yeavering Bell on a guided walk led by the Northumberland National Park Archaeologist.
© *Northumberland National Park Authority*

Far left: 16 One of Brian Hope-Taylor's original designs for posters for 'Future of the Past', featuring Father Time. *Reproduced courtesy of the Council for British Archaeology. Photograph: Laura Sole*

Left: 17 Another poster design for 'Future of the Past', featuring 'the archaeologist' alongside the gathering of artefacts that was retained in the 'History from the Ground' campaign. *Reproduced courtesy of the Council for British Archaeology. Photograph: Laura Sole*

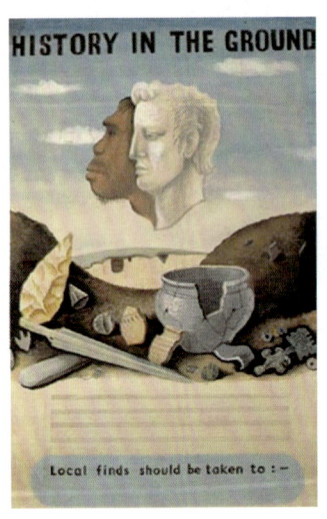

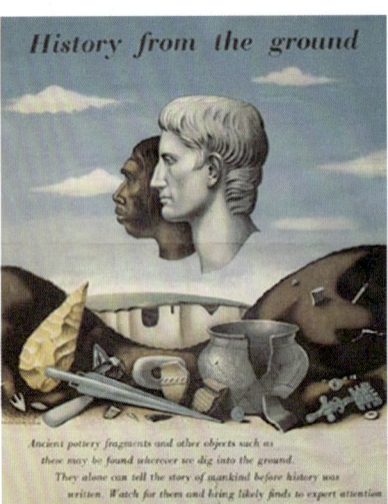

Above left and middle: 18 (a) Hope-Taylor's original design for 'History from the Ground', retaining the collection of artefacts but replacing 'the archaeologist', and (b) its eventual realisation as a poster. *Reproduced courtesy of the Council for British Archaeology. Photographs: Laura Sole*

Above right: 19 A compass point from *Yeavering. From Hope-Taylor 1977, figure 44.* © Crown copyright – reproduced by permission of English Heritage

2

YEAVERING AND AIR PHOTOGRAPHY: DISCOVERY AND INTERPRETATION

Tim Gates

This chapter has two aims: to give an account of the circumstances leading up to Professor St Joseph's discovery of the Anglian site at Yeavering and, secondly, to offer a re-interpretation of certain aspects of the air-photographic evidence both as it was available to Dr Brian Hope-Taylor and as it has continued to accumulate over the 25 years that have now elapsed since the publication of his excavation report.

DISCOVERY

Cropmarks north-east of Old Yeavering, on the site later identified by Hope-Taylor as the seventh-century royal township of *Ad Gefrin*, were first photographed from the air by J.K.S St Joseph on 9 July 1949. Flying in an RAF Percival Proctor aircraft, he used a cumbersome hand-held Williamson F24 air camera, taking 5 x 5in format film, to obtain eight oblique photographs of the site.[1] Amongst other features, these recorded the foundation trenches of more than a dozen rectangular timber buildings, including a series of overlapping halls with projecting annexes and post-holes for external buttresses, an enigmatic group of crescentic trenches later identified as a 'theatre' or grandstand and, at the eastern end of the site, twin ditches marking what St Joseph took to be a native promontory fort. Less prominent was an irregular network of fine intersecting lines which Hope-Taylor later interpreted as the boundaries of a 'Celtic' field system (*17, 18*).

17 Air photograph of Yeavering taken by St Joseph on 9 July 1949 showing the main suite of timber halls and the wingtip of his RAF Procter aircraft. Negative no. DN 49. *Reproduced by permission of the Unit for Landscape Modelling, Cambridge University. Crown copyright*

18 Air photograph taken by St Joseph on 9 July 1949 showing the 'Great Enclosure'. Negative no. DN 51. *Reproduced by permission of the Unit for Landscape Modelling, Cambridge University. Crown copyright*

YEAVERING AND AIR PHOTOGRAPHY: DISCOVERY AND INTERPRETATION

19 Thumbnail sketch of halls at Yeavering drawn from memory by St Joseph in August 1949. Copyright reserved

As it happens, the summer of 1949 was a period of quite exceptional drought and by the second week of July the estimated soil moisture deficit on the Northumberland coastal plain at Acklington was already approaching 190mm.[2] This value is 35 per cent higher than the equivalent figure reached on the same day in 1976 which is widely remembered as one of the driest summers on record. No doubt this is one reason why the cropmarks recorded on the site in 1949 showed with greater clarity than any seen in subsequent years.

In August 1949, within two months of his discovery at Yeavering, St Joseph wrote a long and detailed letter to his friend and mentor Dr Ian Richmond giving a blow-by-blow account of what had been a hectic and exhausting summer's flying.[3] Although mainly concerned with discoveries in the field of Roman military archaeology, a subject in which both men were of course passionately interested, the letter also mentioned many other sites, including Yeavering. Apparently without having seen the photographs, which had yet to be printed, he retained the details of the site fresh in his mind as we can tell from the following description:

> And nr. Old Yeavering another of those supposed 'Dark Age' church sites – just like the one seen last year [at Milfield]: only with several more rectangular buildings, and a big native promontory fort nearby. [Here he inserts a sketch – see *19*] this kind of thing. The buttresses, or post holes recur as last year.[4]

It is evident from this brief account that St Joseph believed that what he had found was some kind of religious or monastic site, an opinion he restated in the first published account of both Yeavering and Milfield, which appeared in *Monastic Sites from the Air* (Knowles and St Joseph 1952) with a representative photograph of each site. While acknowledging that the identity of these sites, whether religious or domestic, could only finally be established by excavation, St Joseph nevertheless laid stress on their ecclesiastical character emphasising the east–west orientation of the timber buildings and comparing the smaller buildings at Yeavering with monastic cells excavated at Whitby. At the same time, however, by describing the newly discovered site as 'close to the site of the traditional Dark Age *villa* of Old Yeavering', he carefully kept open the possibility of a connection of some kind with the *Ad Gefrin* of Bede while stopping short of any claim to have found the *villa* itself. Here the 'Old Yeavering' referred to is presumably the group of cottages and farm buildings lying 0.4km SW of the cropmarked site (*20, 1*), which had already appeared as 'King Edwin's Palace (Supposed site of)' on the first (1866) edition of the Ordnance Survey six-inch map.[5] Moreover, as St Joseph would certainly have known, at least two other alternative locations for Edwin's *villa* had also been proposed. In 1867, Henry MacLauchlan had put forward the site of a 'camp', situated 400m to the north-east of the Yeavering whaleback, in a field known as 'Burrowses',[6] as a more likely candidate for Edwin's residence than the 'Old Yeavering' portrayed on the six-inch map, which he rightly regarded as the ruins of a much later building or 'pele' (MacLauchlan 1867a).[7] Then, in 1947, A.H.A. Hogg proposed as yet another possible candidate 'a complex of rectangular enclosures, unlike any other sites in the district' (Hogg 1947). While these earthworks, lying on the north-facing slopes of Yeavering Bell at NT 9252 2980 (*20, 2*), are now accounted for as a native settlement of the Roman period, the fact is that at the time when Hogg and St Joseph were writing, no one knew for certain what a seventh-century royal palace was supposed to look like.

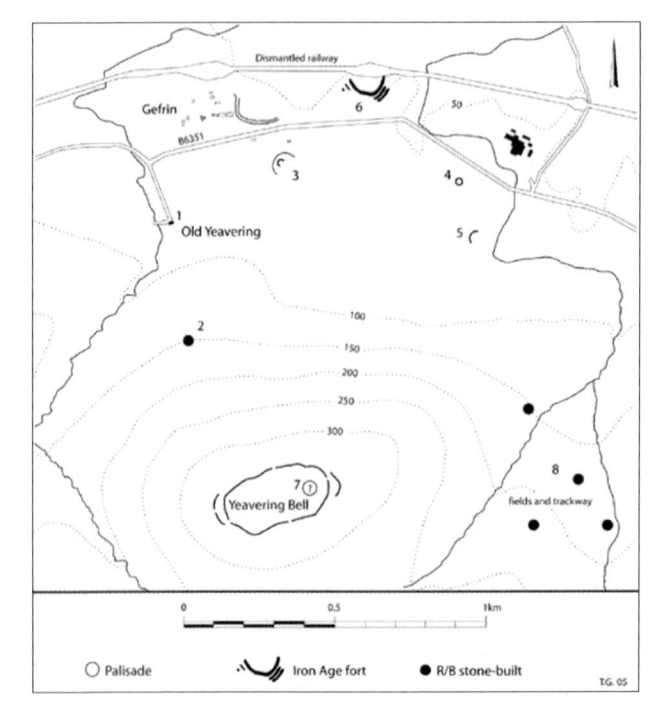

20 Location of sites discussed in chapter 2. *Base mapping reproduced by kind permission of Ordnance Survey.* © *Crown copyright, NC/2005/39729*

Here we may note in passing that most of Hogg's fieldwork was undertaken during the war when he held a Lectureship in Civil Engineering at King's College, Newcastle. At this time of national emergency, strangers who took to wandering alone in the hills were regarded with particular suspicion and ran risks not normally experienced by field archaeologists in peacetime![8]

When St Joseph wrote his long letter to Ian Richmond in August 1949, it was not only because Richmond was a close personal friend and intellectual collaborator but also because he was Chairman of the Christianbury Trust – a Newcastle-based charity set up by Sir Walter Aitchison for the purpose of assisting archaeological survey and excavation in the northern counties of England and in Scotland. To this end Sir Walter, who lived at Coupland Castle near Wooler and whose family owned a successful grocery business, committed himself to provide a sum of £500 a year over a ten-year period commencing in 1944.[9]

As it happens, Sir Walter was not only an enthusiastic amateur archaeologist but was also keenly appreciative of the potential importance of air photography as a technique for finding and recording archaeological sites, an attitude that was no doubt fostered by Ian Richmond with whom he was on friendly terms. It therefore comes as no surprise that during the lifetime of the Trust, from 1945 until 1956, St Joseph received small but useful sums of money as contributions towards the expenses he incurred while making flights over the north of England and Scotland. Additionally, the Trust also paid some or all of the costs of excavation and fieldwork undertaken by St Joseph and Richmond as well as by others who were working in the region. While most of these operations were on a small scale, a surprisingly large number of sites could be involved in any one year. During the summer of 1946, for example, St Joseph alone was responsible for trial excavations on no fewer than six Roman temporary camps, forts and signal stations at scattered locations over southern Scotland for which he received a grant of £250.[10]

In this context it is also worth mentioning that St Joseph had been actively involved in fieldwork in Northumberland and the Border counties of Scotland since the early 1930s, as indeed he continued to be until the start of his war service in July 1942. Particularly in the early years, he worked mainly in collaboration with Ian Richmond though he also received a good deal of encouragement and practical help from O.G.S. Crawford who, with characteristic generosity, regularly supplied him with air photographs and six-inch maps which he was able to take with him into the field. Indeed, while still an undergraduate at Cambridge, from 1931-34, St Joseph spent a good part of his summer vacations in the north, walking Roman roads and prospecting for undiscovered forts and temporary camps. Early successes include the identification, in 1933 or '34, of three new temporary camps – Sills Burn North, Sills Burn South and

Featherwood East – on the line of Dere Street north of High Rochester (St Joseph 1934). Here, as in later years, air photographs taken by the RAF and made available by Crawford were the essential catalyst behind these discoveries, a pattern that was repeated again and again in later years. Although his primary concern was with Roman military archaeology, St Joseph's interests were by no means limited only to sites of this period. For example, writing to Crawford in 1938, he drew specific attention to the richness of the north Cheviot landscape: 'I also had a few days in the Wooler district with your air-photos. The area is of very great interest for the country is thick with earthworks which require weeks of study in detail. I was only able to examine a few particular sites and shall have to go back there sometime.'[11] Unfortunately he gives no details of the sites he visited but it is very likely that Yeavering and the surrounding landscape were included in his agenda.

Even if St Joseph was already to some extent familiar with the northern Cheviots before the war, it was undoubtedly as an expression of personal gratitude and a *quid pro quo* for financial support from the Christianbury Trust that he regularly took photographs of Coupland Castle and its gardens after he embarked on his career as an air photographer in 1945. Most of these airborne visits took place in July or August whilst en route to or from Scotland and it was on just one of these occasions, as he was approaching Coupland, that St Joseph first saw and photographed the Yeavering cropmarks.[12]

If, then, by an act of generosity, as well as by an accident of geography, Sir Walter Aitchison contributed to the discovery of *Ad Gefrin*, it could also be that he had a hand in making the site known to its excavator. For, as Christianbury Trust records show, in 1951 Brian Hope-Taylor received a grant of £28 towards the cost of excavations at the Mote of Urr in Kirkcudbrightshire on Sir Walter's personal recommendation, implying that the two men were already acquainted by this time. Indeed this seems quite likely, as Sir Walter kept open house for any archaeologists who happened to find themselves in the vicinity of Coupland where, at one time or another, Stuart and Margaret Piggott, Kenneth Steer and Angus Graham were his guests, as well as other members of the RCAHMS who were undertaking fieldwork in Roxburghshire for the forthcoming Inventory. Crawford, too, stayed for the weekend after delivering the Rhind Lectures in Edinburgh in October 1943, as also did St Joseph and his wife Daphne as they made their way back to Cambridge in September 1945 after spending their honeymoon in Scotland looking at archaeological sites. On this last occasion it appears that Sir Walter insisted on examining every one of the air photographs that St Joseph had taken in the north that summer, copies of which had been supplied to him as a matter of courtesy, as indeed they were in later years.[13]

INTERPRETING THE AIR PHOTOGRAPHIC EVIDENCE

However it came about, Hope-Taylor (1977, 4) states that he first had an opportunity of examining St Joseph's air photographs of Yeavering in 1951 and it was then that he formed the opinion that the cropmarks could indeed represent the site of the seventh-century royal township mentioned by Bede. In the excavations that followed, Hope-Taylor's initial reading of the cropmarks, as it related to the main elements of the site (the timber halls, the grandstand or 'theatre' and two suspected *Grubenhäuser*) proved well founded. However, there is one aspect of his interpretation of the air-photographic evidence which, with the benefit of hindsight, must now be called into question. This has to do with the 'Celtic' field system and related track or 'fieldway' which Hope-Taylor saw as terminating on the site of a prehistoric or Roman 'settlement' at the NW extremity of the site (*21*). My main purpose here is to suggest that Hope-Taylor's reading of the air-photographic evidence with regard to the 'field system' was based on a misunderstanding and that what he took to be field boundaries are in fact naturally occurring frost cracks of periglacial origin. If this new reading of the cropmark evidence is correct, it has important consequences for our understanding of the overall development and chronology of the site.

The subsoil on the Yeavering whaleback consists of a mixture of late glacial sands and gravels which form a kaim-like terrace extending east to west between Akeld and Kirknewton (Payton 1980; 1992). These deposits constitute part of an extensive delta covering most of what is now known as the Milfield Plain, though subsequent cutting down by the River Glen has left them isolated from the main body of delta material lying further to the north. Whatever may have been the precise mechanism of their formation, it is known that these deposits were certainly in place by 11,000 BP which is to say before the onset of a final period of intense cold lasting from *c.*11,000 to 10,000 BP (Payton 1992 and pers. comm.). Gradually, over the past 50 years or so, air photography has revealed networks of ice-wedge casts covering most parts of the delta surface where this has not been masked by deposits of post-glacial silt. As a result it can now be demonstrated that ice-wedge polygons occur at several other locations on the same formation of sands and gravels which make up the Yeavering whaleback including, for example, two sites within a distance of 1.5km east of the Anglian palace.[14] At the same time, numerous archaeological sites, including settlements, ritual monuments and linear boundaries, ranging in date from the Neolithic to the recent past, have likewise come to light in the form of cropmarks both on the Milfield Plain itself and on the adjacent hillslopes.

For present purposes it is important to note that the existence of periglacial features in Northumberland was not acknowledged in the archaeological

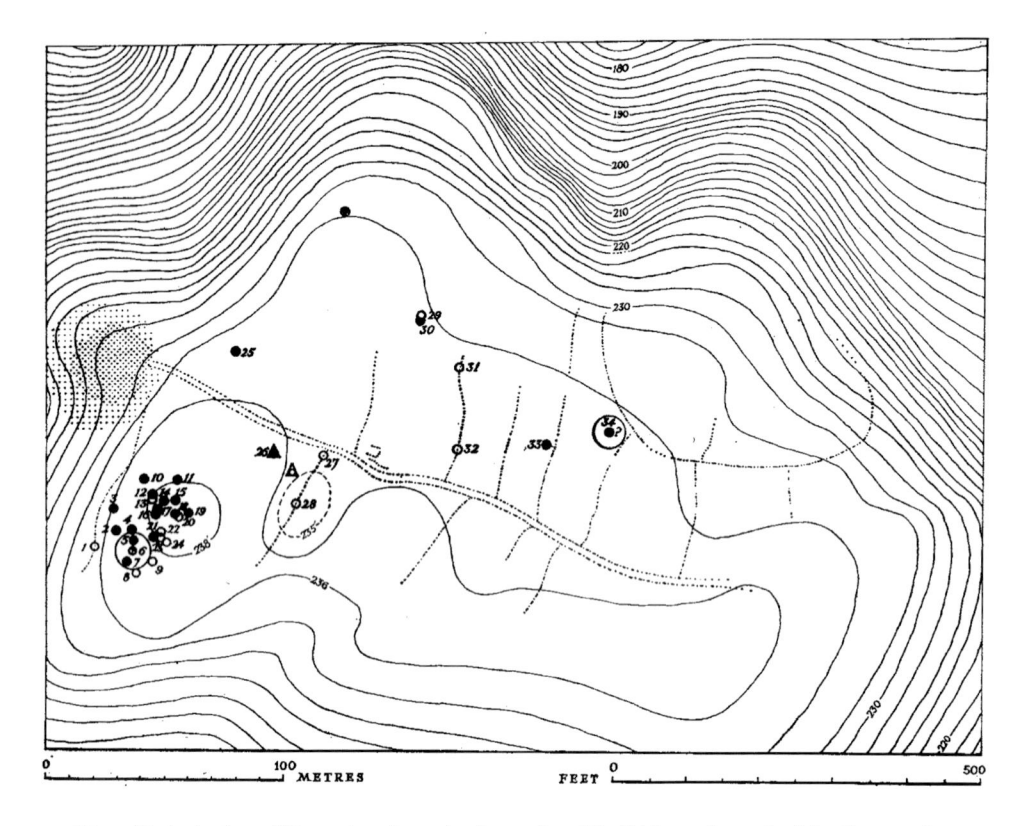

21 Hope-Taylor's plan of 'Yeavering: from the Secondary Neolithic to the end of the Roman Iron Age', showing the 'Celtic fields and fieldway' which we now know to be natural features. The stippled area at the west end of the 'fieldway' denotes what Hope-Taylor believed to be a 'ploughed-out settlement site presumably in use during the pre-Roman and/or Roman Iron Age'. Numbered features are cremation burials, probably mostly of Bronze Age date. Towards the north-east of the site, a possible early phase of the Great Enclosure is tentatively shown: Hope-Taylor believed that this may have begun life 'within the lifetime of the Celtic fields'. *Hope-Taylor 1977, figure 73* © *Crown copyright – reproduced by permission of English Heritage*

literature until as recently as 1971, and even then the potential for confusion with man-made field boundaries was explicitly recognised (McCord and Jobey 1971, 126-7). In these circumstances Hope-Taylor can hardly be held to have been at fault for failing, in the 1950s, to recognise the network of fine lines visible on St Joseph's air photographs for what they were. Nor was he by any means the only archaeologist to mistake these features for the boundaries of a field system.[15]

A sketch plan of the features (*21*) interpreted by Hope-Taylor as boundaries of the 'Celtic field system' and associated 'fieldway' appears in the published volume as figure 73. In the accompanying text these boundaries are described only once, in Chapter Three (1977, 46), in the following terms: 'The ancient field-boundaries that are seen from the air...were found uniformly to be shallow, diffuse gullies with fillings of loamy sand, invariably interrupted at every point of contact with the structures which are now to be described; and accordingly further reference to them will be omitted from this section.' No further account of these features is given in the report nor are any section drawings provided. However, if the air photographs taken in 1949, and in later years, are compared with the sketch plan referred to above, it soon becomes apparent that there is no more than a very generalised resemblance between the network of fine lines visible on the photographs (e.g. *17* & *18*), which are here interpreted as frost cracks, and the alleged 'field system' as portrayed by Hope-Taylor. No doubt one reason for this is the difficulty of producing an accurate large-scale plan from the air photographs available to him, especially as all those taken before 1970 were obliques with an awkward lack of control points common to both photographs and maps.

If the 1949 air photographs are compared with the detailed plans of the excavated Area A, as portrayed in Hope-Taylor's figures 13 and 15, it will be observed that the course of the alleged 'field gullies', represented in outline by dotted lines, is not quite as shown on the more generalised plan (figure 73) presented towards the end of Chapter Three. In particular, it is evident that some of the 'gullies' are *branched* in a manner that would be hard to account for if they were indeed field boundaries but which is absolutely characteristic of ice-wedge polygons.[16]

So far as Hope-Taylor's 'fieldway' is concerned, no very precise description is offered in the published report. Nor can any such feature be made out on any of the air photographs taken in 1949 or in subsequent years. Also, if the outlines of the excavated trenches as shown on figure 12 are transferred onto figure 73 it becomes clear that the 'fieldway' was actually intercepted in excavation in only two places, namely in the extreme SW corner of Area A (figure 13) and over a somewhat longer distance towards the northern edge of Area E (figure 55). In each case the 'fieldway' is simply shown as a linear band of light stippling rather than as the double ditched feature which seems to be implied by its representation on the overall plan (figure 73). In the absence of any textual description of the appearance of this linear feature, we can only speculate as to what may actually have been found though some purely geological phenomenon, such as a relict water channel with a contrasting fill of sand or gravel, could perhaps be invoked to account for what was observed.

According to Hope-Taylor's account, air photographs show that the 'fieldway' led to a 'ploughed-out settlement site' located close to the north-western edge of the whaleback and shown on figure 73 by a roughly circular area of stippling. Elsewhere in the report the same feature is described as an 'area disturbed by occupation' (1977, 267). Like the 'field system' with which it was thought to be associated, this putative settlement was presumed by Hope-Taylor to have been in use 'during the pre-Roman and/or Roman Iron Age'. Although limitation of funds is said to have prevented investigation of the alleged settlement, which 'had been severely damaged, if not destroyed, by recent ploughing' (1977, 267), six small trenches or test pits are indicated in this area, towards the north-west corner of Area A on the general site plan figure 12 (*colour plate 8*, this volume). However the report offers no information on what, if anything, was found in any of these trenches.

Looking again at the air photographs, including those reproduced in the published volume as Plates 3 and 5,[17] the area occupied by Hope-Taylor's 'settlement' will be seen to correspond to a contrasting patch of light tone which, though approximately circular, is completely devoid of an encircling ditch or palisade, or anything resembling interior structures or foundation trenches for circular buildings such as might normally be expected on a late prehistoric or Romano-British settlement site hereabouts. While this would not necessarily rule out the existence of an *unenclosed* settlement of some kind, the absence of rotary quernstones from this or any other part of the site might also be considered somewhat unusual if a native site of late prehistoric or Roman context had existed here, even if it had been subjected to severe plough-damage.

Going back to the air photographs, which, in the absence of corroboration by other means, must remain the primary evidence for Hope-Taylor's 'settlement', the light-toned patch referred to above could perhaps be accounted for as a deposit of coarser gravel. This, being relatively free-draining, would lead to differential parching of the overlying crop in times of drought.

To summarise, there are good reasons to suspect that Hope-Taylor misunderstood the air photographic evidence at Yeavering in certain crucial respects. In particular, because he was not in a position to understand the effects of frost cracking on the underlying sands and gravels, he interpreted what we can now identify as ice-wedge casts as the remains of a 'field system'. At the same time it appears that his proposed 'fieldway' and its associated 'settlement' may have been based on a similar misreading of the underlying geology, both as revealed by air photography and in excavation. It may also be relevant that Hope-Taylor was certainly aware that a complex archaeological landscape, incorporating fields, double-walled trackways and stone-built settlements, some, if not most, of which are demonstrably of late prehistoric or Romano-British context, exists in the form of well-preserved earthworks in a sheltered comb to the east of Yeavering Bell (*colour plate 7*). Indeed he makes explicit reference to this field system early in his report (1977, 21) and it could well be that he already had it in mind as a possible model when it came to interpreting what would otherwise have been the puzzling evidence of frost cracking encountered in excavation.

Until such time as Hope-Taylor's field system can again be tested by excavation, my suggested re-interpretation of the air-photographic evidence must remain to some extent provisional. That having been said, it is nevertheless worth pointing out some consequences of its eventually proving to be correct.

Thus, for example, once the 'field gullies' and the 'settlement' are left out of account then the episode of plough agriculture postulated by Hope-Taylor and envisaged as ending 'somewhere about the second or third centuries AD', disappears also. This being the case, there is then no reason why any of the thirteen *unurned* cremations need be later than the end of the Bronze Age, the only exception being cremations numbers 1 and 27 (1977, Appendix III, 338, 345), each of which was accompanied by a single segmented glass bead of Roman, possibly Gaulish, manufacture. Unfortunately beads of this type are not susceptible to close dating and could have been deposited at any time from the second to fifth centuries AD (Guido 1978), or perhaps even later if they had been treated as heirlooms.[18] On this evidence, therefore, and without prejudice as to the context of the Great Enclosure in its earliest manifestation (see chapter 6), it could perhaps be suggested that there was an almost complete break in both the funerary and the settlement records on the Yeavering whaleback, extending from the end of the Bronze Age until the eventual establishment of the Anglian township. But whether this was so or not, it does not necessarily mean that there was any such hiatus in settlement over the area around the excavated site during this same period. Indeed the opposite seems to be the case, for there are at least two, and possibly as many as four, settlement sites which have been recorded as cropmarks in relatively close proximity to the *villa regia* in the years since Hope-Taylor's excavations were completed and for which dates in the Iron Age or Roman periods are a distinct possibility.

THE PALACE SITE IN ITS LANDSCAPE CONTEXT

The first of these cropmarked sites is a timber-built palisaded settlement lying *c.*100m south of the B6351 Wooler to Kirknewton road at NT 9283 3038 (*20, 3*), which is briefly referred to in Hope-Taylor's report (*23, colour plate 12*).[19] In its original form the site would seem to have been almost perfectly circular with a double palisaded perimeter containing at least one timber-built roundhouse placed slightly off-centre within it. The twin palisades are set 2-3m apart and enclose an area some 75m in diameter. Only the northern half of the site now survives, the rest having been destroyed by retreat of the terrace frontage where the ground dips down to the south into a depression marking the course of a post-glacial meltwater channel. Palisaded settlements of this kind are fairly common in northern Northumberland where they occur both as earthworks in the uplands and as cropmarks in cultivated areas. The excavated site at High Knowes 'A' (NT 971 124; Jobey and Tait 1966) provides a close parallel to the Yeavering settlement and, although undated, would normally be attributed to the early Iron Age. On the evidence of currently available radiocarbon dates, freestanding palisades of this kind can be envisaged as making their first appearance in the Tyne–Forth region early in the first half of the first millennium BC and in any event not later than the seventh century BC as evidenced locally by an uncalibrated radiocarbon date of 690 ± 100 bc obtained from the earliest of two palisaded perimeters which preceded the first box rampart at Fenton Hill, a hillfort located just 7km north-east of Yeavering on the far side of the Milfield Plain (Burgess 1984). At the same time an uncalibrated radiocarbon date of 180 ± 80 bc for the earliest of three successive palisade lines at Murton High Crags, in the Tweed valley near Berwick (NT 964 495), allows for the survival of such settlements into the late Iron Age and conceivably even as late as the first century AD (Jobey and Jobey, 1987). A considerable degree of chronological overlap between palisades and hillforts may therefore be anticipated.

In recent years air photography has located two further curvilinear palisades situated only a short distance south-east of the Yeavering whaleback and close to the foot of Yeavering Bell. One of these, at NT 9341 3032, is sub-circular on plan and its perimeter is formed by a single palisade trench enclosing an area *c*.30m in diameter (*20*, 4). The other site is located at NT 9346 3014 (*20*, 5) and likewise appears to have been curvilinear in plan with a maximum diameter of around 40m, though this remains to some extent conjectural as part of the perimeter is concealed under a belt of trees. Since no buildings, either circular or rectangular, are evident in the interior of either site, their dating can be no more than guesswork though, on balance, contexts in the pre-Roman Iron Age seem likely.

The last of the four is a small, multivallate fort of a type which is becoming increasingly familiar in lowland parts of northern Northumberland, especially in the major river valleys and along the coastal plain, where examples are coming to light in growing numbers, mainly in the form of cropmarks recorded by air photography. This particular site is located 0.5km due east of *Ad Gefrin* at NT 9310 3063 and occupies the summit of a gravel spur with an outlook to the north over the valley of the River Glen (*20*, 6). As mentioned above, it was first recorded by Henry MacLauchlan as a 'camp' situated in a field with the tell-tale name of 'Burrowses' (MacLauchlan 1867a, 24-5).[20] According to MacLauchlan's account, by the mid-nineteenth century ploughing had all but completely levelled the site, reducing the defences to little more than a curving band of lighter subsoil visible as a soilmark on the surface of the recently ploughed field.

YEAVERING AND AIR PHOTOGRAPHY: DISCOVERY AND INTERPRETATION

22 Cropmarks at the Burrowses, photographed on 19 July 1994 by Tim Gates. *Negative no. TMG 15960/47. Copyright reserved*

Thereafter, further damage was done when the site was bisected by a railway cutting and it was not until 1966 that it finally reappeared as a cropmark. Air photographs taken then and on several subsequent occasions show it to have been a defended settlement, more or less circular in plan and with an internal area of approximately 0.75ha (*22*). Where the natural slope is relatively steep, to the north of the railway cutting, the defensive perimeter has consisted of a single bank and ditch. By contrast, on the gentler south-facing slope, where all surface indications of the defences have been erased by ploughing, cropmarks reveal the former existence of three close-set, concentric ditches. As the innermost ditch is somewhat broader than the others, it could be that the site began life as a univallate enclosure and was subsequently strengthened by the addition of another two ramparts and ditches on the south-facing side.[21]

This hint of longevity raises the additional question as to whether or not there may have been a secondary phase of Romano-British occupation on the site of the Burrowses fort. For, as has long been recognised, a substantial proportion of Iron Age forts and related settlements between the Tyne and Forth are overlain by non-defensive settlements of the Roman period in the form of round, stone-founded houses and their attendant stock yards which may overlie or spill out beyond the redundant hillfort defences (Jobey 1964; 1965). Without resort to excavation there is no way of knowing whether such a Romano-British settlement did indeed exist at the Burrowses. On the other hand, as a generalised indication of potential in this respect, it is worth pointing out that no fewer than eight out of a sample of 12 relatively well-preserved hillforts in the north Cheviots that have recently been surveyed as part of the Northumberland National Park Authority's *Discovering Our Hillfort Heritage* project (see chapter 4, this volume) have proved to possess overlying phases of Romano-British occupation. Moreover, where the evidence has not been destroyed by ploughing, it has also been possible to show that these later, stone-built settlements are in turn associated with contemporary field systems incorporating walled trackways and evidence of cultivation, whether this be in the form of cord rig or, less certainly, of stone-revetted terraces on the steeper slopes. So far as the immediate landscape setting of Yeavering is concerned, two hillforts, at West Hill and St Gregory's Hill, possess extensive remains of Romano-British settlement and both are also accompanied by developed field systems (Oswald, Jecock and Ainsworth 2000; Oswald and McOmish 2002).

As the topographical setting of the Burrowses fort is similar to West Hill and St Gregory's Hill, with good potential for agriculture in the immediate vicinity of the site and ready access to moorland grazing on the uplands to the south, there is every reason to suppose that the site would have been equally attractive from the point of view of Romano-British farmers.

A review of the potential for native settlement in the vicinity of Yeavering during the Iron Age and Roman periods must also take into consideration the hillfort on Yeavering Bell itself. The evidence is considered in greater depth elsewhere in this volume by Alastair Oswald and Trevor Pearson and here we need only note that no traces of stone-founded roundhouses have been identified amongst the 125 platforms for timber buildings that are contained within the circuit of the stone-walled rampart (Jobey 1965; Pearson 1998). This being the case, it seems likely that the occupation of Yeavering Bell came to an end in the pre-Roman Iron Age, or at any rate at some time before the mid-second century AD when it is believed that many native settlements in Northumberland were rebuilt in stone (e.g. Jobey 1978). Nor would such a conclusion necessarily be denied by the few scraps of Samian ware and two late Roman coins recovered in small-scale excavations undertaken by George Tate and Hope-Taylor (Tate 1863; Hope-Taylor 1977). Certainly this material is of itself insufficient to demonstrate any substantial occupation of the hillfort in the Roman period and could readily be explained in terms of losses sustained by casual visitors to what must always have been a popular viewpoint. An alternative proposition, namely that there was a settlement of *timber* houses on the hilltop during the Roman period, does not accord with what is known from excavations on hillforts elsewhere in the Cheviots as, for example, at Wether Hill (Topping 2004). On the other hand it would perhaps be unwise to exclude this possibility altogether in view of recent findings at Eildon Hill North where one, or perhaps even two, platforms (HP-1(2) and HP-2), both ostensibly for timber structures, have produced radiocarbon dates consistent with occupation in the Roman Iron Age and extending, at the 67 per cent confidence level, perhaps even as late as the mid-third century AD (Rideout *et al.* 1992).

The sub-circular or polygonal enclosure which occupies the eastern summit of Yeavering Bell (*20*, 7) was tentatively identified by George Jobey as an Iron Age palisaded settlement predating the main occupation of the hillfort (Jobey 1962; 1965). However, its stratigraphic position with regard to certain of the timber house platforms has subsequently been called into question and it has also been suggested that it may be of post-Roman date (Bradley 1987). While recent survey confirms that the enclosure is certainly later than at least two of the hillfort house platforms (Pearson 1998), this does not mean that it cannot be of Iron Age date, particularly if it could be shown that the hillfort had ceased to function as a centre of habitation at a relatively early period. At the same time, what has previously been described as a palisade trench now looks much more like an unfinished ditch. Nor has any convincing evidence been forthcoming to show that the enclosure represents a settlement rather than, say, a ritual or funerary monument, as now suggested by Trevor Pearson (Pearson 1998, 31).[22] Certainly, as presently understood, the earthwork on the eastern summit does not provide a satisfactory basis on which to propose that habitation on the hilltop extended beyond the life of the hillfort itself.

While the question of a native presence on Yeavering Bell during the Roman period is one of many which will only finally be resolved by fresh excavations, the existence of a substantial native population hereabouts in the period leading up to the appearance of the first Anglian settlers at Yeavering can confidently be inferred from the existence of a liberal scattering of stone-built native Romano-British farmsteads which survive in the form of earthworks beyond the limit of medieval or later ploughing (*20*, 8). As indicated above, such settlements would normally be ascribed to a period commencing in or about the mid-second century AD though the evidence for this dating is limited geographically and earlier dates for the introduction of stone-built roundhouses are possible. The existence of organised field systems and walled trackways in association with most of these extant sites may also imply a change in the balance of the farming economy marked by an increased reliance on arable cultivation and the better management of stock.

As already mentioned, three, or possibly four, cropmark settlements have been recorded on the gravel terraces adjacent to the Yeavering 'whaleback' which can, with varying degrees of certainty, be interpreted as native settlements of the Iron Age or Roman periods. Against this background, the rejection of Hope-Taylor's 'field system', while undoubtedly significant from the point of view of the internal chronology of the site, should not be taken as implying a general absence of settlement hereabouts during the Roman period. At the same time, even when the putative Iron Age or Romano-British 'settlement' claimed by Hope-Taylor is similarly discounted, we now have a plausible alternative focus of Iron Age and, more speculatively, of Romano-British occupation, at the Burrowses no more than 0.5km distant from the future *villa regia*. To point this out is not to suggest any notions of 'ritual' continuity of the kind suggested by Hope-Taylor which have in any case already been re-interpreted by Richard Bradley along quite different lines (Bradley 1987).

IMPLICATIONS OF THE REINTERPRETATION

Seen in the narrower context of the excavations themselves, the identification of the 'field gullies' as ice-wedge casts would not only dispose of the 'field system' but also of the phase of plough agriculture, ending 'somewhere about the second or third centuries AD', that was inferred from it. As will be evident from Hope-Taylor's published phase diagrams (figures 58 and 72), it follows from this that the chronology of Yeavering's earliest buildings (e.g. A5-7), and likewise of the palisaded precursors of the 'Great Enclosure' Phase IV (e.g. FP1, FP2 + 3, and FP5), must now be established on their own merits and without reference to the *tempus post quem* previously offered by the boundaries of the 'field system'.

So far as the excavated structures are concerned, Chris Scull has convincingly argued that all the buildings (including A5-8, and D6) can now be paralleled on other Anglian sites and that none need be earlier than the late sixth or early seventh century (Scull, 1991). By contrast, the 'Great Enclosure' is less well understood and in his analysis of the stratigraphy Colm O' Brien (chapter 6, this volume) draws attention to how little we really know about its context and, more particularly, about the chronology of Hope-Taylor's phases GE I (FP5), GE II (FP2 + 3) and GE III (FP1). Indeed only with GE IV, the 'Great Enclosure' in its most dramatic form, do we seem to be on firm ground, for here an origin somewhere in the Anglian period is guaranteed by the fact that its outer foundation trench cuts a line of post-holes ('Palisade 5') which in turn forms a small yard or enclosure projecting eastwards from the end of building A4. According to Hope-Taylor's own model, two of the three palisades which precede GE IV, namely GE II and III, also belong to the post-Roman period. To the extent that both palisades are related in plan, and can also be seen to be concentric with the trenches of GE IV, this does indeed seem likely, even if final proof of their context is presently lacking. On the other hand, the situation with respect to GE I (FP5) is less certain, though Hope-Taylor suggests that it may have originated within the lifetime of his proposed Celtic field system and, moreover, that it should be regarded as the structural precursor of all the later palisades. This at any rate is what seems to be implied by the depiction of FP5 on figure 73 of the published report (*21*) where the palisade trench forms an incomplete, sub-oval enclosure which, if superimposed on figure 77, can be seen to run almost exactly parallel with, and just inside, the inner trench of GE IV. As it is depicted in his drawing, the plan of FP5 is in large measure based on Hope-Taylor's own interpretation of the air photographs taken in 1949 (e.g. *18*). However, in the light of what we now know about the underlying geology, there seems little doubt that most, if not all, of the extrapolated circuit, like the 'Celtic field-system' itself, can be accounted for as a somewhat idealised representation of a network of ice-wedge casts. Certainly an explanation along these lines would account for the otherwise problematic 'junctions' between the 'field gullies' on the one hand and the 'palisade trench' on the other.

Until such time as the validity of this revised interpretation can be put to the test, it may be as well to remain open minded about the chronological context of palisade FP5 and its supposed connection with the Great Enclosure. Indeed, on the evidence so far obtained in excavation, an origin in the pre-Roman Iron Age might even be considered as a possibility. Be that as it may, in present circumstances to speculate further would serve no useful purpose.

FURTHER DISCOVERIES

To conclude this discussion of the part played by aerial photography in our understanding of Yeavering, all that now remains is to consider the results of recent air photography particularly as it relates to that part of the site which lies south of the B6351 Wooler to Kirknewton road.

As Hope-Taylor himself was aware, cropmarks in this area include the foundation trenches of two timber-built halls, the twin-palisaded settlement referred to above, and what later turned out to be a Neolithic henge, excavated

23 Cropmarks south of the B6351 Akeld to Kirknewton road photographed by Tim Gates on 30 June 1994. *Colour 35mm slide. Copyright reserved*

by Anthony Harding in 1976 (Harding 1981; Tinniswood and Harding 1991). All these features were visible on a series of photographs taken by St Joseph in July 1962, one of which was reproduced in the Yeavering report as Plate 6.[23]

Vivid cropmarks south of the road again appeared in the exceptionally dry summer of 1994 when they were photographed by the writer (*23; colour plate 12*). In addition to the above, these photographs reveal several new and important features and also help to clarify what was found in excavation on the north side of the road. They confirm, for example, the existence of a well-developed network of ice-wedge casts covering all parts of the 'whaleback' that are under crop. At the same time there is absolutely no sign here either of Hope-Taylor's 'field system' or of the 'fieldway' whose eastern termination, as depicted in figure 73 of the published report, might otherwise be expected to lie in the area to the north-west of the henge between it and the road.

What is more important is that we can also see at least four (and perhaps more) small, sub-rectangular marks of solid tone which exactly match others at New Bewick, Milfield and Thirlings and can on this basis be recognised as *Grubenhäuser* for the first time (Gates and O'Brien 1988). Interestingly, most of these structures lie 200-300m south and west of the timber halls echoing the position of the *Grubenhäuser* at both Milfield and Thirlings which are likewise situated some little distance from the main suite of buildings.[24] It is also worth noting that these newly recognised *Grubenhäuser* occur in an area of relatively deep silt. This, being less favourable for the formation of cropmarks, is no doubt one reason why these features have escaped notice until now, and also suggests that there may be further structures here which remain undetectable from the air. Though small in number, this group of *Grubenhäuser* is of some importance because it is exactly what would be expected if, as Chris Scull suggests, the *villa regia* developed out of what might be described as a 'normal' Anglian settlement of the type represented locally by the site at New Bewick (Gates and O' Brien 1988). If so, excavation of one or more of these structures might go some way to confirm Scull's belief that the Dark Age site at Yeavering began life in the sixth century AD as a small and quite unexceptional farming community (his Phase I), implying perhaps that its elevation to higher status, however motivated, was a secondary development and not necessarily integral to the original choice of site.

PART II PREHISTORIC YEAVERING

3

YEAVERING IN ITS STONE AGE LANDSCAPE

Clive Waddington

INTRODUCTION

The Milfield basin forms the largest physically contained alluvial flood basin in Northumberland. It also straddles two key communication routes running north–south and east–west with the entrance to Glendale forming the junction of these two axes. Immediately overlooking this naturally defined crossroads is the highest and most prominent hill of the northern Cheviot rim, Yeavering Bell. When viewed from the lower-lying ground of the basin proper, it is the twin-topped hill of Yeavering Bell that stands out most markedly against the southern horizon. Therefore, positioned at a key communication junction, and in the lee of the most prominent hilltop, Old Yeavering (*Ad Gefrin*) clearly occupies a rather special place in the dramatic landscape of the Milfield basin (*24*). Positioned on a gravel terrace immediately above the flood plain, Yeavering remained high and dry on the fringe of a vast tract of fertile land immensely attractive to hunter-gatherer and early farming groups. Stone Age activity from the Mesolithic through to the Neolithic has been discovered at Yeavering and more widely across the basin. It will be argued that 'continuity' at Yeavering should not be considered in terms of whether or not there exists an unbroken sequence of archaeological deposits but rather by considering evidence for long-held 'cultural memory' that attaches importance to a place.

24 The site of Yeavering at the mouth of Glendale with the twin peaks of the Bell behind

LANDSCAPE SETTING

After the dissolution of the ice, the meltwaters from much of the Cheviot ice cap flowed into the low-lying valley we refer to today as the Milfield basin, or 'Glendale' to give it its local name (Clapperton 1970). As the ice retreated the glacial meltwaters flushed huge quantities of sands and gravels down the valley of the River Glen to the low-lying ground of the Milfield plain (Clapperton 1971; Payton 1980). Where the river discharged into the plain a large glacio-deltaic gravel fan was formed (Payton 1980) and beyond this, in what is now the flood plain proper, a glacial lake developed. Referred to by Butler (1907) as 'Lake Ewart', this body of water eventually breached the sandstone escarpment at Etal where the waters cut down to form the gorge through which the River Till still flows today. This breach established the Till as a north-flowing tributary river of the Tweed and allowed Lake Ewart to be drained.

Throughout the Holocene, the Milfield basin has remained the principal flood basin for the north-east Cheviot massif and the Fellsandstone escarpment. It receives water from the rivers Breamish/Till, Glen and Wooler Water, as well as from smaller tributary streams that run off the sandstone. The proximal location of the surrounding upland means the basin is susceptible to flooding and this occurs on an annual basis. Indeed, during the 'great flood' of 1948 the floodwaters

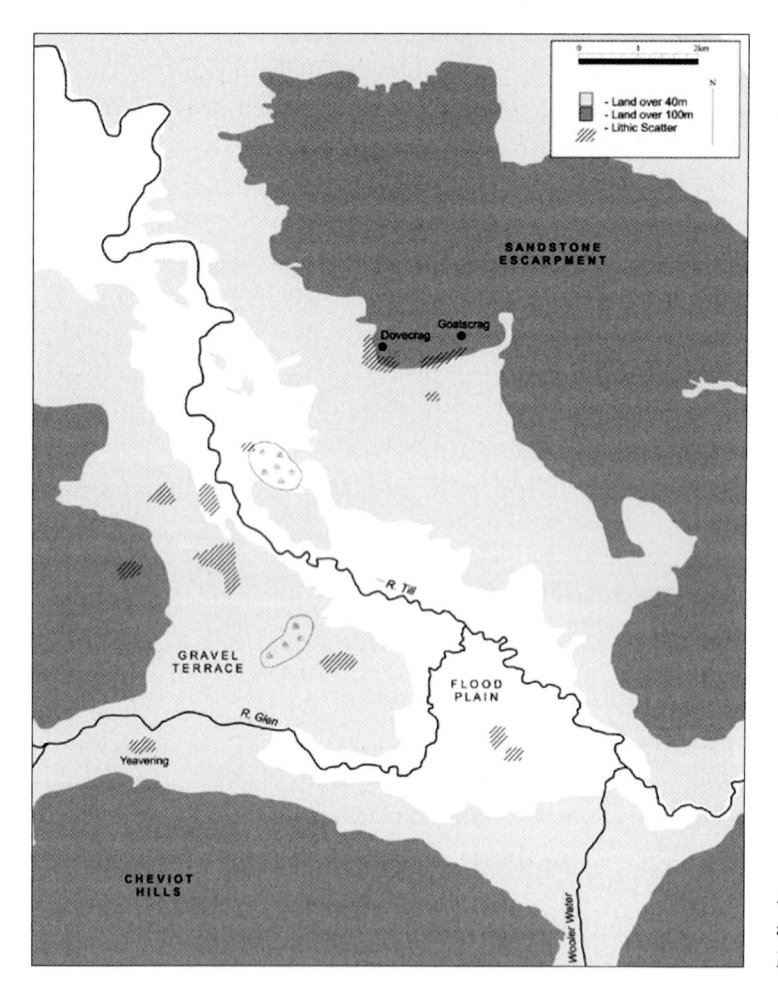

25 The Mesolithic archaeology of the Milfield basin

stretched all the way up Glendale as far as Kirknewton and extended over an area of 6000 acres (Archer 1992). However, perhaps the most important aspect of the glacial legacy was the formation of the raised gravel terraces that fringe much of the flood plain (*25*). They consist of a series of flat, terraced surfaces, set at different levels, and connected by steep scarp slopes. Being composed of fluvio-glacial sands and gravels these landforms are free-draining, and at an average of 10m above the flood plain, are not at risk from flood waters. Therefore, the gravel terraces form an attractive area for settlement, and not just because of their physical properties, but also on account of their location, sandwiched between the rich, riparian environment of the river and flood plain, and the rich soils and woodland of the low Cheviot slopes.

The Yeavering site is located on one of these terraces. However, the location of Yeavering is significant in other ways. The terrace here occupies the point in

Glendale where the valley begins to open out into the Milfield plain and as such controls the entrance to this striking, steep-sided valley, which provides the first east–west route north of the Cheviots. In addition, the Yeavering terrace lies at the foot of Yeavering Bell. Particularly when viewed from the north, this impressive landmark, with its characteristic twin peaks (*24*), further defines the mouth of Glendale where the stream gradient drops. It thus serves to mark out this point as a conspicuous 'place' in the landscape. The Glen can also be forded in this stretch, as witnessed by the ford still in use between Yeavering and Coupland. It is this combination of geographic circumstances that makes Yeavering a discrete and special place in landscape terms. The initial recognition of these qualities by the earliest inhabitants of the basin no doubt contributed to the formation of the special regard in which this place was held over subsequent millennia.

MESOLITHIC

It appears on the basis of the scant evidence so far available that Yeavering was a favoured place for occupation by Mesolithic hunter-gatherer groups. According to Hope-Taylor (1977, 194-6), 'Struck flakes of flint (and occasionally of chert) occurred as stray finds in the overburden, some of them unmistakably Mesolithic; but as there is a lack both of context and of specific forms it would be pointless to illustrate and discuss them.' With only this minimalist reference to Mesolithic activity, little more can be said directly about Hope-Taylor's site other than that it formed a focus for hunter-gatherer groups. This conclusion has, however, garnered further support with the chance opportunity of fieldwalking the Yeavering henge field. This field was ploughed shortly after the Yeavering conference in spring 2003, and was linewalked by the author and a small team at 5m intervals, with all find locations recorded. Although surface visibility was very poor, a total of 30 struck lithics were recovered from the 10ha field, all of which were made from agate, chert or quartz. Many of the pieces were diagnostic Mesolithic types including two scrapers, two retouched flakes, two utilised flakes, 10 cores and a broken microlith. This information, which will be published in full elsewhere, augments the case for the Yeavering 'whaleback' forming an attractive locale for hunter-gatherer settlement.

If we look more widely around the basin we can see that this evidence forms part of a wider picture in which locales on the gravel terraces were selectively chosen for occupation by hunter-gatherer groups. For example, surface lithic scatters have been identified through a fieldwalking programme that has now sampled across 1,000ha, extending from the Cheviot watershed in the west to the sandstone watershed in the east producing 1279 lithics (Waddington 1999).

The highest density of lithics came from the fluvio-glacial gravel terraces upon which the Yeavering site is also situated.

Geological Zone	Area Walked (ha.)	No. Lithics	Lithic density per ha. (100% coverage)
Raised Gravel Terraces	126.9	351	14.7
Cheviot Slopes	269.1	461	10.6
Sandstone Slopes	169.7	310	6.4
Alluvial Gravel Islands	43.3	76	3.8
Boulder Clay	129.9	61	2.4
Alluvial Terraces	214.7	20	0.3
Total	953.6	1279	

Table 1 Lithic densities from different geological zones in the Milfield basin

Concentrations of Mesolithic material were found in areas to the east, south and west of Milfield village and in the areas immediately around the Milfield North henge, Coupland henge and Ewart henge (the material at the latter site was discovered by Joan Weyman). Other Mesolithic sites include two important locations on raised gravel 'islands' set within the flood plain. These slight elevations would have provided small areas of dry ground amongst a perennially wet and boggy area near the river margin, and particularly during the early Holocene while the old lake bed was drying out.

Of the 305 lithics that could be ascribed to the Mesolithic, 63 per cent were non-flint material, including agate, chert, quartz and other rocks that can all be found in the gravel deposits. Most of the flint is a light grey, speckled variety that probably comes from source areas such as the Northumberland coast or north-east Yorkshire. The heavy reliance on locally available stone indicates that Mesolithic groups structured production at a local scale and that a sense of self-reliance prevailed. This kind of strategy mirrors that evidenced at the Northumberland coastal site at Howick (Waddington *et al.* 2003) where virtually the entire stone tool assemblage from the hut (over 13,000 pieces) is made from locally occurring beach flint. The lack of exotic Mesolithic material from the Milfield basin suggests that the groups inhabiting this area did not necessarily range far and wide as part of their annual round. Rather, the concentration of Mesolithic settlement in the basin, structured around the flood plain of the valley floor, implies groups occupying the basin as part of a year-round pattern of residency with occasional movement of settlements within the valley, as well as to logistical camps around its fringe, for specialised activities such as hunting, chert extraction and visits to the coast.

Raw Material	Agate	Flint	Chert	Quartz	Other
% of Mesolithic Assemblage	44	37	12	4	3

Table 2 Frequency of Mesolithic artefacts made from different raw materials

At Goatscrag, on the east side of the basin, evidence was found for a Mesolithic rock shelter site that may have formed one such logistical camp (Burgess 1972). This included post sockets, pits and gulleys and a small assemblage of late Mesolithic flintwork. However, what is remarkable about this site is that carvings of what appear to be four deer were found on the rock face (*26*) within the shelter (van Hoek and Smith 1988). Although the date of these carvings cannot be proven, the employment of representational art in prehistoric Britain is associated with hunter-gatherer groups (such as the horse head on a bone fragment, and the recently recognised rock art showing an ibex and other animals, from Creswell Crags).

Abstract art on the other hand, such as cup and ring marks and passage grave art, is associated with farming groups of the Neolithic and early Bronze Age.

26 The 'deer' carvings inside the Goatscrag rock shelter

Therefore, given the style and location of the carvings, it appears that we have evidence for another special 'place' marked out by the Mesolithic inhabitants of the basin. From Goatscrag there are wide views over the Till valley towards Yeavering Bell, and from the top of the crag the North Sea can also be seen. With regard to the subject of Mesolithic art in the basin it is worth noting the find of a 'rod-like fragment of natural ochre' (Hope-Taylor 1977, 196) that was recovered from the packing soil of the Great Enclosure's final outer palisade trench, and which Hope-Taylor considered to be 'derived from some earlier phase'. Ochre is frequently found on Palaeolithic and Mesolithic sites, as has been demonstrated most recently at Howick, and this raises the question as to whether Mesolithic groups at Yeavering were also making use of this material. Although it has healing properties and is used in the preparation of hides, ochre is also used as a pigment, presumably for art, body decoration or for its symbolic blood-like colour. The association of red ochre with Palaeolithic and Mesolithic burials is well attested in north-west Europe, from the well-known burials in Scandinavia such as Skateholm (Larsson 1989) to British sites such as the Red Lady (actually a man) of Paviland (Aldhouse-Green and Pettitt 1998), where the ochre appears to have been included in the grave as part of a symbolic act. Although this find may seem somewhat unobtrusive and intractable when set against the great Anglian halls, it provides a hint of complex Mesolithic behaviour at the site.

Although at this stage we can only speculate as to the importance attached to Yeavering by Mesolithic groups, it appears to have formed one of a constellation of what are thought to be settlement sites situated on the gravel terraces. With easy access to freshwater and wetland resources (including fish, wildfowl, beaver, otter, birds, eggs, plant foods and reeds), as well as the resources afforded by the surrounding woodland and high ground (including nuts, fruits, berries, birds, mammals, timber, leaves and bark), Yeavering enjoys all the environmental opportunities associated with a Mesolithic 'base-camp' settlement. At the same time though, being situated on the cusp between different ecological niches adds further to the liminal qualities of the place, which have already been mentioned in the introduction, and this must have surely contributed to the concept of Yeavering as a distinctive, and indeed special, place by the early occupants of the basin.

EARLY NEOLITHIC

The Milfield basin is increasingly recognised as one of the cradles of Neolithic settlement in northern England. Excavations at sites across the basin continue to reveal evidence for some of the earliest Neolithic activity in the north (see Waddington 1999). As with the preceding Mesolithic period, both the

YEAVERING IN ITS STONE AGE LANDSCAPE

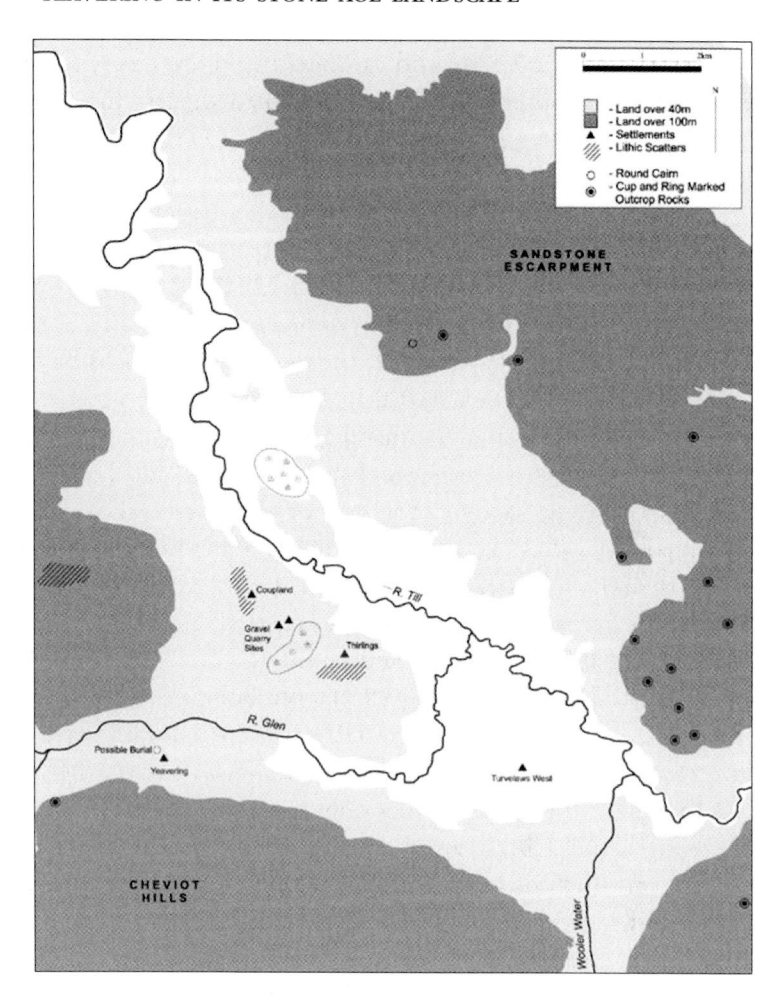

27 The early Neolithic archaeology of the Milfield basin

fieldwalking results and a number of excavations have shown the gravel terraces formed the primary settlement focus in the valley (*27*). Most of the early Neolithic settlements so far known in north Northumberland, a notable exception being the site near Bolam Lake (Waddington and Davies 2002), are situated on the gravel terraces of the Milfield basin and include the sites at Yeavering (Hope-Taylor 1977; Harding 1981), Thirlings (Miket 1976; 1987), the Coupland Henge site (Waddington 1999) and Woodbridge Farm (Waddington 2000 and SMR reports). This excavated evidence is supported by the fieldwalking data which shows greater concentrations of lithics on the gravel terraces, although important areas of activity were also noted in the surrounding uplands (Waddington 1999). At all the sites undecorated carinated ceramic vessels with rolled-over and/or everted rims have been found that fit into the Grimston Ware pottery series. These ceramics were all found in pits, usually with flints, charred hazelnut shells and charcoal. At Thirlings, pits and stakeholes associated with Neolithic structures were found (Miket 1987), while at the Coupland site in situ burning had occurred in the pits suggesting their use as earth ovens or fire-pits (Waddington 1999). However, the deliberate disposal of what appears to be domestic debris in fairly deep pits may have had some sort of symbolic and/or ritual connotations, as it is only some debris that was disposed of in this way. Furthermore, the need to use pits at all for the disposal of domestic waste is unique to the Neolithic. Therefore, although we have assumed over the years that these pits have resulted from settlement occupation, and with this I concur, they should also be seen as the product of what were perhaps symbolically ordered acts. In this way the artifice of our prevailing economic-ritual distinctions is exposed, forcing us to consider that such behavioural boundaries were far more blurred, particularly during the Neolithic, when some routine acts appear to have carried some element of symbolic structuring (Richards and Thomas 1984).

At Yeavering two 'domestic' pits were found outside the east and west entrances of the henge (Harding 1981, 122). The one to the west contained charred hazelnut shells, a sample of which produced an early fourth millennium BC (Cal.) date (2940 ± 90bc, HAR-3063), while the pit outside the east entrance produced 65 sherds of Grimston Ware pottery. At the palace site Hope-Taylor found sherds of Grimston Ware as residual finds in redeposited layers (Hope-Taylor 1977, 345, pit 30, figure 119; 352-3 figure 123) and this again provides evidence for early Neolithic activity at the site. Evidence from the settlement sites at the Coupland henge and Thirlings have shown that emmer wheat, six-row barley and oats were being grown (Miket 1987; Waddington 1999), while at the same time wild foods such as hazelnuts, hawthorn and bramble were also collected. Although there is no direct evidence for the keeping of stock, due no doubt to the poor survival of unburnt bone in this environment, it is reasonable to assume that animals such as cattle and pig were being kept and a similar economic basis can be envisaged for the groups occupying the Yeavering terrace.

Significantly, Grimston Ware sherds were also found at Yeavering in a pit with some burnt bone, implying that the early Neolithic occupants not only lived there, but perhaps also buried some of their dead there. This provides an important parallel with the other early Neolithic burial currently known in the Milfield basin on Broomridge near Goatscrag. Here, a circular cairn investigated in 1858 by Greenwell (1877, 410) covered a primary deposit containing burnt bone that included skull fragments from a child, together with over 200 Grimston Ware fragments (Newbiggin 1935), flints and charcoal. The similarities between the two sites are striking; at both sites the dead were cremated (assuming the Yeavering bone was human) and in both cases the remains had been deposited with fragments of Grimston Ware pottery. This suggests that the occupants of Yeavering shared burial

YEAVERING IN ITS STONE AGE LANDSCAPE

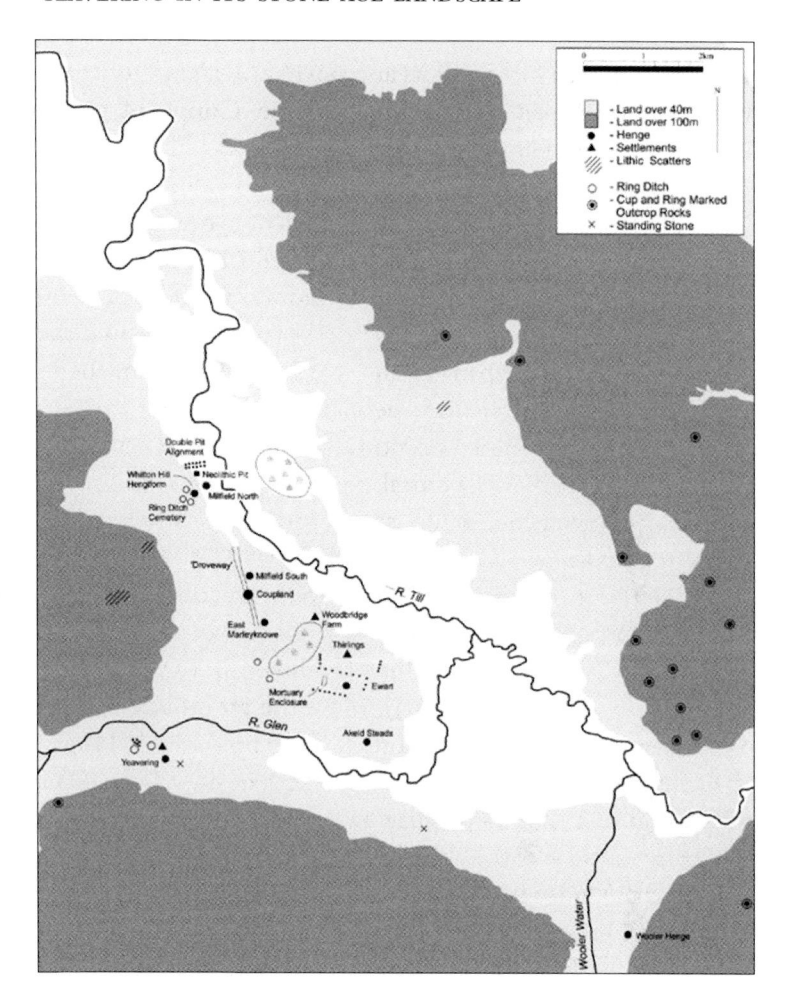

28 The late Neolithic archaeology of the Milfield basin

traditions with other early Neolithic groups around the basin. Furthermore, both sites demonstrate a formalised attachment to a place by Neolithic groups. Indeed it is with this burial that we witness the first unambiguously ritual act at Yeavering; one that makes a special association with the site by creating an ancestral presence (if the burnt bone is accepted as being human).

LATE NEOLITHIC–EARLY BRONZE AGE

As the Neolithic progressed, new styles of pottery and stone tools emerged, but probably the most profound development was the increasing monumentalisation of the landscape as witnessed by the stone circles (Waddington 1999), henges (Harding 1981), pit alignments (Miket 1981; Waddington 1997) and so forth (*28*).

The tradition of placing burnt bone in pits, accompanied by broken pottery sherds, continues throughout the Neolithic. At the Yeavering palace site the 'ritual pit' (to the north of building C1) was discovered containing burnt bone fragments and Grooved Ware pottery of the Woodlands and Clacton styles (Ferrell 1990), together with two flint flakes and charred hazelnut shells (Hope-Taylor 1977, 348-51). These highly decorated bucket-shaped vessels are commonly associated with ceremonial activities, and with henges in particular, and it is at Yeavering, at the foot of the Bell, that one such monument was constructed. It was not until the investigation by Anthony Harding in 1976 (Harding 1981) that the monument was confirmed as a henge. There was no surviving evidence for an internal setting of stones or posts in the central platform. The henge is aligned south-east to north-west with the re-erected standing stone lying 125m to the south-east. Outside the north-west entrance was an oval pit grave with a stone covering. The pit contained a crouched inhumation burial with its head to the south. This is the first evidence of inhumation in the basin, suggesting that burial practices may also have become more complex and varied by the end of the Neolithic. Although no finds were associated with this burial its location and orientation led the excavator to believe it was associated with the henge. This recalls the situation at Woodhenge where the inhumation burial of a child with a deliberately smashed skull was found in a grave outside the entrance to this site (Cunnington 1929). In the latter case the infant is generally thought to be a sacrifice associated with the foundation of the monument. The location of both these burials close to entrances suggests their significance as 'threshold' deposits, marking access into the world of the other within the henge. Passing over such a deposit each time someone entered the Yeavering monument will have reiterated the significance of the offering and signalled the passage from the living, physical world into the spirit world beyond. Being located outside the north-west entrance, the grave at Yeavering was also placed on the axial alignment of the monument that extends to the standing stone and the distant hilltop of Ros Castle (Harding 2000, 272).

I have argued elsewhere (Waddington 1999, 159-64) that the henge monuments of the Milfield plain were situated to form a processional route across the basin, something previously alluded to by Harding (1987, 34, 62-3; 2000, 274). The route is thought to proceed from the northern end of the valley, from the Milfield north henge complex, towards the southernmost henge at Yeavering. The dating, form and functional similarities of the henges strongly suggest that these monuments were likely to have formed part of a contemporary ceremonial complex (Harding 1981; 2000). As all the henges along the route have two or more entrances, this architectural form implies they were monuments intended to facilitate the passage of people (Loveday 1988). The orientation of this proposed route appears to be directed from north to south based on the following argument. On leaving the avenue formed by the Milfield North double pit alignment the participant is deflected by the river, and by turning south would see the Milfield North henge entrance aligned towards the Cheviot hills. Leaving the henge, his view, framed by its southern entrance, is directed towards a stretch of the Cheviot hills with Yeavering Bell visible on the right-hand side of the view (Harding 2000, 272). Having passed through the southern entrance, the participant would see a large timber post on the same alignment as the henge, pointing once again towards the same view, with Yeavering conspicuous as the site of the final henge. This alignment only works for someone travelling in a north–south direction, as the Yeavering henge, being aligned close to east–west, makes no reference to the Milfield North complex in its orientation. Therefore, the alignment of the Milfield North complex suggests that the Yeavering henge was located at the end of a processional route rather than its start. The passage from henge to henge across the valley floor would culminate with a river crossing before reaching the final henge at Yeavering. In this case the participant would have to cross the Glen, perhaps fording it in the reach adjacent to Yeavering, before entering the henge. It is suggested that the henge was entered from the west because the position of the grave in the western entrance could have served as a threshold deposit, and also because by passing through the henge in this direction the participant could experience its alignment towards the standing stone and Ros Castle. If the henge is entered from the east, this alignment is not seen.

The standing stone may have served to draw people to the correct line of site by acting as a focusing device, while at the same time aligning the view from the eastern henge entrance to the hilltop of Ros Castle on the sandstone escarpment. Harding (2000, 272) has previously made the point that virtually all the prehistoric rock art and a number of large cairn cemeteries are located on the sandstone escarpment. The referencing of these hills within the henge architecture is surely an acknowledgement of their importance to the henge builders. If this scenario has even some validity then it would mean that Yeavering formed the climax of a ritual procession based around a planned ceremonial complex that stretched across the length of the one of the most spectacular Neolithic ritual complexes in northern England.

CONCLUSIONS

It is clear that the formalisation of Yeavering as a key ritual centre had been established by the end of the Neolithic, if not before. What is more, it was at Yeavering and the Milfield North complex, at either end of the processional way respectively, that early Bronze Age people chose to locate cremation cemeteries. At Milfield North, ring-ditches were positioned at the base of Whitton Hill very close to the henge (Miket 1985), while at Yeavering the Eastern Ring-ditch was placed on the same alignment as the henge and this formed the focus for a large number of subsequent cremations. This attraction of subsequent burials demonstrates physical continuity of ritual practice into the early Bronze Age. However, it is on the question of continuity that I would like to conclude.

Hope-Taylor framed his argument for continuity around the idea of virtually continuous settlement at Yeavering from the Neolithic to the early medieval periods. Since then this view has been critiqued by a number of authors. Bradley (1987) argued against ritual continuity at the site and made a case for deliberate appropriation by the Anglian hierarchy of a, by then, ancient site to create a mythical sense of continuity with the past in order to promote and protect the interests of a social elite. More recently Scull (1991) has cast doubt on the existence of a post-Roman phase at the site while others have made the point that there is also little evidence for a Romano-British presence on the site as Hope-Taylor's 'field system' has been identified as geological features (ice-edge polygons) by Tim Gates. However, the Romano-British farming settlement at the south end of the site, at the foot of the Bell now provides better evidence for Romano-British continuity.

Although there is currently little evidence for a completely unbroken sequence of activity at the site, and direct ritual continuity is unlikely, there is quite clearly continuity in the way Yeavering was thought of as a special place through the ages. We should not, therefore, envisage continuity at Yeavering in the same presence-absence terms as some previous commentators. Firstly, a physical presence is not required on a site in order for it to remain sacred or important over long time spans. People do not have to live there continuously for the concept of place to be maintained. How many places do we know of in our inhabited landscapes that are referred to by name but which have no cultural traces remaining today? We are talking here about continuity of cultural memory and that is not something that requires a continual sequence of archaeological deposits. Secondly, the fact that Yeavering was repeatedly chosen to be a settlement, ritual and administrative focus over a span of several thousand years, whether punctuated or not, means the importance of Yeavering as a place was maintained in the cultural memory of inhabitants of the region over many generations. Why did the Votadini build one of their largest forts here, why did the Anglian kings of Bernicia choose to build a royal estate centre here, and why was this place chosen for the Christian conversion of the Bernician people if Yeavering was not considered significant in the existing cultural traditions at these times?

Yeavering is a classic example of what landscape archaeologists term a 'persistent place' and this is reflected by the nature of the datable deposits and the significance evidently attached to the place over several millennia. Indeed it is one of the best archaeological examples in the British Isles. Each new era had to make reference to this special place in order to acquire legitimacy, and this could account for the punctuated archaeological record at the site. Moreover it would account for why this place, out of the entire north-east region, was selected time and again to build the most outstanding monuments of each age. Although, as we have seen, geographical setting was a critical component in the initial creation of Yeavering as a place, this does not satisfactorily account for the persistence of that importance through time when it is considered that the landscape may have been used and thought about in different ways in different periods, and that as people modified the landscape other conspicuous landscape settings would have been created. However, continuity of cultural memory, traditions and associations would explain the extraordinary sequence of archaeological monuments at the site, as each age had to redefine itself in relation to this place. This is not to suggest that such cultural continuity should be understood as something that is fixed and unbroken through time, rather it should be seen as part of what constitutes 'culture' and is thus ever changing; being reworked within the context of each generation. It is in this sense that we should perceive continuity at Yeavering and not as an unbroken sequence of pits, pots and post-holes. Brian Hope-Taylor's argument for continuity may, therefore, be valid, though for slightly different reasons than originally thought.

4

YEAVERING BELL HILLFORT

Alastair Oswald and Trevor Pearson

INTRODUCTION

The hillfort on Yeavering Bell was almost certainly constructed at some point in the first millennium BC and subsequently underwent several major modifications before its abandonment as a major settlement, which may have occurred well before the Roman invasion under Agricola in AD 79. It has become almost a truism that the massive enclosure, with evidence for at least 125 roundhouses within its defences, constitutes 'the only true hillfort in the Cheviots'. As such, Yeavering Bell long ago cast a shadow over the rest of the region's Iron Age monumental hilltop enclosures.

Dr Brian Hope-Taylor's recognition and excavation of *Ad Gefrin,* the Anglian royal palace referred to by Bede, inadvertently reinforced this imbalance (Hope-Taylor 1977). For his research turned Yeavering into virtually a household name and so stole the limelight, by proxy, from other hilltop enclosures that might merit our attention. The proximity to the River Glen implied by Bede's account probably explains why the remains of the hillfort had not, at an early date, become associated in folklore with the site of the palace. Yet in many people's minds, Hope-Taylor's research itself established an indirect link between the hillfort and the palace at the foot of the hill that amplified the perceived importance of the hillfort. Ironically, it has even given rise, on rare occasions and amongst people unfamiliar with the region's heritage, to precisely the belief – long-avoided and wholly mistaken – that the palace was built within the prehistoric ramparts. As if all this were not enough, the proximity of Hadrian's Wall has, from the eighteenth century onwards, combined with the apparent dearth of true hillforts to divert energies that might otherwise have been directed towards research into the area's other prehistoric monuments. The cumulative effect of the pre-eminence of the hillfort on Yeavering Bell and Hadrian's Wall is that this region's wealth of other Iron Age settlements and associated remains have never quite emerged from the shadows. This inequality is all the more remarkable given that Yeavering has not, in fact, seen much more investigation than several of the other hilltop enclosures in the region, and a negligible amount compared to the best understood hillforts of southern England. Yet despite the efforts of a succession of individuals and organisations to turn the spotlight onto other sites, the Iron Age in this region has, too often, been treated as a rather unremarkable interlude between rock art and Romans.

Consequently, when the Northumberland National Park Authority initiated its five-year programme of research, conservation and interpretation entitled *Discovering Our Hillfort Heritage*, it was predictable that investigations would begin at Yeavering Bell. The £1.2 million project (largely funded by the European Union and Heritage Lottery Fund) was a partnership between the National Park Authority, English Heritage, the Universities of Newcastle and Durham, and the Northumberland Archaeological Group, with an invaluable individual

29 Aerial photograph of the hillfort on Yeavering Bell from the north-west by Tim Gates, May 1997. © Tim Gates

contribution by aerial photographer Tim Gates (*29*). In 1998, an investigation and field survey of the Yeavering Bell hillfort was carried out by the Royal Commission on the Historical Monuments of England (RCHME) as that organisation's first and last contribution to the project before merger with English Heritage in the following year (Pearson 1998). After five subsequent years of detailed investigations of other hilltop enclosures in the Cheviots, the publication of this paper offers a welcome opportunity to revisit the findings of that initial investigation of Yeavering Bell. There are two interwoven intentions running through this paper: firstly, to re-examine the hillfort on Yeavering Bell in detail as an individual monument, or series of monuments; secondly, to understand the site in the context of other hilltop enclosures in the region.

HISTORY OF RESEARCH

The hillfort on Yeavering Bell has been the subject of scientific archaeological research spanning almost 300 years, doubtless preceded by many centuries of less rigorous speculation. 'Yeaverin Hill' is one of the few summits picked out by name on John Speed's 1610 map of the county (Speed 1610). As early as 1716, John Warburton schematically depicted the perimeter of the hillfort on his map, in a style that linked the monument with the smaller hilltop enclosures that he showed (Warburton 1716). At some point before his death in 1732, John Horsley described the three key elements of the site: a '*tumulus*' on the eastern summit, a 'trench' surrounding it, and 'the remains of an old enclosure or wall' surrounding both peaks, with entrances on the north and south (Horsley nd). He suggested that both the trench and the wall were constructed to protect the *tumulus*. Less than 50 years later, John Wallis recorded, in addition, 'many circular foundations of buildings on the sides or slopes' of the area enclosed by the wall, which he interpreted as a fortification built by the Danes (Wallis 1769). Also in that year, Captain Armstrong, like Warburton before him, depicted the perimeter in the same schematic style as a number of other, smaller, hilltop enclosures (Armstrong 1769).

In 1776, William Hutchinson was so impressed by what he saw on the summit that he drew up not only a heavily stylised plan of the site but also a beautiful semi-bird's eye view (Hutchinson 1778, 246-57; *30*). This technique, popular in the late seventeenth and early eighteenth centuries for showing off the designs of grand gardens, had also been employed previously by the great antiquarian William Stukely. Hutchinson accepted only the entrance on the southern side of the hillfort as genuine, but perceived 'a broad way…three paces wide in a straight direction, as if formed by an even pavement, extending about 30 yards in ascent towards the [eastern] crown of the hill'. He observed that what he termed a 'wall'

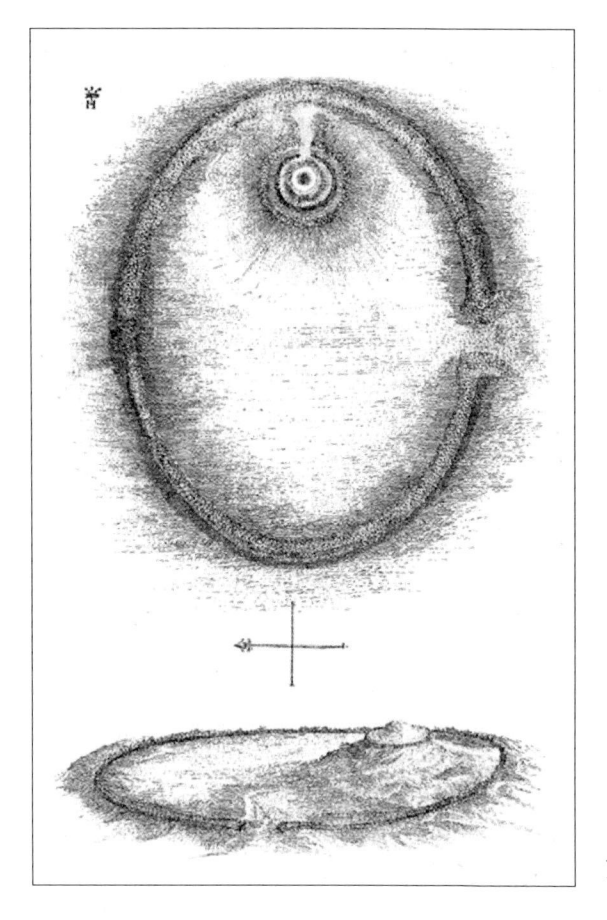

30 William Hutchinson's 1778 plan and view of the hillfort

lying outside the ditch enclosing the summit 'consist[ed] of fewer materials.' It is uncertain whether this conclusion was based simply on the absence of exposed stone, or whether he carried out a trial excavation into the earthwork. He suggested that the site as a whole was 'of very remote antiquity', a form of words widely used at that date to indicate a prehistoric origin, and discussed the possible use of the site by Druids for the performance of various rituals. In the end, however, he pointed to the proximity of the Anglian palace as evidence that all the remains probably belonged to that same era.

Christopher and John Greenwood's 1828 map of the county, whose depiction of the hillfort followed the style of Warburton and Armstrong, represents the last completely schematic portrayal of the site (Greenwood and Greenwood 1828). For, in July 1858, His Grace the Duke of Northumberland funded a large-scale survey by Henry MacLauchlan, the former Ordnance Survey fieldworker and renowned surveyor of Hadrian's Wall (MacLauchlan 1867b, 24; *31*). MacLauchlan surveyed the hillfort with his customary accuracy and observational skill,

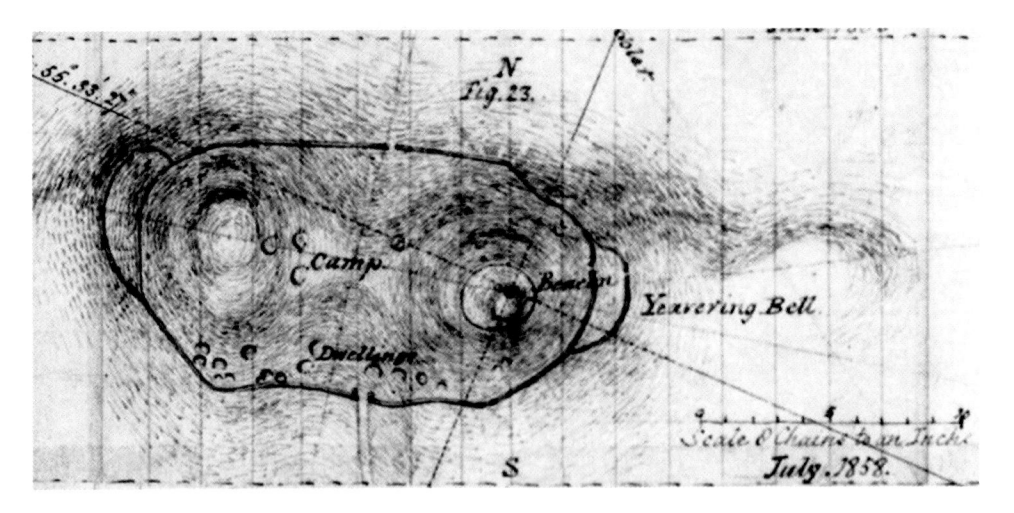

31 Henry MacLauchlan's plan of the hillfort, dated July 1858. Reproduced by kind permission of His Grace the Duke of Northumberland

recording, in addition to the major features noted by previous investigators, the so-called 'annexes' at the eastern and western ends of the main circuit and all the minor breaks in the ramparts. He depicted a broad track approaching the southern entrance and showed the interior of the gateway itself as being flanked by structures that he seems to have interpreted as small guard-houses. The fact that at this stage in his research, MacLauchlan had encountered just the first few of the many prehistoric sites that he would eventually survey in the Cheviots probably explains why he mapped only 24 of the more obvious house platforms in the interior, terming them 'dwellings'. Three years later, partly on the evidence of his excavations, George Tate (1863, 438) was to interpret the platforms as 'a kind of pit dwelling', even though he also termed them 'foundations' elsewhere. If, as seems to be the case, MacLauchlan recognised the possibility that timber buildings had once occupied the platforms, he was well ahead of his time. Examples of timber roundhouses were identified sporadically over the next 80 years, notably at the Glastonbury 'lake village' in the early 1900s (Bulleid and Gray 1911; 1917). Yet it was not really until 1940, when Gerhard Bersu conclusively demonstrated the form of a timber-framed roundhouse at Little Woodbury in Wiltshire, that the once-unshakeable belief in the existence of 'pit-dwellings' suddenly and quietly died out (Bersu 1940; Evans 1989).

In 1860, the Ordnance Survey investigated the hillfort, though their map did not become generally available for consultation until its publication six years later (Ordnance Survey 1866). Terming the earthworks 'Druidical Remains', the mapmakers recorded, in addition to the cairn on the eastern summit and the enclosure surrounding it, four pairs of roundhouses within the main rampart, all

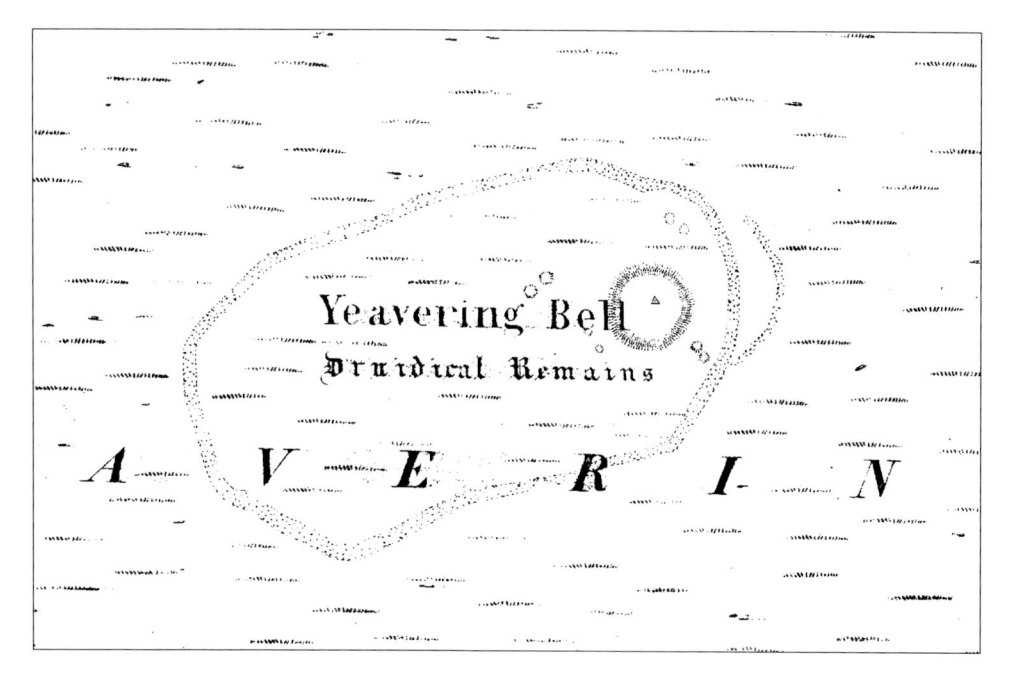

32 Extract from the Ordnance Survey First Edition 25-inch scale map of 1897

grouped around the eastern summit. They also recorded the more easterly of the two outlying stretches of rampart which George Jobey was later to call 'annexes'. Despite the subsequent production of larger scale maps, there was no significant change to the Ordnance Survey depiction for more than 60 years, when the number of house platforms shown in the interior was revised to 51; even then, the western 'annexe' was still omitted (Ordnance Survey 1897; 1924; see also *32*).

Three years after MacLauchlan's survey, His Grace sponsored excavations by George Tate of Alnwick, the remarkable polymath who was, amongst other things, Secretary of the Berwickshire Naturalists' Club (Tate 1863, 431-8). Tate appears to have begun by resurveying the site at the same scale as MacLauchlan, for the plan that accompanies his account of the excavations differs slightly in various details. He identified gateways at the four cardinal points around the circuit, again interpreting that on the south as the principal entrance. He also dug into the rampart in three places, probably at and adjacent to the southern, eastern and northern entrances. Describing the enclosure surrounding the eastern summit, Tate dismissed the suggestion, made by Hutchinson 85 years earlier, of a 'paved way' approaching its sole entrance on the eastern side. Certainly, no possible trace of any paving can be seen today, so Tate may well have been correct in suggesting that natural outcrops had been mistaken for an artificial surface. Although he mentions 'many circular foundations' (of roundhouses), his survey recorded only 13, plus the two 'guard-houses' inside the southern gateway. This makes his total significantly lower than that reached by MacLauchlan three years earlier, suggesting that Tate did not have access to his predecessor's work. However, the distribution pattern of the platforms around the eastern summit is very similar to that on the Ordnance Survey map surveyed in 1860 and Tate acknowledges Sir Henry James, then Director General of that organisation, for providing a copy of the mapping (five years before its eventual publication). He apparently singled out six platforms for excavation: three by digging narrow trial trenches and three by means of 'clearing' – as he put it – the whole platform. He noted 'evidences of occupation' on all of them. His plan shows that three of the platforms investigated lay on the eastern slope of the western summit; traces of spoil and trench edges make it possible to identify two of them on the ground today. In the event, the results of his excavations rather belied the primitive connotations of the term 'hut', for the majority of the circular buildings he excavated proved to be between 24ft and 30ft (7.3m to 9.1m) in diameter. He also excavated the more westerly of the two stone-built structures he supposed to be guard-houses, recovering charcoal and the lower stone of a quern 12in (30cm) in diameter, made of local sandstone.

The handful of artefacts Tate unearthed and recorded from the roundhouse platforms are potentially of great significance, especially in view of the virtual absence of any records of later finds (Tate 1863, 436-8) 5). He was confident in ascribing the hillfort as a whole to the 'Celtic' period, a term whose accuracy we might quibble with today. Yet, ironically, while he was undoubtedly correct in essence, none of the finds he records can actually be securely dated to the earlier Iron Age. Three 'oak rings' of a dark brown colour with 'a bright polish' are perhaps shale bracelets; these might be Iron Age, but objects of this type were manufactured over a considerably longer span of time. A 'copper' (probably bronze) *fibula* pin might be late Iron Age, but could be later. Near the southern gateway, a flint flake, which Tate describes as a 'knife', was found 'in a cutting outside of the wall' at a depth of 3ft (0.9m). This considerable depth suggests that it may have lain beneath the tumbled mass of stone against the outer face of the rampart, which has evidently been exposed over a distance of several metres to the west of the gateway. Three more pieces of flint, which Tate describes as 'the rough material out of which weapons and instruments were manufactured', were found on a house platform. While there is admittedly a growing body of evidence that flint continued in occasional use into the Iron Age, at face value it would seem unreasonable to assume these pieces to be of that date, rather than Bronze Age or Neolithic. A flat rotary quernstone, 18in (46cm) in diameter and only 1in (2.5cm) thick, is not illustrated but seems likely to be Roman Iron Age in date; Tate – an accomplished geologist – also recognised that the stone was not from a local source, but could not identify that source. He also describes a sherd of soft, 'bright red' pottery made of fine clay, which could perhaps be a form of *terra sigillata*, the high-quality Roman tableware also commonly (but misleadingly) known as 'Samian'. The only sherd illustrated is thick, hand-built and with signs of a possible collar, and could well be part of an early Bronze Age funerary urn. A jasper ball 3in (7.5cm) in diameter is also likely to be Neolithic or early Bronze Age and might again come from a funerary context, though it was again found on a house platform.

On the eastern summit, Tate also excavated what he describes as a 'small enclosure' 13ft x 10ft (3.9m x 3.0m), apparently unaware that this earthwork had been dug into by Hutchinson 85 years earlier, although he refers elsewhere to 'Hutcheson's' observations. Tate's description of the 'small enclosure' tallies perfectly with Hutchinson's comment that 'The center of the kairn is hollow like a bason, six paces from brim to brim'. As far as can be judged from what still survives today, the earthwork does indeed seem to equate to the heavily disturbed remains of a burial cairn, as Hutchinson suggested explicitly and Horsley before him had implied. The cairn, which would probably once have been a simple circular mound approximately 8m in diameter and at least 0.6m high, is presumably of early Bronze Age date. The centre of the monument has been subject to such thorough robbing that what survives resembles part of a ring-shaped bank, as both Hutchinson and Tate described in their different ways. It would therefore seem that the robbing had taken place long before Hutchinson's investigation. Some additional disturbance must have been caused by the establishment of an Ordnance Survey trigonometrical station on top of the mound in the mid-nineteenth century. In dismissing the popular interpretation of a large stone as a Druid altar, Tate seems to draw attention to a feature of the cairn that is no longer identifiable, perhaps the capstone of a cist. Yet Hutchinson had previously expressed disappointment that no such 'altar' was present and it is difficult to explain away its absence today, if it indeed ever existed. It would seem, again both from Tate's description and from what can now be seen on the surface, that he emptied (or probably re-emptied) a rectangular rock-cut pit at the centre of the cairn, which might represent the remains of just such a cist. At a depth of 15in (38cm), he encountered a layer of charcoal and burnt material. This confirms Hutchinson's earlier observation that 'After removing the turf and soil for a little depth, we found the stones reduced to a sort of *calx* [that is, burnt stone], and everywhere retaining a strong impression of fire'. Given the natural prominence of the summit, this deposit might conceivably relate to a 'beacon' as Hutchinson went on to imply, rather than residue from prehistoric cremations. However, there is no documentary evidence for the existence of any beacon on the summit, for even MacLauchlan's annotation in 1858 of a

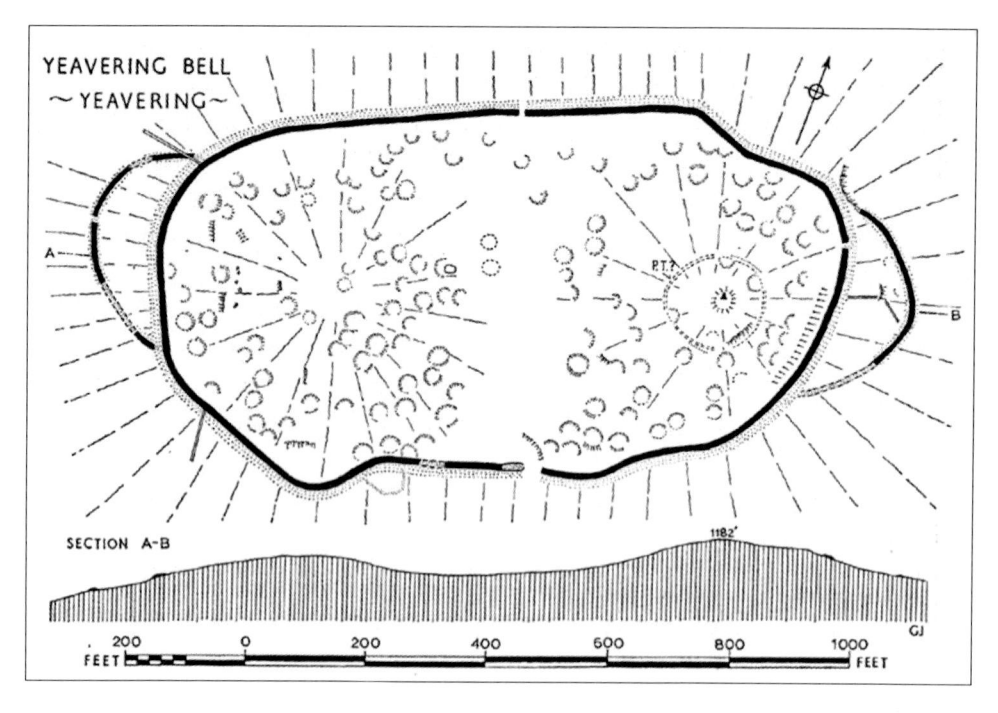

33 George Jobey's plan of the hillfort. Reproduced from Jobey 1965, figure 7

beacon there may derive from Hutchinson's speculation. Radiocarbon dating of the charcoal deposits today would not necessarily offer a clearer picture, for it is highly likely that, even it was not used as an 'official' beacon, the summit may have been the site of any number of unofficial bonfires. Some may even have been commemorated, for a small block of stone lying at the foot of the natural eminence and possibly originally located on the summit itself, bears two inscriptions: one includes the date 1809, but the other is weathered to the point of illegibility and is presumably much earlier.

In the late 1950s or early 1960s, George Jobey undertook what might be termed the first truly analytical earthwork survey of the hillfort (Jobey 1965, 31-5; *33*). In the interior, he recorded 125 house platforms, estimating the real total to be slightly higher. His main concern initially was to point out the constructional differences between 'ring-groove' and 'ring-mound' types, examples of which he surveyed at large scale, concluding that both forms of building were prehistoric (Jobey 1965, figure 8). Ring-grooves represent the foundation trenches dug to support continuous lines of upright posts or planks, while ring-mounds may have acted as sleeper walls, supporting a timber 'collar' on which the conical roof would have been supported. Undoubtedly influenced by Stuart Piggott's concept of 'Celtic cowboys', Jobey also interpreted the outlying arcs of rampart at the western and eastern ends of the hillfort as 'annexes', in which he believed the cattle of the occupants would have been corralled (Jobey 1965, 43-4). In a subsequent article he went on to suggest, in keeping with his conclusions at many other hillforts, that the circuit of ditch enclosing the eastern summit was the foundation trench for a timber palisade (Jobey 1966, 97-8). This, he argued, predated the construction of the hut platforms and by extension the stone-built rampart. In this, he was following the model of the so-called 'Hownam sequence', which was based on the findings of Margaret Piggott's excavations at Hownam Rings in Roxburghshire (C.M. Piggott 1950). Piggott's interpretation, in turn, ultimately derived from Christopher Hawkes' theory of successive invasions by peoples he termed the Iron Age A, B and C cultures (Hawkes 1931). As with so many hillforts in the Cheviots, Jobey's collected observations have remained the most widely accepted interpretation of the site to date, passed on without critical reappraisal in such influential general works as *The Northern Counties to AD 1000* (Higham 1986, 120).

In 1958, five years after the first season of excavations on the site of the Anglian

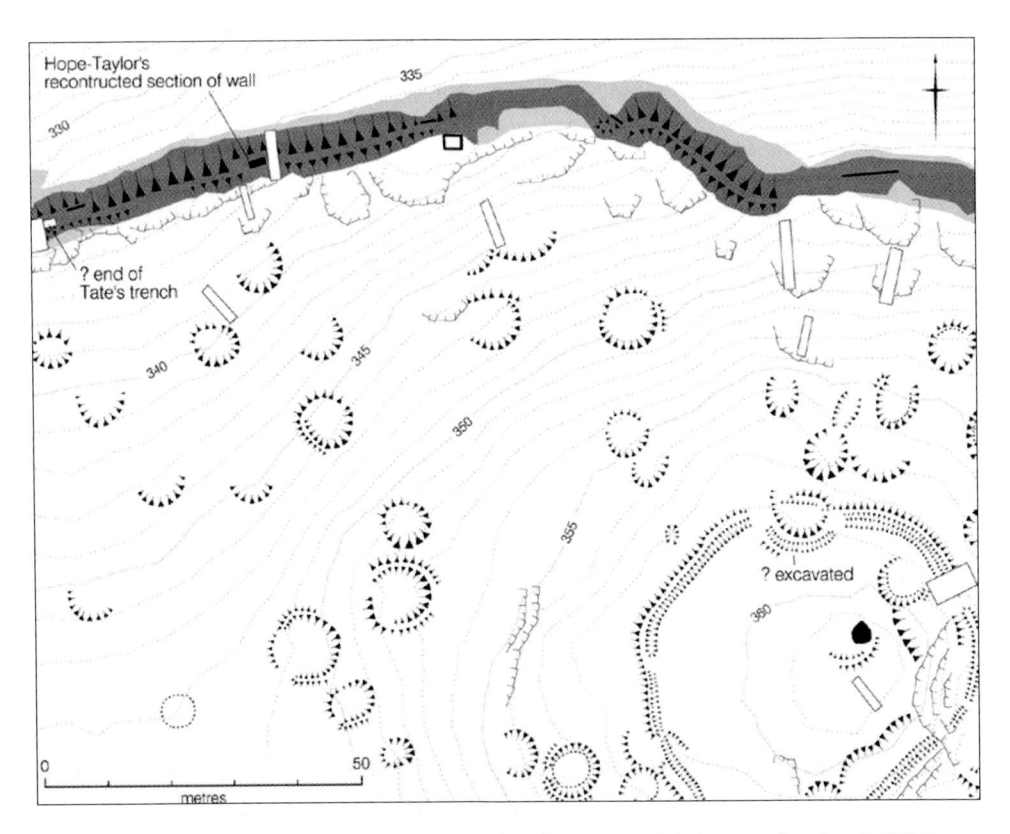

34 Transcription of Hope-Taylor's excavation trenches shown on aerial photographs taken by J.K.S. St Joseph on 16 July 1958

palace, Dr Brian Hope-Taylor excavated on the hilltop seeking evidence of contemporary activity (Hope-Taylor 1977, 6-9). The textual account of these excavations is sketchy, and the trenches were omitted from the published plan, which was based on Jobey's survey (but see this volume's Appendix for a statement by Hope-Taylor regarding the number of trenches excavated). An aerial photograph taken by J.K.S. St Joseph on 16 July 1958 shows 10 trenches on the northern slopes of the eastern summit, targeting the supposed northern gateway of the hillfort, the rampart itself, the northern side of the entrance into the enclosure on the eastern summit, and several house platforms (St Joseph 1958. *11, 34*). However, the photograph does not record the full tally of Hope-Taylor's trenches, for it does not show one placed in order to investigate building foundations just west of the hillfort's southern gateway, a view of which was later published (Hope-Taylor 1977, Plate 11). It is unclear whether Hope-Taylor was aware that Tate had excavated the same structure almost a century earlier, interpreting it as a guard-house (Tate 1863, 436). On the northern side of the circuit, adjacent to the trench dug to investigate the structure of the rampart, whose position can still be identified on the ground, a short section of walling 0.8m high was reconstructed on top of the rubble bank; this too survives (Welfare 1992, 638-9).

Though Roman control over the territory north of Hadrian's wall did not last much more than 80 years in total between Agricola's conquest in AD 79 and the retreat to Hadrian's frontier in about AD 185, the artefacts recovered from three of the houses included three sherds of what Hope-Taylor called 'Samian' pottery and two late Roman *minimi* coins. The coins are of such small denomination that it is not impossible that they were casual losses effectively irrelevant to the dating of the actual occupation of the hillfort. Hope-Taylor referred to 'desultory, small scale use or occupation of its interior during the second, third and fourth centuries' (Hope-Taylor 1977, 267). Yet without the finds themselves, it remains impossible to pin down the date, or dates, of the so-called 'Samian' sherds more accurately than the span between the mid-first century AD and the end of the fourth century AD. Therefore, these too could be written off as unhelpful, if not entirely irrelevant, in terms of dating the actual occupation of the hillfort. Thus, in a strange echo of Tate's work, Hope-Taylor's evidence did not – as far as we can now tell – fully support his conclusion that the hillfort was constructed at the end of the first millennium BC and reached its heyday by the first century AD.

George Jobey was sometimes called a 'one-man Royal Commission', but in 1986 the real Royal Commission called into question one of his most important observations: that the hillfort had been preceded by a palisaded enclosure around the eastern summit (RCHME 1986). Instead, it was observed that the so-called palisade trench actually cut through those house platforms with which it came into contact, suggesting it to be of later origin than the hillfort and therefore

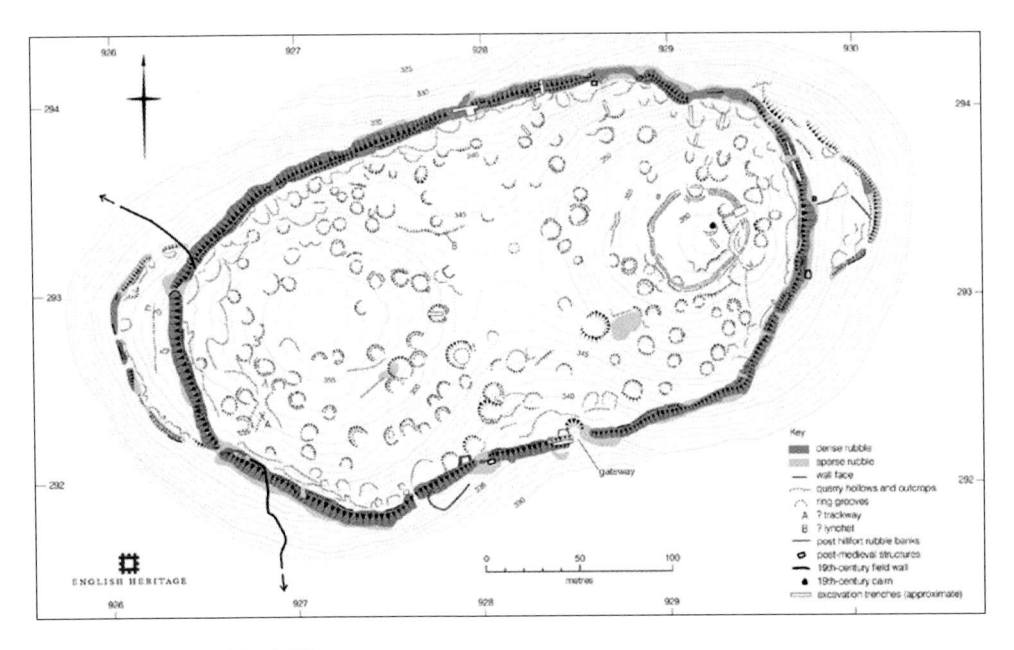

35 RCHME plan of the hillfort

potentially one of the Anglian structures that Hope-Taylor had sought in vain. Richard Bradley had reached the same conclusion on the basis of a field visit in the early 1970s (Bradley 1987, 10 and pers. comm.) and the idea has been raised repeatedly since (Welfare 1992, 639; Frodsham 1999a, 198). The Royal Commission's work also began to record the wealth of remains – notably settlements, cultivation terraces and field systems belonging to the Roman Iron Age – surviving in the landscape around the hillfort. Further field survey is still required to flesh out this picture.

Given the intensity of research that Yeavering had seen (at least by the standards of sites in the Cheviots), it might have been expected that the analytical field survey carried out in 1998 as the opening salvo of the *Discovering our Hillfort Heritage* project (35) could have achieved little beyond dotting the 'i's and crossing the 't's left by previous investigators. Yet, while it is perhaps true that the latest depiction of the earthworks differs only in detail from plans published in the past, the new research has given rise to a number of important advances in understanding.

THE RAMPART, GATEWAYS AND SO-CALLED 'ANNEXES'

As George Tate observed, the 9m-wide bank of rubble that defines the perimeter today seems to represent the tumbled remains of a massive drystone wall, around

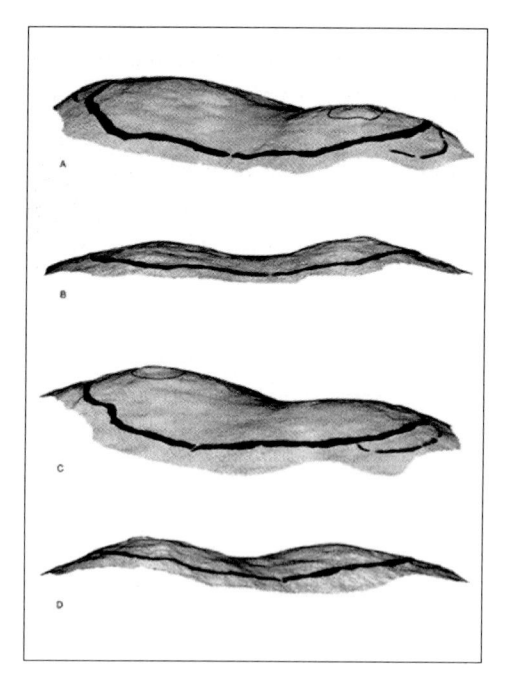

36 RCHME digital terrain model of the hillfort rampart in relation to the natural topography

3m broad at the base and with an outer face probably once standing to at least 2.7m in height. This rampart is clearly an investment of labour in defensive architecture that can justifiably be compared with the monstrous multivallate hillforts of Wessex. It stretches for just over 900m – only slightly more than the half mile estimated by Horsley in the early 1700s. It does not follow the contours precisely, but has a vertical range of about 16m, as digital terrain modelling clearly demonstrates (*36*). In plan, though it follows a smoothly curving course along much of its northern side, in a few places elsewhere there are sharp changes of angle, in at least one instance perhaps representing a response to a change in the natural gradient of the hillside, although this issue is discussed in more detail below. The circuit encloses an area (not taking account of the gradient) of 5.6ha (13.8 acres), slightly less than the 16.5 acres estimated by Hutchinson in 1776. Around the whole circuit, later structures ranging from the foundations of small, rectangular shepherds' huts, probably of medieval or later date, to obviously modern grouse-shooting butts and walkers' shelters have been crudely built from the tumbled rubble of the Iron Age wall.

The material used in the construction of the rampart was the local andesite, a hard, granite-like rock which would have been a bright orangey/pink colour when first split, as has been noted elsewhere (for example, McOmish 1999, 118; Frodsham 2004a, 38). Though the rubble includes a few rounded boulders that may already have been exposed on the surface, the majority of the building stone seems to have been laboriously quarried from a hollow just behind the rampart. The wall has collapsed so completely that there are few indications of its original form. At several points around the circuit, however, short stretches of the outer face, which is rather roughly built and stands at most two or three courses high, can be seen within the mass of tumbled rubble. The strip immediately behind the line of this outer face generally contains a much higher proportion of small stones, which presumably represent the core of the wall. It is not inconceivable that the structure was deliberately demolished, but it seems much more likely that it was ultimately the victim of the instability inherent in its design in relation to the natural slope. For the wall was built essentially as a terrace projecting out from the slope, which would have put much greater pressure on the outer face, potentially leading to precisely the type of apparently sudden collapse that appears to have occurred. The slight batter in the outer face, noted by Tate, may well have been an attempt to counteract that pressure. The inner face, though perhaps as much as 1.2m high on the north-west of the circuit, may not have been much more than 0.5m high for most of its length. However, the only visible evidence for actual facing along the back of the wall is a line of three massive boulders at the western end of the circuit.

Of the four original gateways identified by Tate, those at the eastern and western ends of the circuit can be categorically dismissed as being breaches which post-date the collapse of the rampart. The southern entrance is the only one that is incontrovertibly genuine. Like the possible northern entrance, it is sited on the line of the saddle between the two summits, so that the approach is relatively gentle. Indeed, this is the only approach suitable for horses or carts (and then only with effort), so the fact that the gateway is oriented towards the summit of Hedgehope, the second highest peak in the Cheviots, is not necessarily significant (Frodsham 2004a, 38). At around 4m wide, the entrance is almost double the width of the possible northern entrance, and of the entrances into most other hillforts in the region. It seems likely that the passage would have been barred by a massive timber double gate, which would constitute an exceptionally monumental design. It was probably Tate, rather than Hope-Taylor, who was responsible for removing a strip of rubble to the west of the gateway, apparently in a search for the outer face of the rampart wall, for the disturbance is indicated on Jobey's plan, which was probably made prior to Hope-Taylor's investigations. The same technique was used on either side of the northern and eastern entrances; Hope-Taylor is only known to have examined the northern entrance, while Tate (1863, 435) states that he excavated the 'gateways' (plural).

Tate excavated what he referred to as a 'guard-house' set inside the western terminal of the southern gateway: this was later reinvestigated by Hope-Taylor. Tate, like MacLauchlan before him, depicted two such structures, one on each side of the gateway, and the remains of both can still be discerned, though the excavated one is now clearer. Rather than being Iron Age guard-houses, the structures seem to post-date the collapse of the rampart, which probably accounts for Hope-Taylor's decision to dig here. As observed below, the two structures are almost the only ones that could be assigned to the Roman Iron Age on the evidence of their morphology. Tate's discovery in the western structure of a small quernstone, made of local sandstone, may support that possibility, at least to the extent that it speaks of domestic life rather than the ceaseless vigilance of guards.

The evidence for the northern entrance is more equivocal. Here, a 2.4m-wide passage through the rampart is almost entirely clear of stone and the western terminal of the rampart is defined by several large earthfast boulders, a construction technique typical of genuine hillfort entrances elsewhere, but also of entrances created or remodelled in the Roman Iron Age. The hollow immediately behind the entrance, presumably worn down by passing feet, is also a feature of some other Iron Age gateways on steep slopes, but more often of those that were reused in the Roman Iron Age. Hope-Taylor's published photograph of the trench he excavated here seems to show a line of stones, defining the rear edge of a degraded stony bank, running across the inside of the passage, which could indicate that the wall was originally continuous (Hope-Taylor 1977, Plate 12).

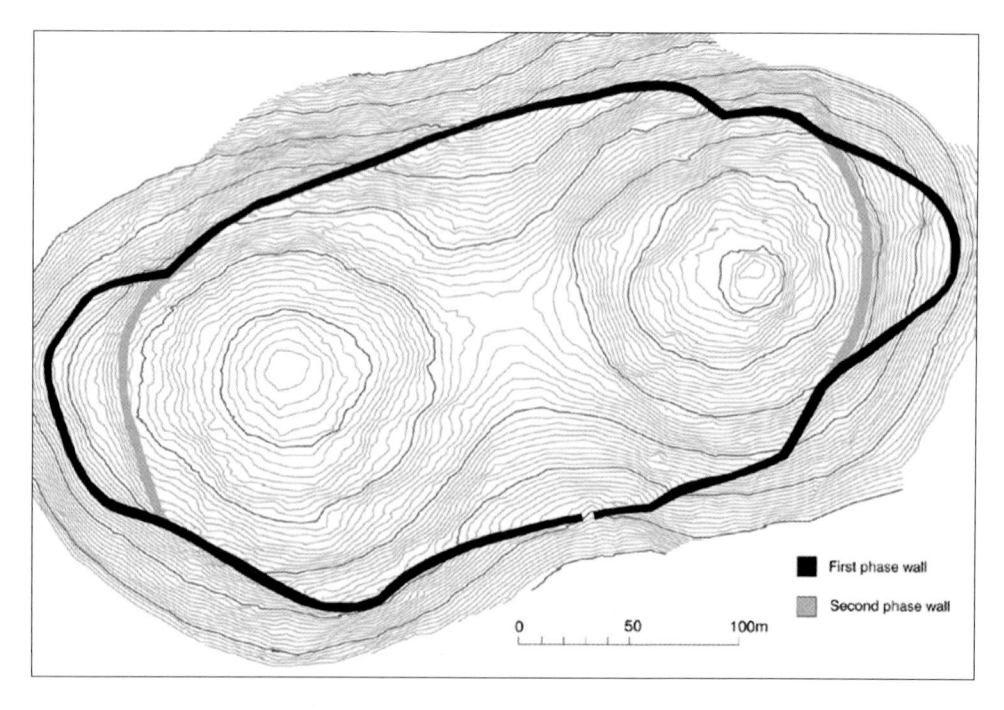

37 RCHME plan of the early enclosure

In short, the entrance might be of great antiquity, perhaps even dating to the Roman Iron Age, but it is probably not original in the strict sense.

What George Jobey interpreted as 'annexes' for corraling cattle at either end of the hillfort can now be shown to be abandoned remnants of an earlier and considerably larger circuit (37). It is worth adding that, since the suggested entrances at the east and west ends of the hillfort seem to post-date the collapse of the second-phase rampart, even the possibility of the reuse of these subsidiary enclosures as corrals seems remote, for they would not have been easily accessible from the interior of the second-phase hillfort. A similar process of contraction, leaving abandoned an enclosed space which would have been inaccessible from the hillfort, has been recognised by recent field survey at the much smaller hillfort nearby on Great Hetha (Pearson and Lax 2001). These and other examples collectively add up to the dismissal of what has long been seen as a key piece of evidence for Iron Age livestock management, removing an important pillar of Stuart Piggott's long-accepted idea of 'Celtic cowboys' (S. Piggott 1958, 25; see also Topping 1989).

The new interpretation of the so-called 'annexes' also testifies to a time depth for the hillfort itself for which there was previously precious little evidence. At the south-west and north-east of the hillfort, the points at which the second-phase circuit diverged from the earlier line are marked by sharp changes of angle. Indeed, these angle changes and the inferred overall plan of the first-phase circuit are so awkward that it is tempting to speculate that there may, at some early stage, have been two smaller hillforts on Yeavering Bell, one occupying each of the twin summits. There is no discernible evidence for the course of earlier ramparts within the later circuit, except – perhaps – in the distribution of the house platforms. Certainly, house platforms are notable by their absence on the saddle between the two peaks. Furthermore, with the eye of faith, a concentric pattern can be discerned in the siting of the house platforms on the south-east side of the western summit, which might betray the former presence of a stretch of rampart following the natural contours. On the south-west side of the same summit, a short length of what appears to a slight hollowed trackway seems to predate one of the house platforms and therefore could conceivably relate to an earlier line of defence and perhaps an earlier gateway. The abandoned lengths of the earlier rampart outside the main circuit, particularly close to the points where the remodelled line diverges from them, were evidently robbed of stone, presumably to provide construction material for the stretches that replaced them. It is not totally far-fetched to suggest that within the main circuit, more conveniently upslope from the new construction work, the robbing may have been so intensive that every vestige of an earlier line was completely erased.

THE HOUSE PLATFORMS

The 1998 survey confirmed Jobey's tally of 125 house platforms. Given the high degree of earthwork preservation and the nature of the topography, it seems likely that this number may fall not far short of the actual maximum. However, it is probable that some additional roundhouses – perhaps as many as 20 – may have occupied the quarry hollow behind the rampart, their stances now impossible to distinguish, without excavation, from the cuttings left by the stone quarrying. We have already mentioned the curious absence of settlement traces on the saddle between the two summits, a piece of level ground which might be assumed to be amongst the most suitable parts of the hilltop for settlement. This absence cannot be satisfactorily accounted for by the nature of the vegetation cover, as previously suggested (Jobey 1965, 32). However, a short length of what seems to be a slight positive lynchet on the north-western side of the saddle hints that there may have been some form of cultivation across at least part of this apparently blank area, so some caution is still necessary in interpreting the distribution. If the absence of roundhouses is genuine and does not reflect the development of the settlement pattern over time, it is tempting to infer that the saddle was reserved for some special activity, presumably communal in nature.

It remains to be seen whether all the circular buildings were truly domestic houses. Even more crucially, it is impossible to gauge how many were in contemporary use. There is not a single clear instance of one roundhouse platform impinging on another, so it is not impossible that all were in use simultaneously. In this context, it is interesting to note that only one probable house platform has been identified within the two fairly large areas left abandoned by the contraction of the rampart from its earlier course. In other words, the first-phase enclosure (or enclosures, as speculated above) may have been larger in area, but may also have been more sparsely settled. Notwithstanding this uncertainty, Yeavering's tally certainly represents a respectable number of houses, even by the elevated standards of Wessex.

Of the total number, 77 examples (62 per cent) definitely employed the 'ring-groove' construction technique, which is generally held to be associated with timber roundhouses of the earlier Iron Age and late Bronze Age. The majority of a further 40 roundhouses probably employed the ring-groove technique, even though traces of the actual grooves can no longer be discerned on the surface. Only eight examples (6 per cent) are 'ring-mounds', a construction technique which Jobey (1965, 32) suggested might represent more substantial roundhouses, but contemporary in date with the ring-groove types. Since then, similar earthworks elsewhere have been shown by both excavation and field survey to be of Bronze Age date (Gates 1983; Jobey 1981; 1983; 1985). There are as yet no grounds for ruling out this possibility on Yeavering Bell; such buildings might well belong to a phase of unenclosed settlement predating the hillfort by some centuries.

The ring-mounds are emphatically not the low, stony banks with occasional upright facing stones that are generally considered typical of the period from the mid-second century AD onwards (termed Romano-British by Jobey, but here called the Roman Iron Age). Almost the only possible examples of this type of building are the two so-called guard-houses set inside the southern gateway. The sole stone-built structure in the interior of the hillfort, as first noted by Jobey (1965, 32), is rectangular and likely to be of medieval or later date. Equally, there are few signs of the subsidiary yards, compounds and other subdivisions which the recent surveys of other sites have confirmed are characteristic of Roman Iron Age settlements. Two small enclosures are identifiable: one within the abandoned stretch of the first-phase rampart at the eastern end of the hillfort and one against the outside of the rampart some 50m west of the southern gateway. Both seem to post-date the collapse of the second-phase rampart, but both are apparently associated with rectangular structures likely to be of medieval or later date.

However, the findings of the excavations at Eildon Hill North have somewhat alarming implications for this straightforward template for dating settlement remains. There, it would appear that timber roundhouses, very similar in design to those which are generally accepted as prehistoric in the Cheviots, were occupied during the second century AD by people who used Roman ornamental items (Owen 1992, 69). In view of the Roman artifacts from Yeavering Bell, which are few but apparently widely scattered, it may be worth reflecting on whether the use of the hilltop during the Roman Iron Age was really so 'desultory and small scale' as Hope-Taylor suggested.

Amongst the 50-odd roundhouse platforms where probable doorway orientations are discernible, there appears to be a real pattern, with most directed towards somewhere between south-east and north-east (*38*). Clearly, in such a windswept location and on gradients where topography must have been an important factor in influencing the design of roundhouses, this pattern could be interpreted in purely pragmatic terms. Yet it is noticeable that within this distribution, there are concentrations towards south-east and due east, the directions corresponding to sunrise at the equinoxes and at midwinter, which is typical of roundhouses of the earlier Iron Age, both regionally and nationally (Gates 1983, figure 3; Oswald 1997a). It is also worth noting that two of the largest roundhouses seemed to have been sited immediately above the southern gateway, one on either side, with their entrances facing towards the gate. A very similar pattern is evident on Hambledon Hill in Dorset, the two large roundhouses there (perhaps dating to the late Iron Age) sited in relation to a fork in a trackway leading from the gateway into the interior of the hillfort (Oswald

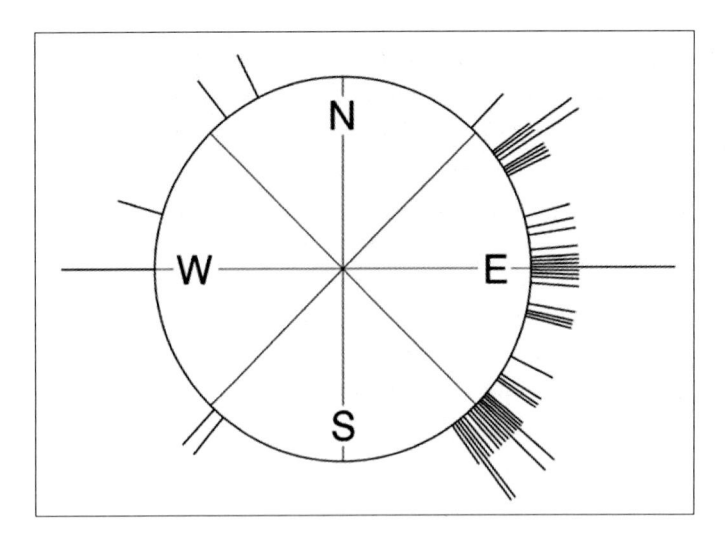

38 Orientation of the roundhouse doorways

1997b). If these two apparently equally important buildings were the homes of two equally important individuals – rulers, warrior champions, or Druids, for example – it would raise interesting questions about the exercise of power in Iron Age society. It has often been observed that it is generally very difficult to distinguish powerful individuals on the basis of excavated evidence. At Yeavering Bell, the surface traces may testify to some form of 'bi-archy'.

THE ENCLOSURE ON THE EASTERN SUMMIT

The roughly circular enclosure on the eastern summit comprises a ditch up to 0.3m deep with an external bank up to 0.4m high, surrounding an area of less than 0.18ha (0.45 acres). Noted by antiquarians from Horsley onwards, the monument was certainly excavated by Tate in 1861 and by Brian Hope-Taylor in 1958, the former leaving more informative records of his work. While St Joseph's aerial photograph (*11, 34*) shows that Hope-Taylor examined the terminal of the ditch to the north of the east-facing entrance, no other records are known to survive. Presumably, no dating evidence was recovered, or Hope-Taylor would have mentioned it. Tate, on the other hand, does not record exactly where he located his trench, but gives the dimensions of the ditch as 5ft (1.5m) deep, diminishing in width from 5ft (1.5m) at the top to 2ft (0.6m) at the bottom. In view of its size, Jobey's interpretation of the ditch as the foundation trench for a timber palisade seems difficult to sustain and Tate explicitly rejected this possibilty. Furthermore, though a slight spread of material might be expected to be cast down slope from such a foundation trench, the size and regularity of the external bank in this case argues that it was deliberately constructed as an integral part of the earthwork. The size of the ditch as recorded by Tate, compared with the shallow depression now visible, might prompt speculation that an internal bank may have been deliberately razed and pushed back into the ditch, as perhaps occurred at the hillfort on Wether Hill, overlooking the Breamish Valley (Topping 2004, 197). However, at Yeavering Bell, not only is there no evidence to positively support this idea, but the excellent preservation of the house platforms immediately within the lip of the ditch actually seems to indicate that they were never overlain by any bank.

Despite excavations having taken place twice in the past, dating of the enclosure remains reliant on the earthwork evidence. The 1998 investigation upholds the conclusion of Bradley and subsequently the Royal Commission over that of Jobey: the enclosure stratigraphically post-dates all the four house platforms with which it comes into contact. As a result, the conclusion sometimes drawn from Jobey's observation that Yeavering constitutes an example of the 'Hownam sequence' of expansion and conversion from timber to stone is no longer tenable.

In one instance, on the northern side of the enclosure, the surface traces need particularly careful scrutiny, for at first glance the stratigraphic relationship might seem to be the opposite, because a length of the ditch spanning the interior of a house has been levelled up, as though by deliberate in-filling, thus implying the house to be later. Closer inspection, however, reveals that the earthworks defining the perimeter of the house are cut by the enclosure. While it is possible that differential silting alone is responsible for the condition of the ditch within the circumference of the house, other explanations are worth considering. It is possible that a strip across the house, encompassing the ditch, may have been archaeologically excavated and subsequently backfilled, for it should have been clear to any archaeologist from the time of Tate onwards that excavation of this area would offer the clearest possible indication of the chronological relationship between the platform and the enclosure. Since he wrongly concluded that the enclosure predated the hillfort, Hope-Taylor can apparently be ruled out, though it is conceivable that his interpretation of the sub-surface stratigraphy might have been dictated by Jobey's reading of the surface traces. As mentioned above, the location of Tate's trench is uncertain, but it is perhaps worth reflecting on his statement that 'in another [house platform] near to the Fortlet [that is, the small enclosure], charred wood was found on the floor at the depth of 4 feet' (Tate 1863, 437). This seems an extraordinary depth: could it be that Tate had targeted this house platform, but eventually reached the base of the ditch, which he then took to be the floor of a 'pit-dwelling'?

Yet even the conclusive demonstration of the stratigraphic relationship hardly reduces the number of interpretative possibilities. Certainly, the fact that the enclosure post-dates the house platforms should not automatically lead to the conclusion that the enclosure is of early medieval origin, although that possibility has been raised again since Hope-Taylor's investigations and must certainly still be considered (Bradley 1987, 10; Welfare 1992, 639). For since the date of the house platforms themselves is uncertain, the fact that the enclosure is later need not rule out an early – perhaps prehistoric – origin for the enclosure. As already discussed, it is also open to question whether all the house platforms are contemporaneous with the stone-built rampart. In this context, the relationship of the enclosure to a small quarry below the summit assumes greater importance, for the quarry can reasonably be inferred to have been a source of building material for the hillfort rampart. Yet, while it is clear that the enclosure overlies and therefore post-dates the quarry, since the quarrying may have been contemporary with the first phase of rampart construction, it remains possible that the enclosure chronologically overlaps with the second-phase rampart. Possibly, the fact that the entrance into the enclosure faces towards the breach in the rampart at the eastern end of the hillfort may indicate that the second-phase rampart had also fallen into disuse by the time the enclosure on the summit was built.

At this point, having muddied the chronological waters sufficiently to show that the enclosure could belong to practically any period from the Iron Age onwards, it is worth stepping back to consider its morphology in greater detail. Bradley, returning to Hope-Taylor's original suspicion of a connection with *Ad Gefrin*, has pointed to two possible early medieval parallels, one near the Anglian palace at Milfield (Bradley 1987, 10). However, this remains undated and other examples are hard to find, though admittedly, rarity in itself does not invalidate Bradley's suggestion, given the equal rarity of sites such as *Ad Gefrin* itself. All the same, his argument relies heavily on the similarity between the ground plans; the enclosure on the summit of Yeavering Bell is perhaps less markedly polygonal than suggested and its plan may well reflect other factors, including the topography and the intractable nature of the bedrock, to a greater extent than the two proposed parallels. It is also worth observing that the easterly orientation of the entrance into the enclosure and the supposed approach through the breach in the second-phase rampart at the eastern end of the hillfort do not, at face value, support the notion of a link with the palace to the north. In view of the presence on Yeavering Bell of Roman artefacts, the possible existence of an undocumented beacon built into the remnant of the Bronze Age round cairn on the summit, and the fact that the hilltop is intervisible with both the coast and the Roman signal station on the summit of Eildon Hill North, comparison with the defensive enclosures built to surround Roman signal stations is almost unavoidable. However, those Roman enclosures which are circular are generally smaller in area and perfectly circular, rather than approximately so.

While the scale of the bank and ditch on Yeavering Bell is not dissimilar to that surrounding the signal station on Eildon Hill North, the fact that the bank lies outside the ditch seems difficult to accommodate. However, as will emerge from the following discussion, the enclosure also shares certain characteristics with some of the smaller Iron Age hilltop enclosures of the Cheviots, which have also conventionally been termed 'hillforts'. The enigmatic monument may, therefore, be of Iron Age date. At this point, it is appropriate to broaden the scope of our enquiry.

YEAVERING BELL IN ITS REGIONAL CONTEXT

If the hillfort on Yeavering Bell is indeed the only 'true' hillfort in Northumberland, it arguably becomes even more important to understand the character of the large number of enclosures that have conventionally been called hillforts, yet are not true ones. It also follows that we should ask whether it is proper to continue using the term 'hillfort' to describe such monuments, not least because we can no longer state with confidence that all were built on hills. Six decades of past aerial survey, and continuing research by Tim Gates, confirm that the smaller enclosures conventionally classed as hillforts in Northumberland are merely the tip of an iceberg that extends well into the lowlands, the few left stranded above the high-tide mark of the most intensive medieval and later arable agriculture. It remains to be seen how much further the development of a more elaborate classificatory system, based at this stage primarily on morphological characteristics, will take us in understanding the chronologies and functions of these enclosures. In Scotland, the term *dùn*, once used loosely to refer to a similarly large and diverse category of monuments, has undergone just such refinement over the last three decades (Feachem 1977, 175-7 and 100-4). However, this publication is not the place for that debate and here we will continue to use the long-accepted term 'hillfort' as a convenient and elegant tag. On the other hand, it has been pointed out that even in Wessex, small enclosures, which have never been termed hillforts, dominate the settlement record and need to be recognised as the background to the major monuments (McOmish 1989; 1999, 114). Therefore, while the criteria under which the hillfort on Yeavering Bell has qualified for acceptance are undoubtedly borrowed from Wessex, they may still represent a valid yardstick: huge size; apparent defensive strength; supposedly dense settlement; alleged central economic importance; assumed political dominance. In recognition of this, Hope-Taylor favoured the term *oppidum* to describe the major hillfort on Yeavering Bell. In fact, all these characteristics have been held up to question over recent years and collectively these critiques add up to an undermining of the conventional definition of what the major hillforts actually are (Bowden and McOmish 1987; 1989; J.D. Hill 1995; 1996). But let us turn a blind eye to those objections for the time being and see how smaller hillforts in the Cheviots compare.

Great size, in terms of both internal area and scale of defences, is arguably the most immediately striking characteristic of the hillfort on Yeavering Bell and the Wessex hillforts; it is also the most striking contrast with the local norm. Until field survey by English Heritage in 2002 at Norham Castle, overlooking the River Tweed, led to the recognition of a possible underlying Iron Age promontory fort, which may have enclosed an area of 6.6ha (16.3 acres), the hillfort on Yeavering Bell was by far the largest known in Northumberland (Pearson 2002). The only other hillforts in the region that are in the same league in terms of area are those on Traprain Law, the Dunion, Hownam Law, Woden Law and Eildon Hill North (Rideout and Owen 1992). It has been argued that there are grounds for treating the hillfort on Traprain Law as a focus primarily for ritual activity rather than settlement, but that conclusion has recently been refuted (P.H. Hill 1987; Erdrich *et al.* 2000). By contrast, most hillforts in the Cheviots enclose less than 1ha, many being less than half that size. In this context, the enclosure on the eastern summit of Yeavering Bell would not be too small to be another Iron Age hillfort. The hillfort on the summit of Staw Hill, for example, is slightly smaller (Ainsworth, Oswald and Pearson 2002).

Even where the stone-built defensive walls or earthen ramparts *appear* formidable when seen from the exterior and down slope, the construction technique was evidently designed to make best use of the topography to conserve effort, rather than to expend it on a lavish scale. Most stone-built ramparts, like that of the second-phase hillfort on Yeavering Bell, seem to be between 2m and 4m wide at the base. But, to judge from the quantities of tumbled rock at most of the smaller hillforts, it seems highly unlikely that this impressive breadth was maintained to the full height of the wall. Rather, we may imagine something more akin to an expertly-built drystone field wall, forming a parapet along the front edge of a broad basal platform or terrace. As a result, the outer faces of the rampart walls may once have stood somewhere between chest- and head-high; indeed, at Sinkside Hill the external face of the rampart still survives to waist height in places. However, at Sinkside and elsewhere the inner edges may have stood barely higher than ankle height. Where more than one rampart exists, the interval between the two circuits is often not a ditch, but merely a narrow strip of level ground. Though doubtless partly masked by later infilling with tumbled rubble and silt, whatever ditch or quarry hollow originally existed cannot have been very deep.

In this respect too, the enclosure on the eastern summit of Yeavering Bell has something in common with the region's small hillforts. Seen from down-slope, and notwithstanding the form of whatever superstructure existed, it is not clear that the barrier is actually formed by a bank outside a ditch. Around much of the perimeter, the sharpened scarp of the rising ground within the ditch gives the impression of a slight internal rampart, although there appears never to have been one, with a counterscarp bank outside the ditch. In this way, the line of the circuit seems to have been designed to make good use of the crest visible to people ascending the surrounding slopes. Yet there are also key differences between the small enclosure on Yeavering Bell and typical Iron Age hillforts. Firstly, the scarp within the ditch is not impressive: even its highest sections are only just on a par with the least imposing defences of small hillforts. Secondly, the absence of any proper stone-built rampart is remarkable, especially in view of the abundant reuseable stone just down slope, in the form of the (apparently) dilapidated and disused second-phase rampart. Recent field surveys carried out as part of the *Discovering our Hillfort Heritage* project suggest that such walls are the latest incarnation of the Iron Age defences at many sites.

Yet, if the hillfort builders conserved effort in terms of the design of individual ramparts, it is appearing increasingly likely that at many sites, successive generations were determined to make their mark on the form of the defences, leading to numerous episodes of rebuilding. Not every episode produced a massive bank and ditch or stone-built wall: some, particularly those where a timber superstructure formed the main barrier, resulted in a fairly slight earthwork. Many of the recent field surveys have demonstrated such developmental sequences, but excavation would almost certainly reveal more complex histories. At Wether Hill, overlooking the Breamish Valley, where, as a result of a long campaign of survey and excavation, the sequence is currently best understood and dated, at least five redesigns seem to have taken place over a period of perhaps 250 years between the third and mid-first centuries BC (McOmish 1999; Topping 2004). The single radiocarbon dates obtained by Jobey from the hillforts on Brough Law and Ingram Hill suggest that these sites were in use at a broadly similar period to that on Wether Hill (Jobey 1971; Burgess 1984, 174). The enclosure on Ingram Hill, radiocarbon dated to 220 ± 90 cal BC, may be of greatest relevance to the discussion of the small enclosure on the eastern summit of Yeavering Bell. Jobey admitted that the enclosure, comprising a diminutive bank and ditch perhaps associated with one or more palisades, did not fit easily into the 'Hownam sequence', commenting that 'it is perhaps salutary to have this suggestion of something later' (Jobey 1971, 91).

Most Cheviot hillforts – that on Great Hetha, for example – unquestionably occupy commanding locations, although there are notable exceptions, such as that at Glead's Cleugh, which are dominated by higher ground within easy slingshot. The staggered designs of entrances, at Ring Chesters for example, may be interpreted as evidence that their gateways were designed with defence in mind (Oswald, Pearson and Ainsworth 2002). However, in this case, the low, stone-revetted banks of the bivallate fort that preceded the stone-built inner circuit seem never to have been intended as insurmountable barriers in their own rights, but rather to have acted as foundations for hedges or timber palisades. It is now widely accepted that the massive ramparts of the Wessex hillforts were in part intended as architectural displays of power. The mere existence of ramparts should therefore not be taken as proof that warfare was endemic throughout Iron Age society, or even that the function of the hillfort was primarily military. This observation perhaps applies even more to the smaller defences of hillforts in the Cheviots. Around the northern sector of the perimeter of Ring Chesters, for example, the steep natural slope has evidently been deliberately harnessed to lend the defences on that side of the bivallate fort, flanking the entrance, the illusion of great strength. This contrasts with the diminutive size of the earthworks on the south, although that sector, where the perimeter breaks away from the contours to run across a stretch of level ground, would arguably have been far more vulnerable to attack.

One characteristic found repeatedly is that circuits were not built so as to closely follow the contours, but to tip slightly across them. As a result, the monument is effectively tilted towards a specific aspect, often towards an extensive tract of lower-lying ground. This might be interpreted as the 'territory' of the hillfort, whether in terms of land tenure or political hegemony. This is true of both the hillfort on Yeavering Bell and the enclosure on the eastern summit. Indeed, apart from the sheer size of the monument and the settlement within it, this is the only evidence – admittedly slight and questionable evidence – that the site was a seat of power. At Ring Chesters and other smaller hillforts, just as at Yeavering Bell, the architectural elaboration of the more commanding entrance, together with the greater size of the flanking ramparts, also hints that each hillfort was designed to be seen and approached from a specific direction. This display may well have been intended to convey the wealth or social status of the occupants, rather than (or as well as) military dominance. Turning to the later phase of Ring Chesters, it is clear that its massive stone-built rampart and single narrow gateway could be regarded as defensive in character. However, the near-circular plan laid out with little regard for slight variations in the topography is common to so many smaller hillforts in the Cheviots – for example, the inner circuit on West Hill and the sole circuits on Brough Law and Fawcett Shank – that it may be interpreted as in part a stylistic motif which is more than strictly functional. Turning once more to the enclosure on the eastern summit of Yeavering Bell, its circuit is almost circular and there too, it is notable that the size of the earthworks increases towards the entrance. The entrance also seems to have been oriented towards the slope which affords the longest approach without a blind spot, whether for the security of those within the enclosure or to impress those ascending the hill, or both.

In terms of intensity of settlement, most hillforts in the Cheviots were clearly far from the so-called 'proto-towns' of Wessex. Even if tightly packed with domestic buildings (as is the case at Mid Hill, for example), such tiny areas cannot have supported very large populations. The hillfort on Staw Hill can have had no more than three Iron Age roundhouses in its interior, while even the relatively impressive defences of Ring Chesters surrounded a similar number (Ainsworth, Oswald and Pearson 2002; Oswald, Pearson and Ainsworth 2002). In most cases, although we may justifiably suspect the existence of more Iron Age buildings than we can identify from the surface traces, what evidence is actually available seldom allows for more than a handful of Iron Age roundhouses. Against this background, the apparent presence of only a single roundhouse within the enclosure on the eastern summit of Yeavering Bell might not be such a stumbling block to its interpretation as a minor hillfort. Admittedly, however, it remains uncertain whether the construction or use of this house was contemporary with the enclosure, given that all those in the vicinity evidently predate it.

With interiors up to 100m^2 in area, the few roundhouses within each hillfort are impressively spacious by comparison with the buildings of the Roman Iron Age, few of which are much more than one quarter as large. It has been suggested that this size, together with the apparent absence of subdividing boundaries (at least, of Iron Age date) in the interiors of hillforts, suggests that there may have been relatively few occupants, with a close social bond between them – perhaps an autonomous extended family group – within a social structure with no pronounced hierarchy (Ferrell 1997, 233-4). If we make the assumption (perhaps unwisely, as already observed) that all the 125 or more roundhouses within the hillfort on Yeavering Bell were in contemporary occupation, it is noticeable that most of the buildings would have been well separated from each other. Predictably, it would seem that the social relations between the occupants of such a large settlement were rather less intimate.

The nature of settlement in the Roman Iron Age, or the Romano-British period as it has often been termed, is a subject in its own right that there is not space to deal with in full here. However, one notable outcome of the current programme of research should be mentioned. Jobey's work established a clear distinction between Iron Age timber roundhouses represented by ring-grooves and stone-founded houses of the Roman Iron Age, supposedly built from the second century AD onwards, represented by low penannular wall-lines and stony banks. He saw the transition from one type to the other as a progression suggestive of continuity of settlement. Apart from the striking differences of size and construction technique, the new analytical surveys have repeatedly shown that Roman Iron Age settlements in hillforts represent the reuse of sites that were apparently already entirely dilapidated, implying long intervening periods of abandonment. At West Hill, St Gregory's Hill and Monday Cleugh, to take examples close to Yeavering Bell, at least two phases of Roman Iron Age settlement post-date the collapse of the Iron Age ramparts (Oswald, Jecock and Ainsworth 2000; Oswald 2004; Oswald and McOmish 2002). All these three have also now yielded convincing stratigraphic evidence that the outer corral enclosures are contemporary with the Roman Iron Age occupation and not, as Jobey believed, with the Iron Age. In every case, the evidence points to the landscape being far more intensively used in the Roman Iron Age than in the Iron Age. This is matched by the density of settlement remains within the hillforts, although tightly clustered earlier settlements such as that at Mid Hill should give us pause for thought about how many ring-grooves the Roman Iron Age activity may have masked. At a time when settlement in the wider landscape is characterised by a preference for sheltered locations, the decision to reoccupy ruined hillforts is an intriguing one. Perhaps the ruinous earlier monuments were enshrined in folklore or were consciously mythologised in order to deliberately reclaim them as symbols of ancestral achievement and power, a process similar to that proposed by Richard Bradley (1987) for the foundation of the Yeavering palace itself.

And at this point we should turn again to Yeavering Bell, for this is another respect in which the site is strikingly different from the local norm. While the landscape around the hillfort contains abundant evidence for Roman Iron Age activity, in the form of trackways, settlements and enclosed fields, all surviving as earthworks, the interior of the hillfort itself has only two possible examples of roundhouses, and no boundaries, that we could reasonably attribute to that period on the morphology of the earthworks. Yet it may be that the northern gateway was created at this time. How should we interpret this striking and anomalous pattern?

DISCUSSION

The single most important gap in our knowledge of the hillfort on Yeavering Bell is the question of the site's chronology, a satisfactory answer to which has eluded archaeologists from Hutchinson onwards. Although it has long been generally accepted that the hillfort originated in the earlier Iron Age and continued in use into the late Iron Age, there is really no hard evidence to support that hypothesis. Since the findings of the recent analytical surveys of other hillforts in the Cheviots point to a prolonged period of disuse between the collapse of hillfort ramparts and the reoccupation of the interiors, putatively in the second century AD, the theory that Yeavering and other, smaller hillforts were occupied till the end of the Iron Age must now be open to doubt. The small enclosure on the eastern summit cannot readily be classified as a standard Cheviot hillfort, but it has aspects in common with that class of monument, and is perhaps an example of a late Iron Age type described by George Jobey with apt vagueness as 'something later'. If the breach in the second-phase rampart at the eastern end of the hillfort is linked to the construction of the small enclosure, and if that enclosure is indeed comparable in date to the one on Ingram Hill, the occupation of the second-phase hillfort may already have ended before the third century BC. At this point, it is again appropriate to draw a parallel with the hillfort on Eildon Hill North, a monument which is comparable to Yeavering Bell in terms of area, scale of defences, number of roundhouses and setting in relation to the topography; the two sites are also intervisible (*colour plate 6*). Modern excavation there, although admittedly of a tiny sample of both the defences and the roundhouses, has revealed that there may have been a late Bronze Age precursor to the outer rampart, while two of the four roundhouse platforms excavated proved to have been first constructed in the ninth century BC (Owen 1992, 66-8). It is tempting to conclude that the first-phase hillfort on Yeavering Bell might also have originated in the late Bronze Age, thus allowing for several centuries of occupation and modification before the latest defences fell into ruins, and a prolonged hiatus before the enclosure on the eastern summit was built in the later Iron Age. By analogy with other sites recently investigated, the enclosure on the eastern summit may itself have been abandoned long before the second century AD.

Paul Frodsham (1999a, 200) has accepted Hope-Taylor's view that 'during or soon after the Roman Iron Age, some part of the function earlier associated with the *oppidum* [that is, the hillfort] had been transferred to the lowland site which emerges historically in the seventh century bearing its name'. Frodsham has also gone further than anyone except Hope-Taylor in speculating that Yeavering Bell may have been such a special place that it retained totemic importance and perhaps remained a focus for monumental building and ritualistic activities spanning millennia, from the later Neolithic to the foundation of the Anglian palace and beyond (Hope-Taylor 1977, 249; Bradley 1987; McOmish 1999, 120; Frodsham 2004a, 38). Such veneration might account for the apparently symbolic function of the enclosure on the eastern summit, whose interior seems devoid of contemporary features, with the possible exception of a single roundhouse. It might also begin to account for the curious absence of settlement straightforwardly attributable to the Roman Iron Age. A sacred place might even be expected to be the focus of offerings of small denomination Roman coins like those unearthed by Hope-Taylor. In this context, the damage caused by unlicensed metal detectorists in 2003 is all the more tragic, for it may have removed the best hope of understanding the role of the site at that date.

Yet continuity of symbolic importance and/or ritual practice is notoriously difficult to prove: we always run the risk of manufacturing a continuum by a process of 'joining the dots' and disregarding the intervening gaps. The calculated creation of fictional continuities in the past by this same process, sometimes for political ends, may deceive us all the more effectively because it speaks directly to our desire to find continuity (Bradley 1987, 1-5). On Yeavering Bell itself, the evidence is perhaps beginning to point to a more complex history of monumental construction than has previously been recognised, but a history punctuated by prolonged episodes of disuse. Tim Gates' reappraisal of the cropmark evidence on the river terrace below also undermines Hope-Taylor's view that the Anglian palace was the evolutionary end-product of an 'unbroken thread' of continuous ritualistic activity in the area (Gates, this volume). In short, it remains to be seen whether we are looking at genuine continuity, or a series of essentially disconnected constructional episodes, some, perhaps, motivated by the desire to create an appearance of continuity. It would seem wisest to await more secure dating evidence before pushing the discussion much further.

ACKNOWLEDGEMENTS

The authors would like to thank Tim Gates for commenting on a draft of this chapter in a typically generous spirit of cooperation. Thanks also to Iain Hedley for presenting the paper on which this chapter is based to the 2003 Yeavering conference.

PART III EARLY MEDIEVAL YEAVERING

5

EARLY MEDIEVAL BURIAL AT YEAVERING: A RETROSPECTIVE

Sam Lucy

The burial sequence at Yeavering is a complex one, stretching across three millennia and encompassing cremation and inhumation, north–south and east–west burial, potentially 'pagan' and Christian. Leaving aside the prehistoric cremation cemetery, the inhumation tradition appears to have been in use from the late or post-Roman period until the abandonment of the site, probably in the seventh century, but possibly later. The Yeavering cemeteries have always been rather enigmatic: with their variations in orientation, clustering around (and sometimes within) specific structures, these predominantly unfurnished burials clearly do not fit comfortably with other 'Anglo-Saxon' burials of the sixth to eighth centuries. This chapter aims to present a clear account of the burial sequence, based on that published by Hope-Taylor in 1977, along with a discussion of how Hope-Taylor interpreted these burials. I shall then review the relevant parallels and interpretations in the light of 25 years of more recent excavations in north-east England and south-west Scotland (and in light of recent theoretical discussions on the meaning of burial ritual), in order to see if a broader context for Yeavering can be offered.

Some comment must first be made about the nature of skeletal remains and the excavation procedure. The acidic soil destroyed all but some tooth enamel in general (dental remains being clearly visible on original plans), but body outline (from soil staining and skeletal traces) was recorded in some instances, from which Hope-Taylor estimated skeletal heights. The 1977 publication was not intended as the full publication of the cemeteries: this was planned to follow, but, to my knowledge, never did; as a result, only a handful of burials are numbered and described fully in the text; all others are just depicted in outline on a number of plans, and summarily described. Bodies with more or less detailed plans were reconstructed from a series of layers, *cf.* the description of the excavation of grave AX:

> Delicate skimming and brushing of the underlying level of the grave-filling revealed powdery traces that represented a human skeleton. These were examined and plotted in successive, thin levels, and the record which was thus built up showed that the body had lain on its back, inclined towards its left side, in a slightly flexed position, arms drawn up and head to the west. A small section of the sinciput and a few cappings of enamel from the teeth were the only portions of the skeleton which retained their structure. (Hope-Taylor 1977, 69)

THE YEAVERING BURIAL SEQUENCE

The first phase of inhumation burial on the site appears to be that associated with the Western Ring-ditch complex (Hope-Taylor 1977, 109-116) (*39* & *40*). Within the area defined by a probable circular bank (this associated with a former stone setting in a ring-ditch surrounding a cremation burial and orthostat) lay a group of 31 burials, all but three of which were radially aligned to the central point (perhaps now defined by a wooden post in place of the orthostat). There were four cases of graves intercutting others, suggesting use over a span of time. Orientation was therefore varied, with the three exceptions having an east–west alignment (two of these having iron knives as grave goods). The majority of these burials, moreover, appear to have been made within a rectangular post-setting, *c.*8.0m x 7.5m, though the latest burials in the sequence cross its alignment, suggesting its ultimate decay. These were the first burials to be excavated on the site, and the former presence of bodies was at first not recognised; it was only with the discovery of tooth enamel in a number of cases that the destructive effects of the acidic soil became apparent. These traces enabled some indication of skeletal position: probably all of the primary (radial) graves within the rectangular post-setting had been placed feet towards the centre. Of the secondary graves, one lay with head to east, and the others had heads to west. Presence of daub in these secondary burials was interpreted by Hope-Taylor as possible evidence that the post-setting had consisted of weather-screens, with the structure open to the sky. Its position in the stratigraphic sequence places it among the earliest buildings on the site, indicating that the ritual associations of the site began long before the construction of the great halls.

The Western Ring-ditch complex was superseded by the inhumations of the western cemetery (Hope-Taylor 1977, 102) (*39*): with one exception, these were

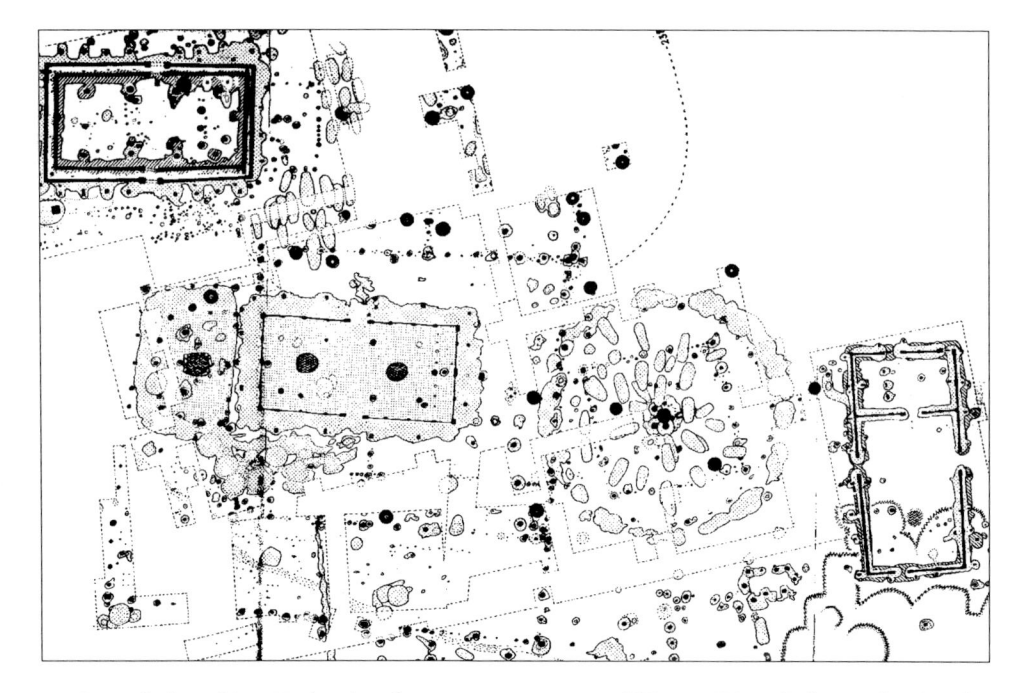

39 General plan of Area D, showing the western cemetery and Western Ring-ditch complex (north is to the left). *Extract from Hope-Taylor 1977, figure 41.* © *Crown copyright – reproduced by permission of English Heritage*

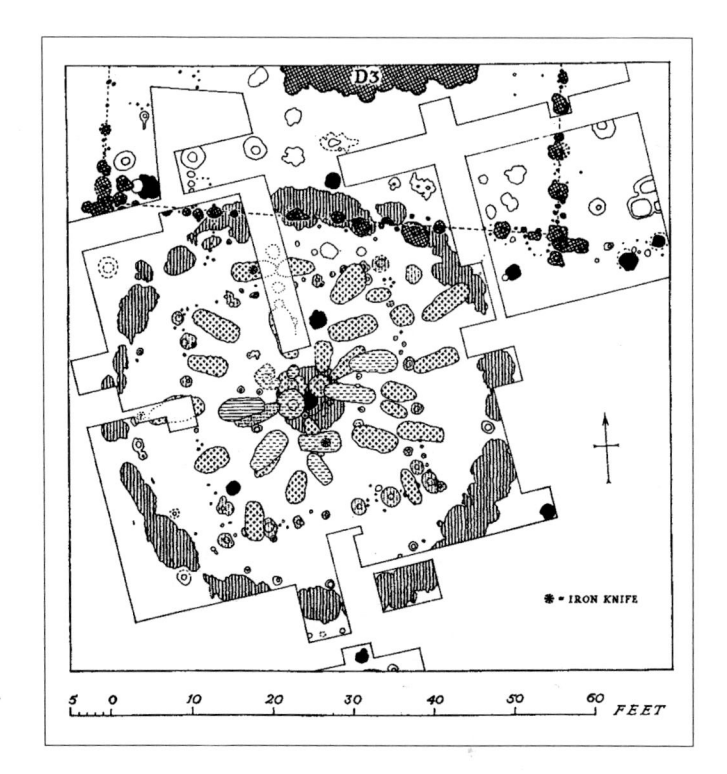

40 Plan of the Western ring-ditch complex. *Hope-Taylor 1977, figure 50.* © *Crown copyright – reproduced by permission of English Heritage*

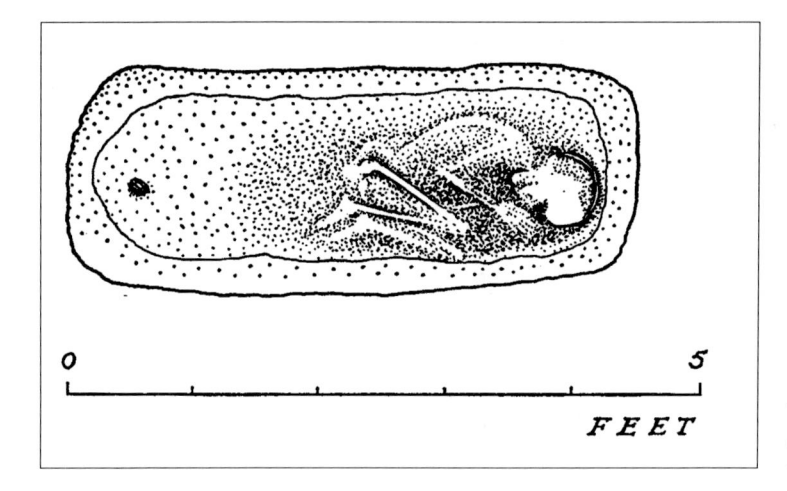

41 Plan of crouched burial close to Building D2's south-west corner. Hope-Taylor 1977, figure 46a. © Crown copyright – reproduced by permission of English Heritage

strictly east–west burials with heads to the west (as in the latest inhumations of the former). In terms of sequence, the northernmost burials respect Building D2 (with Building D2(b) appearing to be a structure of special significance) and its southern enclosure, and presumably post-date their construction; the exceptional burial lay at the south-west corner of the building (perhaps just protruding into a gap in the western side of the associated enclosure (Blair 1995, 18)) and contained a relatively well-preserved child's skeleton crouched on the left side with head to the east, occupying only the eastern half of the grave; in the western half was found a solitary ox-tooth lying directly on the floor of the grave (*41*).

The size of the western cemetery is unclear from the publication: while figure 77 (here reproduced as *42*) shows a cemetery which eventually occupied an area *c.*40m by 20m (and presumably contained numerous graves), the excavation plan figure 41 shows only around 35 clearly identifiable burials, those most closely associated with Building D2. However, Hope-Taylor talks of 'an aggregation of native graves so great as to be more fairly comparable in size with the pagan Anglo-Saxon cemeteries common in other regions of England', thus implying that these burials number in the hundreds, as does his figure 77; the introduction to the volume also points out that the investigation of the western cemetery was less extensive than was wished. Hope-Taylor places this cemetery firmly within the pre-Christian tradition, and sees it as something 'conceived by a pagan or semi-pagan upper class in the new, politically more ambitious, Anglo-Saxon age' (1977, 249).

Burials associated with the eastern area of the site (numbering at least 365) were divided by Hope-Taylor (1977, 70-78) into five distinct phases: the first of these consisted of what he termed 'string-graves' (*43*), sequences of linearly

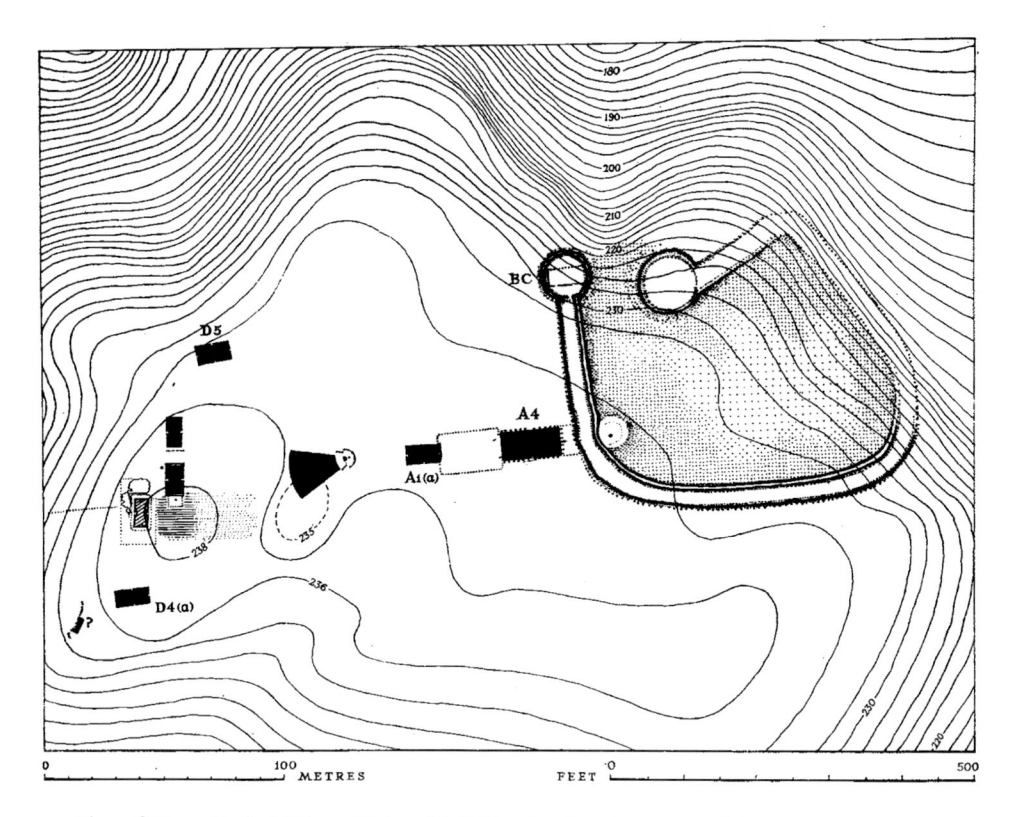

42 Plan of Hope-Taylor's 'Phase IIIc' at Ad Gefrin, *showing the extent of the western cemetery area which continued to expand during this phase. Hope-Taylor 1977, figure 77. © Crown copyright – reproduced by permission of English Heritage*

aligned burials, which appeared to reference standing posts and a primary burial in Grave AX. This grave appeared to be associated with Building A4: it was clearly aligned on its eastern doorway and was situated in a small palisaded area. On excavation, very fragmentary remains of a flexed skeleton with head to the west were associated with a decayed wood and bronze object, tentatively interpreted by Hope-Taylor (1977, 200–3) as a form of *groma* (used by Roman land surveyors for setting out alignments and right angles), perhaps a ceremonial one (*44*); intriguingly (given that the name Yeavering means 'hill of the goats'), also associated with this burial were the fragmentary remains of a goat's skull. The subsequent string-graves which appear to use this grave and post BX and others as foci are different in nature: these appear to represent localised excavations within different linear trenches. As a result, their orientation varies, though heads (where in evidence) were generally in the western spectrum.

Hope-Taylor sees these burials (around 70 in number) as clearly referring to existing graves and features at the site (Grave AX and post BX). They are thus

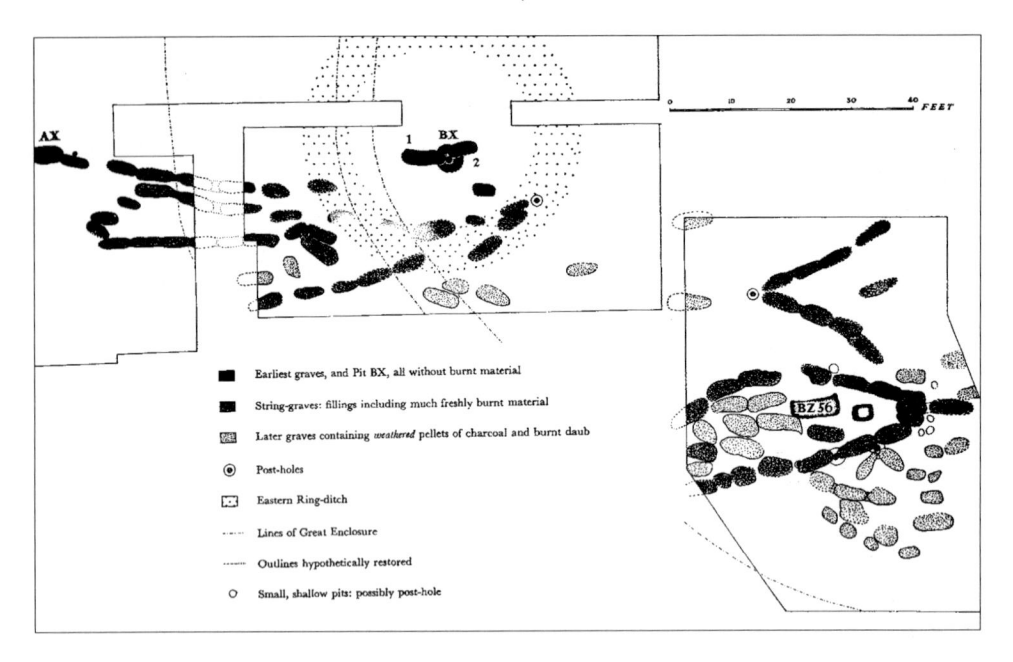

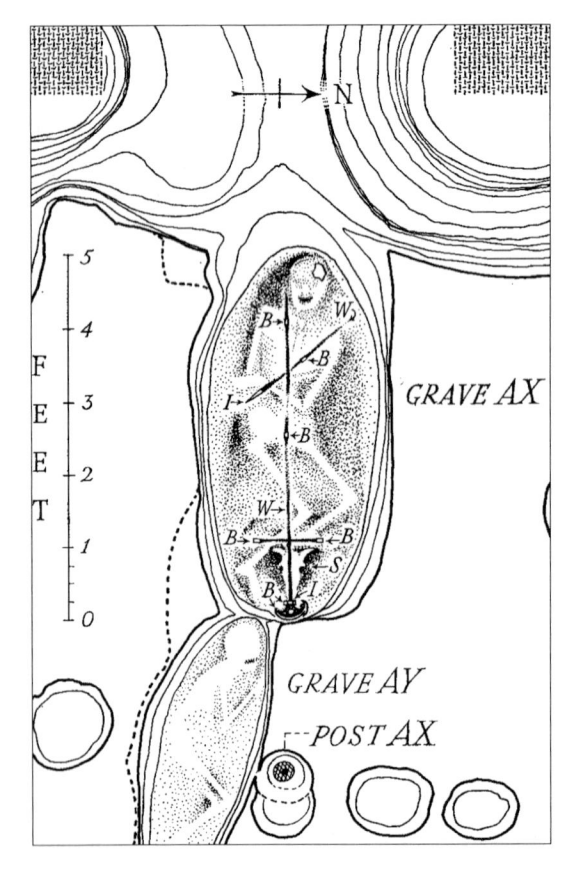

Above: 43 Plan of the string-graves in the eastern cemetery. *Hope-Taylor 1977, figure 31.* © *Crown copyright – reproduced by permission of English Heritage*

Left: 44 Plan of Grave AX. *Hope-Taylor 1977, figure 25.* © *Crown copyright – reproduced by permission of English Heritage*

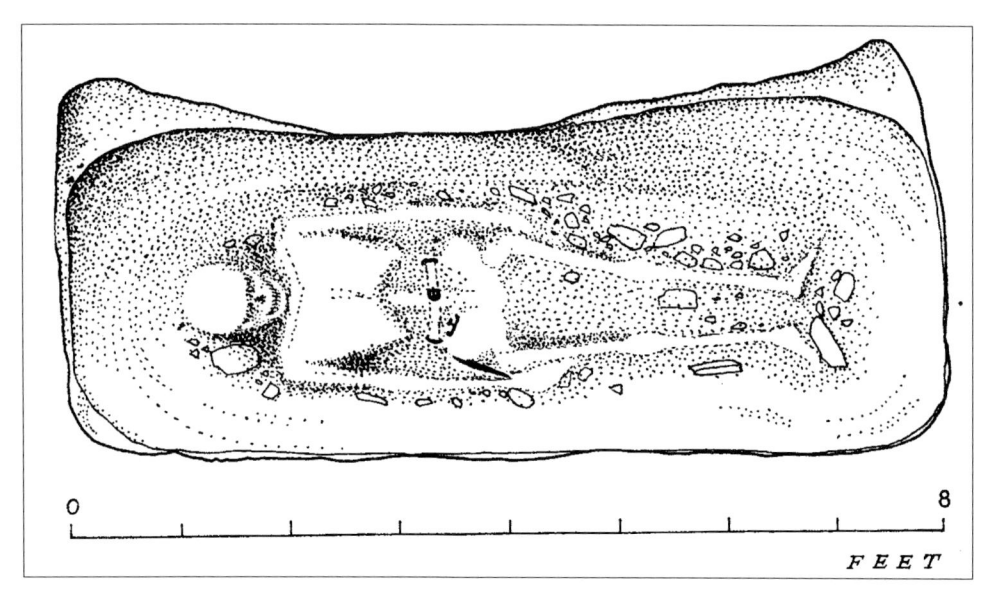

45 Plan of Grave BZ56. Hope-Taylor 1977, figure 35. © Crown copyright – reproduced by permission of English Heritage

interpreted as the graves of defeated native defenders, with inclusions of burnt material in their grave fills indicating that they had been buried soon after timber and daub structures had been burnt down (1977, 70, 251). One of these graves was BZ56, buried with an assemblage of iron and bronze objects: a buckle, two belt-loops, a knife and a 'purse-mount' (though three similar finds on site were interpreted as fastenings for shutters or doors (*45, 46*); it is perhaps possible that BZ56 may have been brought to burial on a door, a shutter or a lid of a chest (1977, 187)). Estimated stature for this individual was suggested as unusually tall for the site at 5ft 9in (whereas other burials were estimated as 4ft 11in to 5ft 4in).

Subsequently, the area of the eastern cemetery saw more systematic burial, within a fenced enclosure; burials (numbering over 250) were laid in closely packed, parallel straight lines (*47*). This cemetery was associated in its later phases with a rectangular annexed wooden structure (Building B); its foundation trenches cut through only a number of 'string-graves' in the area. Hope-Taylor sees this phase of the cemetery and its associated building as unambiguously Christian: the building is a church and the fenced enclosure a churchyard (1977, 252, 258). Certainly the density of burial in this area resembles that found in Christian cemeteries: 'the soil in and around the foundation trenches of Building B was so densely packed with the powdery traces of successive, uncoffined interments that, not infrequently, several sets of teeth, manifestly *in situ*, would be found within a few inches of each other, vertically and horizontally' (1977, 74). Not all the

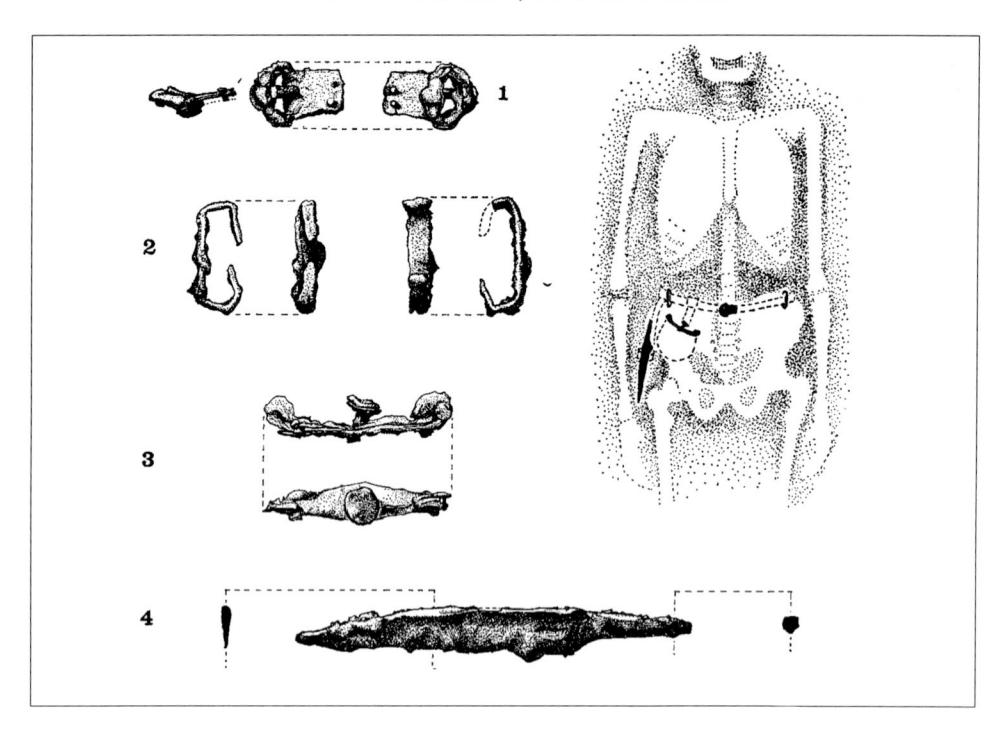

46 The grave goods from BZ56. Hope-Taylor 1977, figure 87. © Crown copyright – reproduced by permission of English Heritage

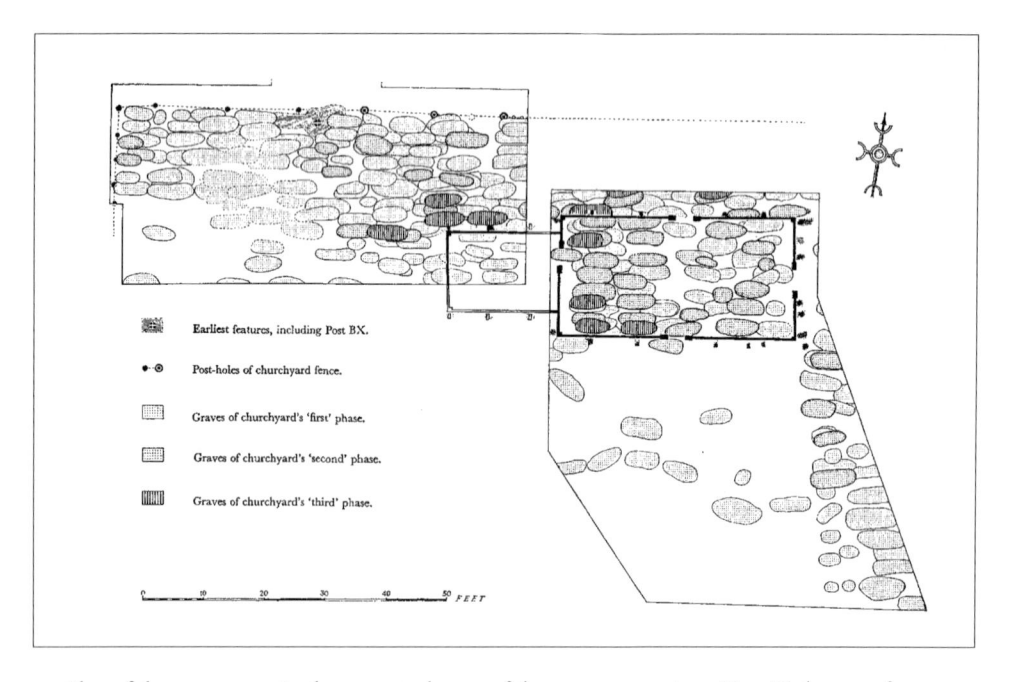

47 Plan of the row-graves in the excavated areas of the eastern cemetery. Hope-Taylor 1977, figure 33. © Crown copyright – reproduced by permission of English Heritage

cemetery was excavated, with the southern and eastern limits not reached.

REGIONAL CONTEXT AND COMPARISONS

Hope-Taylor (1977, 246–7) recognised that the inhumation burials from Yeavering did not conform to 'normal' Anglo-Saxon practice at the time, with only a handful of burials (Grave BZ56, with belt and knife, and two others in the Western Ring-ditch complex with just knives) apparently belonging to this tradition,[1] and another (Grave AX, with goat's skull and *groma*), 'a ritual half-breed, perhaps, in its own curious limbo'. Otherwise, Hope-Taylor placed all the burials firmly in a native British tradition, while recognising that, at the time of his writing, such native traditions were virtually unknown through lack of evidence: he was not even sure if the burial tradition north of the Tyne in the post-Roman period was inhumation or cremation (he was, however, correct in arguing that only unfurnished inhumation would leave so few traces in the acidic soils of the north). He posed the question whether unfurnished inhumation could have already become established as a 'pre-Saxon and non-Saxon fashion'; a question which we are now in a better position to answer.

While Hope-Taylor was familiar with the long-cist cemeteries of lowland Scotland (characterised by extended inhumation, absence of grave goods, a tendency to linear end-on alignment, stone grave-linings and association with standing stones or posts), and rightly pointed out that the Yeavering burials only lacked stone linings for them to correspond with this tradition (1977, 252), there is now a wider body of excavated data for comparison. In the late 1960s, the known distribution of these cemeteries was confined to north of the Tweed, with a particular concentration along the Firth of Forth and in the Edinburgh area, but also stretching up to and beyond the Firth of Tay (1977, 254, figure 111). The only given exception to this was Bamburgh, where in the nineteenth century a gale had exposed a few cist graves, but the evidence was too slight for Hope-Taylor to rule out their being prehistoric. The distribution is now known to be more extensive (*48*).

Hope-Taylor wondered if this apparent division between the Tyne–Tweed and Tweed–Forth regions might have had a geological basis, with the screes from the sea-cliffs of the northern area offering plentiful supplies of stone which could be broken easily into the slabs needed for such graves (1977, 254). However, he also pointed out that the distribution of long-cist cemeteries did not (at the time) correspond exclusively with the geological spread of such resources. The difference, he suggested, may ultimately have been a religious one (1977, 258).

Thus, Hope-Taylor's interpretation of the cemeteries at Yeavering can be seen to be rather a sophisticated one, which comfortably accepted notions of

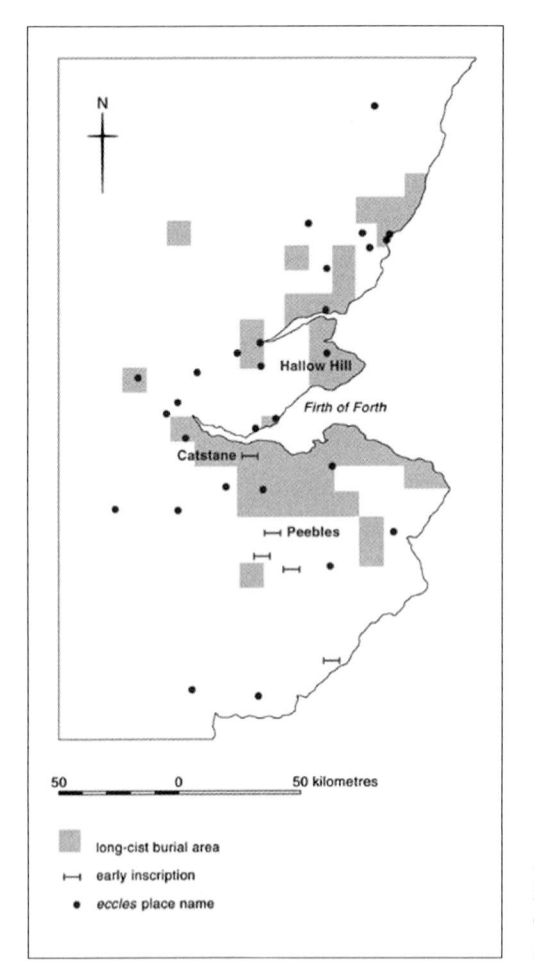

48 The distribution of long-cist cemeteries in lowland Scotland. Foster 2004, figure 66. © Crown copyright – reproduced by courtesy of Historic Scotland

cultural influence, and was happy to downplay received ideas of documented Anglo-Saxon political domination as resulting from large-scale movement of population:[2] 'if there was, despite appearances, any considerable Anglo-Saxon element in the population of Yeavering's successive inhumation-cemeteries, it must have surrendered its archaeological identity through a distinctively one-sided process of cultural exchange' (1977, 247). He saw the cemeteries here, and elsewhere, as 'deeply revealing local entities'. The text for the Yeavering report was submitted in 1969: excavations since then can offer a wider context within which its cemeteries can be interpreted.

Hope-Taylor already knew of the discoveries at Howick in Northumberland, but thought these inconclusive (1977, 26). Here in the 1930s a series of objects, associated with skeletons, were discovered during topsoil clearance in a quarry: these comprised two small opaque green glass cylindrical beads, an opaque brown glass bead with white spiral markings and blue bosses, along with three iron knives and an iron spearhead recorded with three or four of 10 recorded skeletons, although at least five more were present. Orientation was variable, and further stray finds comprised a knife and a fragment of a Roman trumpet brooch (Keeney 1939).

Likewise, he dismissed Hunter Blair's (1954) account of early Anglo-Saxon presence north of the north Tyne valley as 'a weak one, based almost entirely on the presence of iron knives and spears which could equally well be representative of the Celtic population' (Hope-Taylor 1977, 26). In fact, Hunter Blair's evidence is entirely consistent with the burial record of the seventh century as we understand it: as well as those stray brooch finds from Corbridge, Benwell and Whitehill in the Tyne valley itself, he lists further brooches from Corstopitum and Birdoswald, the Capheaton hanging bowl, and further possible finds from Barrasford, Hepple, Sweethope, Lowick and Tosson, although freely admitting that 'the entire body of this material from Northumberland would be scarcely equivalent to the contents of six well-furnished graves from, for example, the Cambridge region' (1977, 149, n1). Although not specifically mentioned by Hope-Taylor, the 1852 burial from Galewood, near Milfield, with paired annular brooches, a bead, plus further associated and stray finds (Keeney 1935) is a convincing candidate for a sixth-century burial.

In fact, Hope-Taylor was working too hard in his efforts to demonstrate that the burial record of north Northumberland was dramatically different from that of other nominally Anglo-Saxon areas. By 1983, opinion was already changing, in the light of emerging archaeological evidence: Rosemary Cramp (1983, 263), in her review of Anglo-Saxon settlement in northern Britain argued that Bernician settlement was usually considered less intensive, and on the whole later than Deiran (further to the south), and that it was concentrated in the Coquetdale area and along the Tyne Valley, with other major centres at Bamburgh and Yeavering. The few, small cemeteries and the poverty of the grave goods were argued to represent small numbers of settlers. More recent excavations have revealed evidence for a number of sites that would not look out of place in a late sixth- or seventh-century context further south.

Close to Yeavering, just 3km to the north near Milfield, excavations in 1975 and 1977-8 of two prehistoric henge monuments revealed that both had been reused for the site of early medieval cemeteries (Scull and Harding 1990). Milfield North revealed five grave cuts, with another burial indicated by a chatelaine complex, knife and buckle from a section of the henge ditch; it is probable that further shallow burials were likewise placed in the monument ditch, but had been removed by ploughing. Bone survival was extremely poor, but four of the five graves produced grave goods (including annular brooches, buckles, knives, a pin, a spearhead and a possible girdle ornament). The earliest date for these burials is argued to be the late sixth century, it being quite possible that all date to the seventh century.

A more extensive cemetery was revealed in the henge monument to the south; of 45 possible or certain graves revealed within and around just part of the henge, 24 were excavated. As at Milfield North, skeletal remains at Milfield South were scarce: human bone was recovered from just three graves, and grave goods from just one (though further goods – an iron blade fragment, probably from a sword, and an iron spearhead – had been dispersed by the plough, these presumably from at least one disturbed grave). The furnished grave was a double burial, with two iron knives, an iron ring and a possible sharpening steel associated with the upper burial, and an iron knife, an iron buckle and a lace-tag or strap-end from the lower (Scull and Harding 1990, 13–21). The excavators noted (1990, 22) slight differences of alignment within the burials, and drew parallels with the 'string-graves' at Yeavering which are succeeded by the row-graves of the eastern cemetery: at Milfield South graves in the henge entrance were of a different orientation and were less intensively clustered and ordered than those of the henge interior. The general lack of grave goods, together with the date ranges for those that were recovered suggest a date for the cemetery of the later seventh or earlier eighth centuries. Intriguingly, and again showing parallels with Yeavering, the two cemeteries lie north and south of the major early medieval settlement at Milfield, revealed by aerial photos, and identified with the *villa regia* at *Maelmin* documented by Bede. The photos show timber halls (some buttressed and one annexed), a great enclosure and other smaller enclosures, and other marks which appear to indicate the presence of sunken-featured buildings (SFBs) or *Grubenhäuser*, as was confirmed by the excavation of a similar feature at New Bewick (Gates and O' Brien 1988, 5–7, figure 1).

Excavations by the Bamburgh Research Project since 1998, just to the south of Bamburgh Castle, have revealed an even more extensive cemetery[3] which has so far produced around 100 inhumation burials, around a fifth of which have produced grave goods, including beads, knives, buckles, latch-lifters and a bone comb. Two of the burials have produced radiocarbon dates of AD 560-670 and AD 640-730, suggesting that this cemetery belongs firmly within the 'final phase' or 'conversion-period' tradition of burial of the later sixth to early eighth century. The range of burial rites is interesting: the graves are a mixture of cist graves and dug graves (as indicated by the original nineteenth-century excavations); the cist graves (consisting only of slab-linings rather than full cists) so far excavated have produced only animal bones as grave goods. Crouched, supine and prone burials have all been identified, these with a range of orientation.

INTERPRETATIONS

The Yeavering cemeteries do not fit comfortably with the earlier, predominantly seventh-century phase of burial in this area that is represented by Milfield North and Bamburgh (and which also displays great similarities with cemeteries of this date further south, for example those in East Yorkshire (Lucy 1998)); its eastern cemetery is more similar to the probably late seventh- to eighth-century burials excavated at Milfield South. This creates problems for the accepted dating, however. The generally accepted date ranges for the Yeavering cemeteries are much earlier than this. Hope-Taylor (1977, 258) sees the string-graves as dating to no earlier than 632-3 (representing 'a spontaneous reversion to paganism immediately on Edwin's death'), with use of the eastern cemetery not ending until after the middle of the seventh century (1977, 245).[4] As Scull and Harding point out (1990, 22), this discrepancy can be partly resolved by seeing the eastern cemetery remaining in use for longer than the excavator would allow. However, in a Northumbrian context as we now understand it, the eastern cemetery would fit more comfortably into a late seventh-, but predominantly eighth-century (or even later) context. It is worth remembering that Hope-Taylor's dating for the end of the eastern cemetery rested solely on Bede's statement that the Yeavering township was deserted 'in the reign of subsequent kings', being replaced by Milfield. Yet, given the recent archaeological evidence which suggests a longer occupation of the latter site, it is not inconceivable that some forms of activity at the two centres may be concurrent (cf. Alcock 1988, 8-9). Given the extended burial sequences seen at other sites in the region (see below), the continuation of burial in the eastern (and perhaps also the western) cemetery at Yeavering into the eighth century and perhaps beyond, must remain a possibility.

One issue is the presence in the eastern cemetery of burials within the structure interpreted as a church. While the site at Sprouston revealed on aerial photos shows a remarkably similar burial arrangement, with at least 380 graves, the majority oriented ENE/WSW, focused around a timber building at the south-west edge of the cemetery, no burials were present within that structure (Smith 1991, 280-1), and the use of the cemetery probably encompassed a large part of the seventh century, and perhaps beyond (1991, 288). Indeed, no contemporary churches from Britain have been identified with internal burials, other than those of the religious or secular elite, and doubts have been voiced as to whether Yeavering Building B can really be considered a church (Elizabeth O' Brien, pers. comm.).

There are examples where later churches have been constructed over earlier cemeteries, apparently with particular reference to the location of a 'special grave', for example at Capel Maelog, Llandrindod Wells, Radnor, where earlier burials underlie the walls of the first (stone) church on the site (James 1992, 98-9, figure 10.6), and at Thwing, East Yorkshire, where a number of burials within a Bronze Age ring-work were sealed by a rubble platform which may have formed the hard-standing for a timber church (Geake 1997, 159). However, the stratigraphic sequence of the eastern cemetery at Yeavering presented by Hope-Taylor (1977, 73-4, figures 28, 33), suggests that the structure had only cut through the preceding 'string-graves', with all the other graves with which the building was in contact being cut into the packing soil around its walls. This density of burial within a putative Christian church is unique for its accepted dating, with intramural burial only becoming a common feature of Christian church burial after the Conquest.

Turning to the western cemetery, this was dated by Hope-Taylor from the middle of the sixth century onwards (1977, 244). However, it does not conform to contemporary 'Anglian' burial practice of the mid-sixth to early seventh century at all (though it, too, would not look out of place in the later seventh to eighth centuries). Accepting Hope-Taylor's argument that the use of Area D precedes that of that of Area B, explanations and parallels for the earlier sequence of burials at Yeavering must be sought elsewhere.

One possibility is that they reflect a difference in status: Scull and Harding (1990, 23) wondered if the lack of grave goods in sixth- and seventh-century burials at Yeavering might perhaps reflect status and identity differences between an unfree population tied to a major estate centre and independent farming communities, rather than deriving from a 'native' tradition. This is certainly a possibility, though their argument regarding the use of monuments as acts of legitimisation by a new ascendancy is rather undermined by this being a common practice in early medieval Wales, where no elite change is suspected (*cf.* James, 1992).

Can consideration of the role of the various associated structures help in interpretation? Hope-Taylor argued that Building D2(b) was one of special significance: the contemporary burials of the western cemetery clustered around free-standing posts which appeared to have been kept sacrosanct within the rectangular enclosure at its southern end (Hope-Taylor 1977, 158). This building had been constructed as a 'shell' around D2(a), with distinctive, perhaps religious, usage suggested by the internal three-post setting at its southern end, and the large and intermittent deposits of ox skulls inside the east door, perhaps indicating a custom involving periodic feasts. Blair (1995) and O'Brien (2000) have extended this idea, with the recognition of a tradition of square ritual enclosures, often containing standing posts on which burials were aligned, which had their origins in Romano-Celtic shrines and pre-Roman prototypes. Blair places the square post-setting of the Western Ring-ditch complex, as well as

Building D2(b)'s enclosure, into a group which includes a freestanding structure at New Wintles in Oxfordshire (Hawkes and Grey 1969), a redated Slonk Hill, Shoreham (Hartridge 1978), and the annexe to Cowdery's Down Building A1 (Millett 1983), to which O' Brien adds Thirlings Building C as a further example; four of these enclosures/annexes have central post-holes.

Blair (1995, 3–19) argues that these represent assimilation into English ritual practice, tracing a development from Iron Age and Romano-Celtic shrines in Britain and Gaul, through late and post-Roman grave enclosures, to large square-plan ditched enclosures imposed on prehistoric monuments, which range from Roman to post-Roman in date. Blair's assumption that these phases at Yeavering represent the 'English' as opposed to an extension of the 'native' tradition relies on Scull's (1991) reinterpretation of the Phase I occupation at Yeavering as a modest Anglian settlement of the late sixth century – which itself rests on arguments about the cultural affinities of rectangular post-hole buildings that are much debated (*cf.* Dixon 1982, James *et al.* 1984); I would argue, *contra* Blair (1995, 19), that the archaeological sequence associated with the D2 enclosure is not 'unambiguously…pagan Anglo-Saxon'. While the example from New Wintles is associated with a more typically 'Anglo-Saxon' settlement of SFBs and post-built structures, it should be noted that no diagnostic finds were associated with it (two similar structures from a recently-excavated site at Kilverstone, Norfolk, were found in the same area as a small Anglo-Saxon settlement, but are clearly contemporary with earlier Romano-British occupation; Garrow *et al.* forthcoming). In short, there is little evidence that these square and rectangular structures at Yeavering belong to an Anglian pagan tradition, rather than a sub-Roman milieu.

Driscoll (1998) argues that the very idea of focusing a royal centre on a prehistoric monument is a feature of the northern and western Celtic regions (especially Ireland and Scotland), and not of those areas further south that subsequently became Anglo-Saxon England; interestingly, he sees Northumbria as following the Celtic pattern. He gives a number of examples of sites where, following conversion, older monuments such as henges and barrows become the focus of Christian burial (1998, 148-9), arguing that this can be seen as an attempt to establish a physical relationship between recently dead kin and an ancestral past; situating royal activity at such sites enabled claims of political ownership and historical legitimacy (1998, 155). Foster (1998, 10-22) argues that Pictish and British kingdoms in Scotland possessed a similar range of settlement hierarchy to areas further south, aimed at the collection of tribute, with principal royal residences, a series of important major farms and ceremonial centres (as do Alcock and Alcock 1987, 135). In this light, Yeavering's origins do still make sense (as Hope-Taylor argued) within such a non-Anglian, northern British, context.

What, though, of the burials?

Contemporary rites in southern Scotland are now better known. Hope-Taylor was right in his educated guess: inhumation burial is now known to have been introduced in the early centuries of the first millennium, both crouched and extended, although after a few centuries extended long-cist burial in more or less extensive cemeteries appears to have become a fairly standard pattern (Close-Brooks 1984, 87-9), with typical radiocarbon dates of the late fifth to mid- to late seventh centuries (Dalland 1992, 204). These may, or may not, be Christian burials (1992, 204-5), with some definitely producing pre-Christian dates (Proudfoot 1996, 443). At least 48 long-cist cemeteries are known from the Lothians, with a further 25 in Fife to the north (Rees 2002, 344-6). Southern Scottish rites do, however, exhibit a great deal of variety, with the use of short and long cists, cairns and square- and circular-ditch features around graves (2002, 89-94, 103-5). What is also now becoming apparent is that dug graves (i.e. without cists; recent examples have been found associated with four-post structures and log coffins (Rees 2002)) are also present in some of these cemeteries: they have been found among the long-cist graves of the extensive Hallow Hill cemetery, St Andrews, Fife, (Proudfoot 1996) for instance. A more recent example comes from Castle Park, Dunbar, where at least 26 cist graves and 21 dug graves were recovered in trial excavations near the Anglian period royal settlement: these were unfurnished, generally west-east oriented and, interestingly, the cemetery was probably in use until the twelfth or thirteenth century (Perry 2000, 283-93).

Indeed, cemeteries which consist almost entirely of dug graves seem to be a particular feature of south-west Scotland, for example at St Ninian's Point, Bute; Ardwall Isle, Kirkcudbrightshire; and Camphill, Trohoughton, Dumfriesshire (Perry 2000, 95-6; Alcock 1992, 125-128). While long-cist cemeteries are not generally associated with churches (although a rectangular post-hole building appeared to be respected by graves at Hallow Hill), cemeteries consisting mainly of dug graves usually are. At Ardwall, graves were oriented west-east, and were parallel and close to the long walls of the chapel, suggesting a definite relationship. Christian burial is more tentative at Trohoughton, where orientation was also more variable, and no associated structure was identified, but the *c.*60 dug graves were the final phase of activity within an Iron Age hillfort (Simpson and Scott-Elliot 1964). Of perhaps more relevance for Yeavering, excavations at Kirkhill St Andrew's, just 2 miles from Hallowhill have produced a long sequence of dug graves, the earliest of which date from the seventh or eighth centuries (Youngs and Clark 1982, 219).

CONCLUSION

What conclusions can be drawn from this brief review of contemporary burial practice? Firstly, despite years of discussion on these issues, the key debate seems to return again and again to the question of whether archaeological affinities (of buildings, graves or artefacts) are 'British/native' or 'Anglo-Saxon'. Once again, we are forced to ask if this is the most productive way to address the problem. Recent work on early medieval cemeteries and settlements in southern Britain is starting to explore ideas of syncretism: taking elements of different cultures and fusing them into a new 'Anglo-Saxon' culture, which does not necessarily indicate the geographical origins of its users (Lucy 2000; Hills 2003). In this respect, Hope-Taylor, with his emphasis on cultural influence, rather than domination or replacement, seems ahead of his time (leaving aside his approaches to physical morphology). He clearly argues against the assumption 'that Anglo-Saxon power in Bernicia was won by force of arms, and that its achievement necessarily involved immediate and extensive settlement by a considerable body of "typical" pagan Anglo-Saxons' (Hope-Taylor 1977, 26).

In fact, the interpretation of Yeavering as essentially a British estate/ceremonial centre is not particularly at odds with the historical sources: such centres would have been managed by a dependent population, with occasional royal visitation for the collection and consumption of tribute. With the political takeover of Northumbria, there would have been little reason to abandon the site immediately (*cf.* Alcock and Alcock (1992, 266), who argue that the incoming Angles took over a British system of administration, which also included fortified royal centres, as a going concern). Indeed, it would have made powerful political sense to continue to use it in much the same way, as this would help to legitimise the new elite (*cf.* Bradley 1987, and similar arguments by Alcock and Alcock (1992, 236-8) for the royal site at Forteviot, Perthshire, and also Driscoll in this volume). Using an existing ceremonial and burial centre as a focus for conversion would also have been politically expedient. Construction of the great halls and the amphitheatre would have served to reinforce the political domination of the site, by physically altering its appearance (although it should be restated here that the Anglian character of rectangular timber halls is still something which has to be demonstrated beyond doubt: questions about their ethnic affiliation do remain).

The fact remains that the Yeavering burials fit more comfortably into a northern British context than they do in a more southerly Anglo-Saxon one, unless they do in fact date to the late seventh century and beyond. Whether this is a function of the status of the people buried there is something that may never be resolved, unless future excavations of comparable cemeteries at Sprouston or

Philiphaugh (Smith 1991) produce enough skeletal material for independent scientific methods to be employed (something which is currently underway for the Bamburgh Bowl Hole burials). Analysis of stable isotopes preserved in tooth enamel can offer the potential to study aspects of individual life-histories, such as place of childhood origin, and diet (*cf.* Budd *et al.* 2004 for some initial results from other early medieval cemeteries). Combination of these results with high-precision radiocarbon dating would enable the chronological issues to be resolved.

6

THE GREAT ENCLOSURE

Colm O'Brien

The idea, and the image, which dominates general perceptions of Yeavering is that of the royal palace (*colour plate 10*), the term usually used to translate Bede's *villa regia*; it is, above all, as a result of Brian Hope-Taylor's excavations that we have such a clear sense of the kingly site and its architecture. Yet to think of Yeavering simply as a palace would be to miss the wide-ranging scope of Hope-Taylor's study of the site. For he used his 1977 monograph (276-234) to develop a thesis on the origins of the Bernician state and its kingship. The stratigraphic sequences which he elucidated in his excavations were, he suggested, too long to be compressed into the seventh century; they must have earlier beginnings. This led him to question the then-prevailing view (e.g. Stenton 1971, 74-6) that before about AD 600 and the reign of Aethelfrith, the Bernician state was hemmed into its Bamburgh stronghold by hostile neighbours. Turning the argument on its head, he suggested that the hostile campaigns by neighbouring British states arose out of weakness in the face of a robust Bernicia: acts of desperation. Yeavering, for Hope-Taylor, demonstrates contact; it 'testifies to the meeting of two major cultural groups ... and to the vigorous hybrid culture which that produced' (1977, 267). It is the place at which an incoming Angle elite, small in numbers, came into contact with an indigenous population. This is the key idea on which he builds his understanding of this place.

There are three strands to the contact thesis. First is the architectural tradition and Hope-Taylor's concept of a hybrid style. The cultural affinities of building styles have since been addressed by other commentators (Dixon 1982; James *et al.* 1984; Hamerow 2002) and the basis of Hope-Taylor's argument in this respect has been questioned by Miket (1980) and Scull (1991). The second strand is the evidence of burial and ritual practice which led Hope-Taylor to argue (1977, 249) for 'an immensely long continuity in local ritual observance' from the Bronze Age to the Anglo-Saxon period. But this understanding of continuity must now be modified in the light of Richard Bradley's (1987) idea of the creation of continuity.

The third strand concerns the Great Enclosure. Or perhaps this is the first strand; for the first appearance of this structure marks the beginning of the stratigraphic sequences. In conceptual terms also, this comes first. In one of those discursive passages in which Hope-Taylor used his text to think out loud, he debated whether the Great Enclosure or the Theatre (the Auditorium) is the key feature, eventually concluding that 'perhaps, after all, it is this long-cherished palisade work, not the later "theatre", which is the true key to understanding of the regard anciently shown for this obscure place in the northern Cheviot foothills' (1977, 280).

In the light of this, what do we really know about the Great Enclosure? The answer is not as much as perhaps we think. We need to take a close look at the stratigraphic evidence and to assess this against two points: first Chris Scull's (1991) reassessment of Yeavering Phase I; and second, Tim Gates' observations in this volume on the 'Romano-British' field system.

To begin with, Hope-Taylor's analysis. The double palisade which is evident as a cropmark represents a rebuilding and elaboration, during the lifespan of Building A4 and its associated structures, of a feature which by then 'had passed through at least four or five structural phases' (1977, 153). The double palisade suffered destruction by burning and, apart perhaps from a hastily-built and short-lived revival, GE V, this was the end of it. Though it is often referred to as being 'fort-like', given its position perched on the terrace-edge, 'it would be absurd to see the Great Enclosure as a permanent, military work' (1977, 280). 'Viewed as a communal cattle-corral, the Great Enclosure becomes entirely comprehensible'; it may be seen as the 'officially recognised scene of traditional events' (1977, 157). Different comments are made in different sections of the text but the overall sense of the use of the Great Enclosure is that it serves communal functions, being the fundamental institution for periodical markets and festivals and 'something roughly equivalent to the Scandinavian *Thing*' (1977, 280).

STRATIGRAPHIC ANALYSIS

But what are the elements of this multi-phase feature and how do they fit? Let us look at the stratification. Hope-Taylor excavated at the terminals which

THE GREAT ENCLOSURE

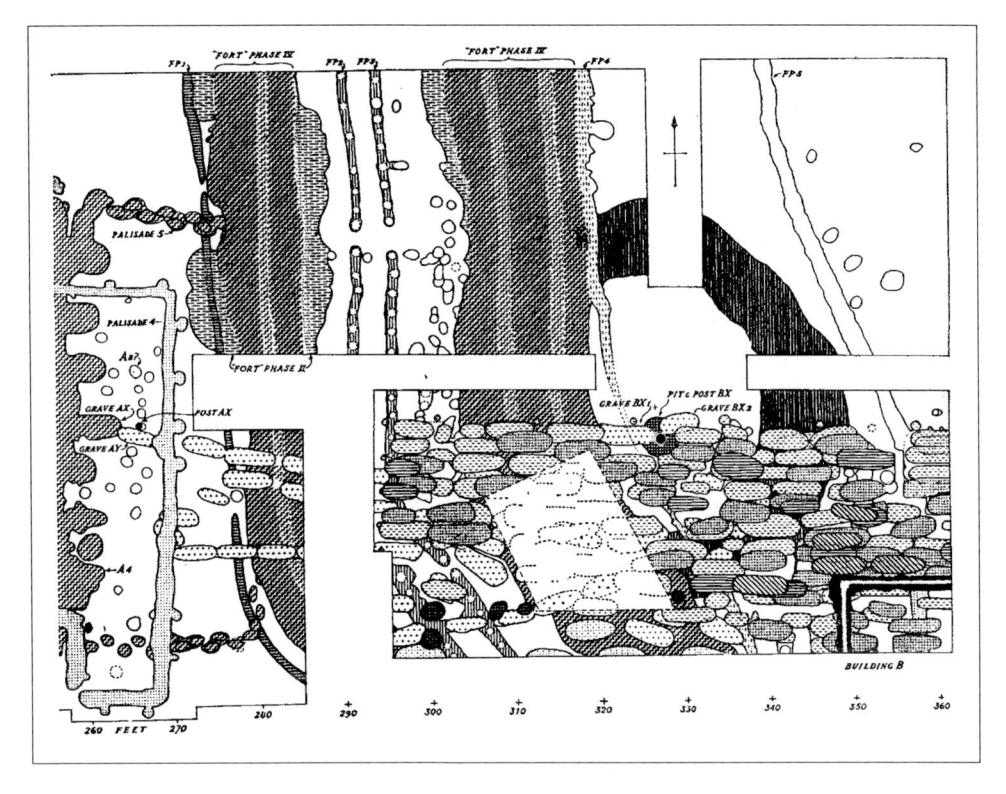

49 The Great Enclosure and adjacent features, plan view. Hope-Taylor 1977, figure 26. © Crown copyright – reproduced by permission of English Heritage

were seriously degraded by erosion of the terrace edge. He apparently opened a narrow trench from the east terminal some way into the interior. This is on the evidence of his figure 12, though there is no mention of it in the text. We must, I suppose, assume that it was devoid of features. And he opened an area along the west side where the Great Enclosure came into contact with the central complex of buildings of Area A and with the graves of the East Cemetery, including the string-graves and others (figure 26, here reproduced as *49*). This is the key area for analysis.

Prominent on Hope-Taylor's drawing are the two broad bands of the inner and outer palisades of Phase IV. Also visible are the narrow palisade trenches FP1, 2, 3, 4 and 5 which are assigned to different phases and the bulges around the outer (left side) Phase IV palisade. These are marked 'Fort Phase II' and in the text are called 'early discontinuous trenches'. A bulge on the edge of the inner Phase IV palisade is called an 'intermittently visible palisade'. On the left edge are palisades associated with the set of buildings of Area A; centre right, the Eastern Ring-ditch; and graves cover much of the southern half.

Here, and continuing westwards across Area A, Hope-Taylor has elucidated a sequence from an awesomely complex stratification of inter-cuttings and from this he developed a model for phasing and chronology (*50*). This can be read as a normal site matrix with the lines down indicating sequence (from later to earlier); the double horizontal lines indicate associations of features.

The overall model is built thus: from the stratification; from such few datable objects as there are (I have indicated these on the right hand edge of *50*); from the sequence of buildings which is determined in part by the stratigraphic evidence of Area A, in part by an assessment of stylistic evolution; from the two fire episodes which form, as it were, two horizontal datum lines; and from the assigning of fixed historical dates which depend on the proposition that the first fire episode represents an attack in AD 633 by Penda and Cadwallon and the second an attack by Penda in AD 651 or 655. There are no radiocarbon dates. The historical dates are derived from events described in Bede's *Ecclesiastical History* but it should be noted that there is no direct evidence from this narrative that *Gefrin* was attacked on either occasion.

At the centre of all this is a sequence of phases of the Great Enclosure (GE I – GE V) tied in to the A building sequence. The destruction of GE IV in Fire Episode 1 fixes the end of the sequence; the abandonment of the Romano-British field system the beginning. The arithmetic analysis by which Hope-Taylor derived the formula for the starting date of AD 375 $\pm$?125 is tortured and we can almost see him throw his hands up in despair when he admits to the 'appalling shortcomings of that arbitrary, arithmetical approach' (1977, 212). Nonetheless, it is a working proposition, and any criticism must acknowledge that Hope-Taylor himself recognised that further excavation is needed to sort out the Great Enclosure (1977, 205). Between the beginning and end points, he then assigned the phases of the Great Enclosure and pulled Building A5 into the scheme on the argument of similarity of construction technique (1977, 153).

Soon after Yeavering was published, Roger Miket (1980, 301-303) questioned Hope-Taylor's proposition that the Style I buildings (A5, 6, 7 and D6) were 'British' as opposed to 'Anglo-Saxon' and the linking of these buildings with the middle phases of the Great Enclosure. This critique was further elaborated by Chris Scull (1991) who developed a closely-argued reassessment of the post-Roman Phase 1 from an analysis of stratigraphic information. The designation 'British' depends on dating the Style I buildings before AD 550 and that in turn depends on associating A5 and D6 with Phase II of the Great Enclosure which has been dated by Hope-Taylor's arithmetic. There is no need here to look at the detail of this argument; the point which we can take from Scull is that A5 need not be associated with GE II. Having detached the buildings from the palisades, Scull was then able to reconsider the buildings in their own right. The other side

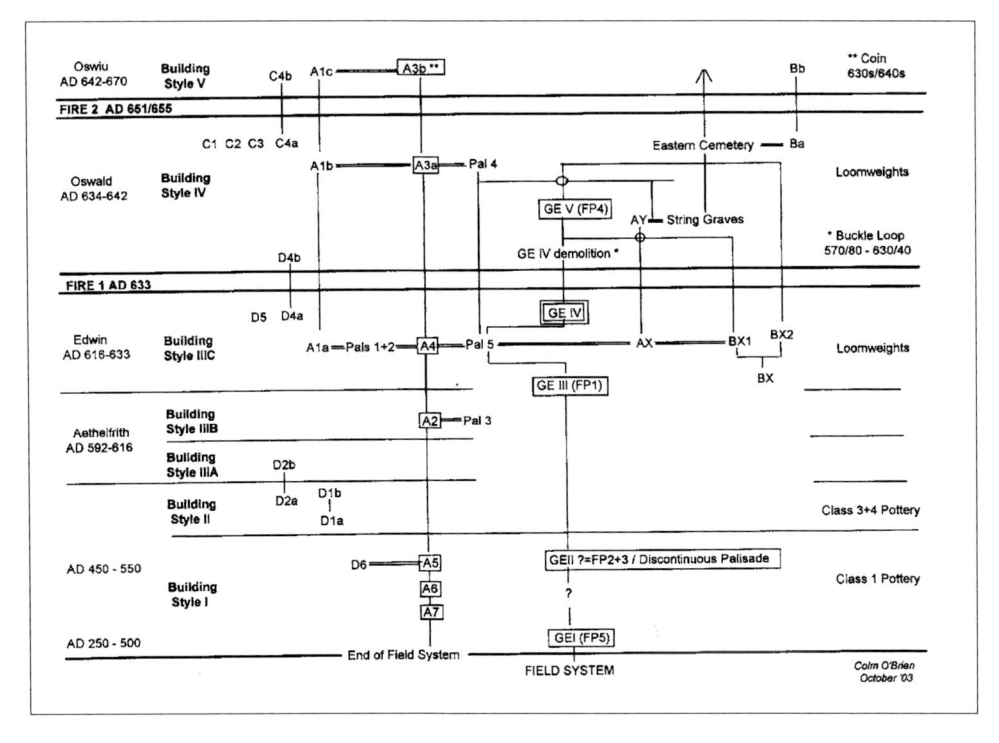

50 Phasing and chronology: Hope-Taylor's model

of that coin is that the Great Enclosure also floats free and we can look at that too on its own terms.

This can be seen in the second chart (51). This is a minimalist view in the sense that it uses only the strict stratigraphic evidence of intersections, but it does separately identify each individual element of the Great Enclosure.

The two most striking points about this analysis as compared with the Hope-Taylor model are, firstly, that there is no direct contact with the building sequence earlier than palisade 5, which is part of the A4 building complex. Scull had said (1991, 58) that the evidence linking the earlier building, A5, with GE Phase II 'is not compelling'; Miket (1980, 301) that it was 'tenuous': this analysis shows that it has no basis in stratification. Secondly, that the strong linear sequence of GE phases has broken down. Stratification does not define any connections between the two GE IV palisades and FP2 and FP3; and as for FP5, out there in stratigraphic isolation, all that can be said is that it predates Phases 2-5 of the Eastern Cemetery, as does everything else. There are two sequences of three elements: the outer palisade of GE IV is later than FP1 which is later than the outer part of the 'early discontinuous trench'; FP4 is later than the inner palisade of GE IV which is later than the 'intermittently visible palisade'. And

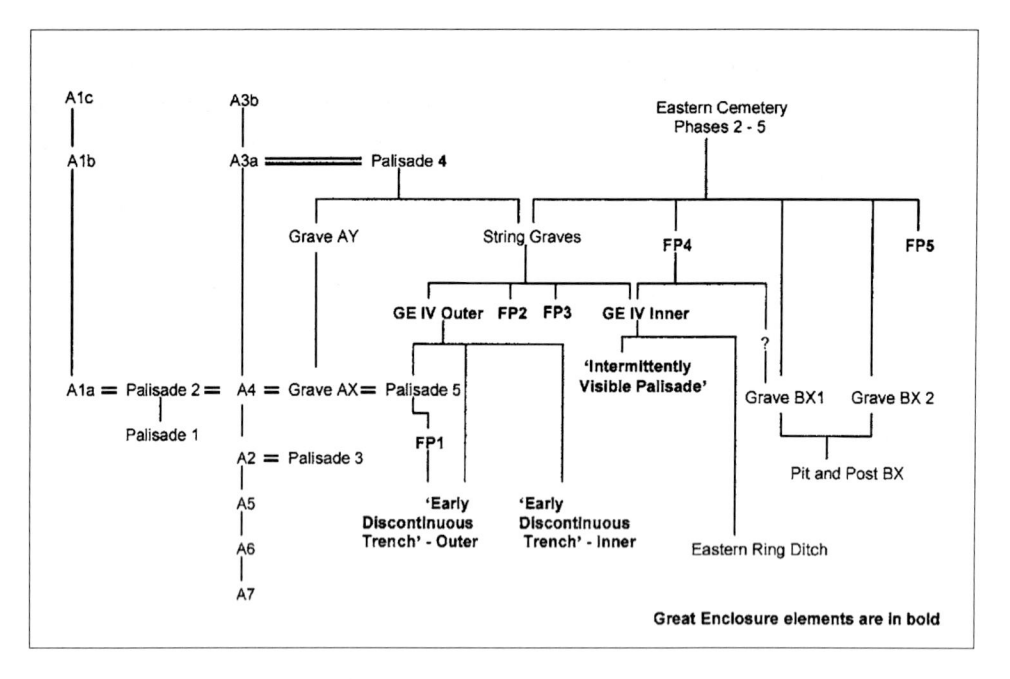

51 The Great Enclosure: stratigraphic analysis

since we know from the terminals that the two large palisade trenches of GE IV are two elements of a single structure, this gives a sequence of four stages: FP4 is later than GE IV, which is later than FP1, which is later than the outer part of the 'early discontinuous trench'. But what are we to make of this 'early discontinuous trench'? It seems an optimistic reading of the evidence as we have it to classify it as a phase in its own right, 'Fort Phase II' of figure 26: why do the outer parts not appear again south of the baulk? And how intermittently visible is the 'intermittently visible palisade'? Apparently, it appears only once in the area of excavation.

Hope-Taylor defines the beginning of the Great Enclosure by reference to the Romano-British field system. But Tim Gates has now shown in this volume that the field system is a misreading of naturally-formed periglacial features – there is no field system. The implication of this is simply stated: that for most of the elements under examination there is no *terminus post quem* (or at least none beyond quaternary geology) and so the beginning of the Great Enclosure is not fixed. The intersection of GE IV with Palisade 5 defines the *tpq* for this phase; its intersection with the Eastern Ring-ditch adds nothing significant to the analysis.

Then, to look beyond this excavated area, are we to suppose that all the palisade lines follow much the same course as the pair which make up GE IV? We do not know this for sure. Is the interior really devoid of features? Maybe so;

but this understanding depends on the non-appearance of cropmarks and until this negative evidence is further tested, we cannot know that it is evidence of absence and not just absence of evidence. Why have discussions of the palisades at Yeavering made little reference to another double palisade, south of the road, close to the henge which Anthony Harding excavated (Tinniswood and Harding 1991)? Did this have the same function as the Great Enclosure? Were the two in use together? Were they occupied at different times? We do not know. And what of the small ditched enclosure around the eastern summit of the Bell? The most recent ground survey (Pearson 1998) 'has assembled compelling evidence' that it post-dates the occupation of the hillfort. General understandings of enclosure or defence at Yeavering have not taken account of either of these.

These revisionist comments do not prove that Hope-Taylor is wrong with regard to the Great Enclosure; but we do not know that he is right, and we need to know. His is but one possible reading of the evidence and reference back to strict stratigraphic analysis gives a datum point from which to begin a re-evaluation. We need to know because the Great Enclosure matters. It matters locally for understanding the interplay between what happened at the top of the hill and what happened at its foot. It matters, indeed it is central, to Hope-Taylor's thesis of Yeavering as a place of contact.

A CONTEXT FOR THE GREAT ENCLOSURE

To establish a wider context for Yeavering's Great Enclosure, Hope-Taylor invoked the idea of a northern palisade tradition (1977, 205-9). He referred in particular to Hownam Rings and Hayhope Knowe in Roxburghshire and to Harehope in Peeblesshire. He proposed, by an argument from typology, that the terminals of GE Phase IV were a development of Harehope I and II. The latter, with its entrance towers, he judged, showed the influence of Roman military architecture and therefore cannot be assigned to a date earlier than the second half of the first century AD. This was a clever way to try and bridge the gap between late prehistory and the seventh century AD; however, it is not convincing. Hope-Taylor himself seems almost to have admitted as much when he acknowledged the difficulty in arguing for a date as late as the third or fourth century AD for Harehope II. With hindsight, one could say that a typological analysis of entrance features is too contrived a method and too narrow a basis for assessing these structures.

Despite this weakness in method, Hope-Taylor's search for a northern palisade tradition may have been soundly based, as Leslie Alcock's researches would suggest (1988; 2003). The large double palisades of Yeavering GE IV and those at Milfield and Sprouston are to be seen as an Anglian development but there is support for the idea that palisaded defence was inherited from earlier British tradition (1988, 3-9; 2003, 233-5). Alcock assembled evidence, as recorded in eighth- and ninth-century written sources, which shows that the names of a number of places associated with Bernician kingship are adaptations or alterations of names in the British language. Coldingham, *Coludi Urbs* in Bede, derives from something like *Caer Colud in which the second element may be a personal name, while the *Caer element indicates a fortification. Dunbar, *Dynbaer* in the *Life* of Wilfrid, derives from a Cumbric term *Dinbarr*, meaning something like a summit fort. The *din-* element indicates fortification. In his own excavations, Alcock demonstrated (Alcock *et al.* 1986) a sequence of defences on Kirk Hill, Coldingham; and now the headland at Dunbar has evidence of both defences and buildings (Perry 2000). Nennius (*Historia Brittonum*: 63) gives the information that Bamburgh (*Bebbanburh*) was named for Bebba, wife of King Aethelfrith; previously it was called *Dinguoaroy*, with the British *din-* element again. Yeavering (*Gefrin*) derives from the British *gevr-rinn*, the 'hill of the goats' and Milfield, *Maelmin* in Bede, another British name, means 'decayed river bank' or 'marshy edge' according to the most recent assessment of the name (Breeze 2001). Thus there is a body of linguistic and archaeological evidence to suggest that the Bernician kings had taken over a set of fortified sites which were places of leadership in the native precursors of the Bernician state.

Perhaps, then, the Great Enclosure will fit into a northern British context in much the same way that Sam Lucy has suggested in this volume for the burial tradition. But we should conclude on a note of caution in saying that the stratigraphic evidence, as we now have it, is not sufficiently well founded to bear the weight of interpretation which has been built upon it. We need a more robust understanding of the Great Enclosure.

7

THE SOCIAL USE OF SPACE AT *GEFRIN*

Carolyn Ware

Yeavering has provoked over 25 years of discussion and debate since publication of Hope-Taylor's site report (1977). Convincing arguments have been made for seeing the reuse of prehistoric monuments in this period, particularly as a focus for burial, as a means of proclaiming an ancestral heritage (e.g. Bradley 1987; Frodsham 1999a). Richard Bradley, for example, has made the case for seeing the reuse of monuments at Yeavering as an attempt by the social elite to create direct links with an ancestral past. He suggests that this system is directly analogous to the creation of fictitious genealogies whereby individuals trace their origins back to a prestigious and perhaps mythical past. Such an argument corresponds well with work conducted in Scotland which suggests that royal activities were situated at ancient monuments to claim a sense of political ownership and historical legitimacy, thus developing exclusive access to positions of authority and securing popular support (Driscoll 1998).

These arguments provide a persuasive model for the importance of *Gefrin*'s location, but it is important to remember that the buildings were not passive or neutral elements in this setting. The presence of buildings marks a significant transformation in activity in the early medieval period. As other papers have discussed, burials and monuments with more overt ritual associations dominate prehistoric activity. The beginning of the post-Roman phase is marked, as Chris Scull (1991) has shown, by buildings that may not have looked out of place on any modest agricultural settlement of the mid-sixth century. This, perhaps, adds weight to Bradley's suggestion that there is no actual continuity of practice at Yeavering. However, the apparently commonplace quality of these buildings does not diminish the significance of the settlement. The very act of building and, in particular, of situating at Yeavering, is charged with meaning.

As an idea, the hall was undoubtedly important to the early medieval social world. In the early (pre-Christian) Anglian period there is little evidence for dedicated public buildings and civic institutions *per se*. Rather, political, economic and social activities were played out at the everyday level of the house or as we seem to prefer to call it in early medieval England — hall. The poetic discourse, which celebrates not simply the hall as a building, but the social system associated with it, underpins this. Although never articulated into any kind of social philosophy, the hall was pictured, for poetic purposes, as a circle of light and peace enclosed by darkness, discomfort and danger (Hume 1974, 65). For example, in *Beowulf*, the hall is the centre of kinship, amity and cosmology, reflecting sacral and magical functions, as well as the deeply serious drink-confirmed reciprocities of the lord-retainer relationship (Hill 1995, 159); while Bede uses the hall as a metaphor for life itself (Bede, *Historia Ecclesiastica*: ii,13).

The positioning of a hall at Yeavering is one of the most salient aspects of the site. The hall was not simply a symbolic ideal but was important as a *place*. The construction of buildings at Yeavering would secure links of a particular lineage or community to the landscape. In the same way that the reuse of monuments secured ownership of the past, it is possible to see the buildings as being just as much an attempt to establish or perhaps enhance the physical relationship between people and place. The relationship of key buildings to other features in the landscape most strongly demonstrates this. Of particular note are the relationships between the north boundary of the inhumation cemetery, with post-pit BX, grave BX, post-pit AX, the 'watcher of the threshold' (burial AX), buildings in Area A and the focal point of the theatre structure locked together in an east–west orientation. Hope-Taylor attempted to identify many such complex alignments (*colour plate 10*). The buildings and other features created an essential and highly visible link between past and present and secured that exclusive access for future generations. The architecture presenced the community or lineage in the landscape and, importantly, created a dominant locale, which would influence interaction and patterns of movement. The buildings were a physical representation of the community, even when the people themselves were not gathered in that place.

The buildings carried a powerful message of belonging, both to outsiders and those associated with it. Prehistorians (e.g. Thomas 1996; Brück 1999) have argued that the act of building is the starting point in understanding the nature of human engagement with their surroundings. Building is a form of transformation and a means of dwelling, of abiding with things and entering into a relationship with them. Through building people establish a connectedness with their world, which lays the conditions in which the unconsidered practice of everyday life (the *habitus*) may proceed. Buildings both bring a world into being and continually reproduce human social relations in that world.

Thus we might consider the way in which even the very act of construction would have drawn people together. Even the early buildings at Yeavering are not particularly small, falling within the size range of normal sixth-century buildings (Marshall and Marshall 1993). It would require many people to provide labour for construction and this could have been a means through which alliances were expressed and indebtedness negotiated. Once built, structures would become a testament to the pooled labour of household or kin groups involved. Building is a strong feature of Yeavering. If we take Scull's phasing of post-Roman Phase I (the initial period with 'buildings') to around the mid-sixth century and also accept Bede's implication that the site was abandoned by the late seventh century – Hope-Taylor (1977, 277) said no later that AD 685 – then that is a lot of building in a very short period. Even if we rely on Hope-Taylor's more extended phasing we gain the impression of a site in a constant state of change. Hope-Taylor attributed this to successive kings each making their mark. Whilst this sort of historical linking is problematic, not least because of the dating problems that exist at Yeavering, seeing the numerous phases of rebuilding as the endeavour of different generations or particular individuals is compelling.

Construction on this scale and the ability to maintain such buildings would be costly and therefore a visible sign of prestige. To undertake such a project was an act of conspicuous consumption: a physical and visible sign of wealth, power and possibly authority. In anthropological examples of societies where the house is at the core of human social relations we frequently find a combination of factors, namely the cooperation of a large group associated with the house and the existence of a social ranking system within which members of an aristocracy enjoy the wealth and power which enable them to undertake impressive construction projects. In such cases the house is designed by its impressive size, distinctive shape and fine ornamentation to give visible substance to a family's claim of superior status and to serve as an enduring sign of their prestige (Waterson 1997).

Each phase of building seems to add some new elaboration to the site at Yeavering. Initial concern may have been to state physical connection to place: their right to dwell; and hence the buildings look (in the archaeological record at least) quite ordinary. They connect to a wider early medieval building tradition (James *et al.* 1984), the attributes of which can be summarised as rectangular, precisely laid out and constructed in substantial earth-fast foundations. The plans frequently employ simple geometric forms or length–width ratios. Most buildings have a door exactly in the centre of each long wall and some have an annexe at one or both ends. Buildings tend to be oriented east–west or north–south and annexes or internal partition walls tend to be located at the east or north end depending on this orientation. From post-Roman Phase III, however, the ordinariness is elaborated to monumental proportions. For example, the architectural form and arrangements of space in buildings A2 and A4 are fundamentally the same as buildings excavated at nearby Thirlings (O' Brien and Miket 1991) but with floor areas in excess of 250m² compared to 70-80m². Such elaboration is then augmented by the complex alignments, and what we might call ritual embellishment of particular locations. For example, situated against the east wall of structure D2 close to the door was a pit layered with ox skulls. The association of this structure with burials and has led to its interpretation as a temple (Hope-Taylor 1977, 277-8). If the ox skulls were stacked up against the walls, as the excavator suggests (1977, 100), then this building might have worked in much the same way as the Indonesian origin house at Toraja (52) in which the horns of sacrificed buffaloes were fastened to house-posts to bear witness to past ceremonies (Waterson 1997, 140). Across the east entrance to structure A4 lay burial AX with body aligned with the axis of the building as though guarding the doorway. A goat's skull and ceremonial staff accompanied the burial.

The form of Yeavering was designed to impress not simply through its sheer wealth and extravagance. Yeavering was a place where people gathered and interacted and the material form of the architecture not only provided the stage but also acted as cue – a mnemonic for behaviour. The built environment regulates personal mobility and access to social and economic resources and this in itself reflects dominant modes of power. Buildings create a certain formality: they structure and regulate interaction in space and time. As constructed spaces, the halls at Yeavering were symbolic forms as much as they were a form of shelter, but several aspects of their design imply that their construction was conventional and set within a wider tradition. The orientation, layout and constituent materials were such that dwelling in them and moving round them would have generated a rich fabric of meaning.

In the study of non-western preliterate societies, anthropologists have noted that where the house form is relatively standardised, it often constitutes a significant medium for the negotiation and reproduction of social relationships. In many cultures, the house acts as an image of society or of the universe. The sets of values, principles and dispositions that structure social life become metaphorically transformed into an objectified spatial order which, through the routines of daily practice, comes to constitute uncontested reality (e.g. Bourdieu's study (1970) of the Berber house).

The familiarity of the architecture at Yeavering says a lot about the nature of social interaction and perhaps therefore the development of early kingship. These buildings were not entirely otherworldly places but drew on a person's everyday knowledge. Social elites appropriated, as a means of legitimising power, symbols

THE SOCIAL USE OF SPACE AT GEFRIN

52 Indonesian origin house at Toraja, with buffalo horns displayed on posts.
Reproduced from Waterson 1997, figure 124, by kind permission of Roxanna Waterson

and metaphors easily recognisable within the wider community. The buildings were designed by their remarkable size, and possibly fine ornamentation (for which no direct evidence exists) and other embellishments to give substance to superior claims of status and serve as an enduring sign of their status. But while Yeavering may have been awesome to those in its presence, inside the hall people would know how to proceed because the rules of interaction were the same as those that governed everyday encounter.

It is interesting to consider how each phase of rebuilding changed the way in which people moved in and around the site. It is clear that the objective of rebuilding was not simply to prove that it could be done bigger and better by the next generation but was, in part, a response to changing needs and requirements for how people could and should interact. The most significant change comes in Phases IV and V. In earlier phases we see a concern to define both interior and exterior space through buildings and enclosures. As discussed earlier, building interiors are generally quite simple, at most divided at one or both ends by partitions. Associated exterior enclosures added an extra depth of complexity to the spatial structure (*53*). It is interesting to note here that burial AX, called the 'watcher of the threshold' by Hope-Taylor, lies within an enclosure at the east end of structure A4 and therefore the entrance he watches is perhaps not the main or most public access point to the building (*53*, Phase IIIC). To enter this space one

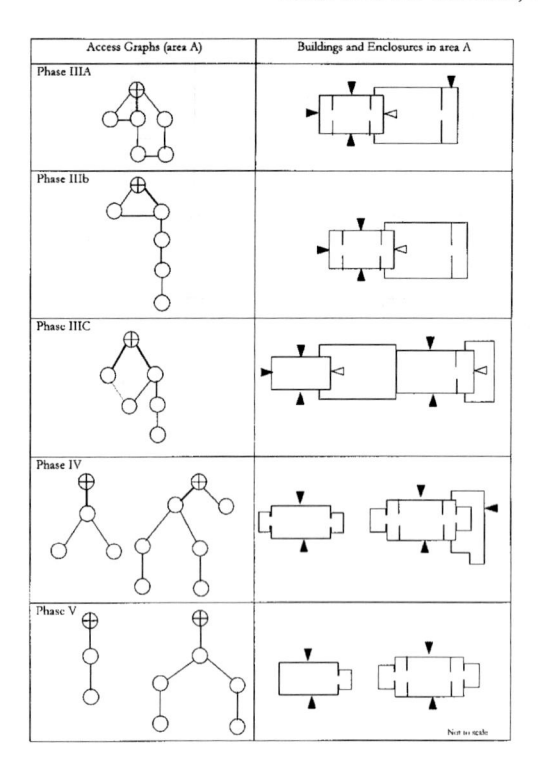

53 Movement through buildings and enclosures in area A at Yeavering

must first pass within the building. From Phase IV the emphasis is placed much more strongly on controlling interior space. The exterior enclosures in Area A disappear. Partitions and annexes, creating a series of separate spaces with access closely controlled from the centre of the building characterise structures A3a and A3b in Phase IV and V (54). The structure of the partitions and offsetting of doorways to each other meant that movement and lines of sight between spaces were directed in a very particular way. Also at this time the Great Enclosure, elaborated in the previous phase to monumental proportions, disappears.

Hope-Taylor suggests that the site is in decline from this point following attacks from Penda and Cadwallon (but see comments by Driscoll in this volume). However, the new structures are certainly not flimsy shacks, despite his characterisation of Style V (1977, 151). Furthermore, if the destruction of the site is due to attack, then why is the response to control interior space more tightly with no apparent effort to make the exterior more defensible? Yeavering remains an open, unenclosed settlement but access and movement within the buildings is increasingly exclusive (54). The scale and form of buildings is much further removed from the dwellings of ordinary folk.

Rapoport (1990) argued that formalising spatial order in such a way often occurs in societies undergoing conflict or change. As built environments are created to

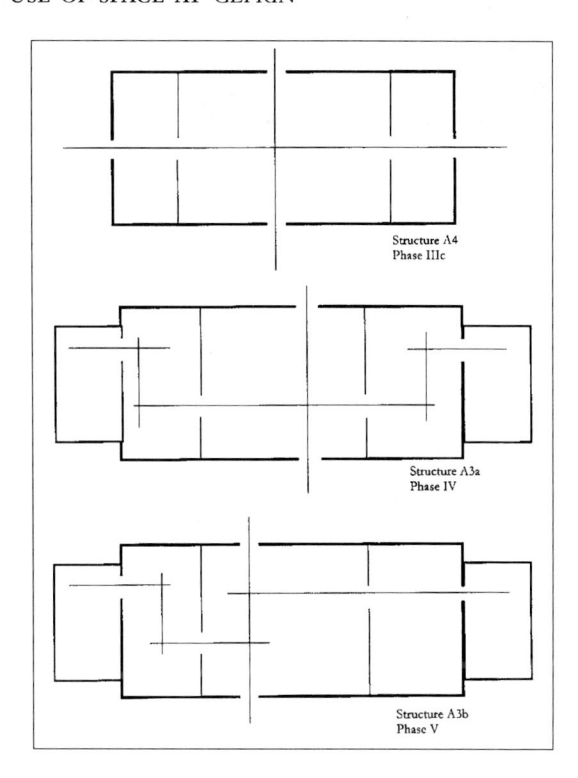

54 Control of space and movement within the buildings in the later phases of Yeavering

support desired behaviour, formalising space in this way can create a sense of stability and limits the capacity to reinterpret or change meanings. Through the sixth and seventh centuries there was a gradual progression towards a more stratified, hierarchical social system. The hall was at the centre of these social and political transformations. As a core institution, the hall could provide an important connection between the emergent dominant elite and ordinary people in society.

In many anthropological examples the aristocracies often come to monopolise 'house ideology' entirely – ordinary people only have shallow genealogical memory and less attachment to houses. Roxanna Waterson (1997) has, for example, looked at how house ideology has served to legitimise 'the enterprises of the great' in societies in the throes of political transition – towards greater concentration of power of a few and a shift from kin-based to more complex political, economic and religious structures of organisation. Her analyses suggest that the correlation between rank and architectural elaboration is often striking. In the early medieval period the social elite appropriated the hall ideal to their own ends. And while the physical substance of the structure is still indicative of the power and prestige of those associated with it, there is perhaps increased mystification of what goes on inside, with certain individuals being removed or removing themselves and their activities beyond the gaze and attention of others.

The experience of being within A3a and b where access to the building's interior spaces is closely controlled contrasts vividly with earlier structures A (54). These changes in spatial organisation suggest that social relations were more complex and hierarchical and that this was being written into the fabric of the architecture. Kingship was exercised less through the *habitus* of everyday knowledge but more through specially sanctioned powers and exclusive prerogatives.

In the end Yeavering is abandoned and the buildings are left to rot. This could mark the ending of a genealogy and lineage – wiping them from memory, as has been argued by Paul Frodsham (1999a). In poetic discourse the ruined and wasted hall is a dark and dire occurrence and can represent a social catastrophe (Hume 1974, 66). Wider social changes in the early medieval period also meant that it was no longer as necessary to retain links with the old seat of power at Yeavering (Cramp 1983, 275). An effect of the Christian Church changing traditional belief systems and removing ceremonies from the everyday dwelling was that attitudes to temporality also changed. The origins of later Anglo-Saxon kingdoms have been attributed to successful descent groups who had the ability to attract followers (Scull 1993). The process began with the formation of ranked lineages and the competition would have resulted in the emergence of local hegemonies with chiefs. Competition between such local chiefs would at first lead to cyclical or regional hegemony and then to more permanent dynasties with a political hierarchy. Yeavering would have played a critical role in such a process but as such hegemonies became established would *this* place remain so important?

CONCLUSION

While there may have been no actual physical continuity, Yeavering was a place of recurring importance: a place that has repeatedly drawn people to it. The situating of buildings here in the early medieval period engaged people in a particular way. As well as marking the people in the landscape it changed the way in which people interacted with it and with each other. Increasingly those with the wealth and influence to do so sought to assert their prestige through Yeavering and this also enabled them to control how people interacted in that space. In this way Yeavering became bound up with the enterprises of the social elite. Through time this monopoly perhaps also led to Yeavering's decline as the now-established elite moved towards new forms of expressing authority. It is certain that as Christianity claimed a hold on society, new ways of expressing power, heritage and ancestry grew in importance. The technology of writing to record histories and events is one powerful example. Ironically, this is also what saved Yeavering itself from being lost when Bede committed it to memory in the *Historia Ecclesiastica*.

8

AD GEFRIN AND SCOTLAND: THE IMPLICATIONS OF THE YEAVERING EXCAVATIONS FOR THE NORTH

Stephen T. Driscoll

Few excavations in England have exerted as much influence on our understanding of Early Historic Scotland as Yeavering; only Sutton Hoo and Coppergate have been as significant. In part, this is because Yeavering is the only Dark Age royal centre on the east side of Britain (i.e. between York and the Brough of Birsay) to have seen large-scale excavation. The exceptional evidence for timber architecture adds to its value because, as we have come to realise, most of the high-status sites of this period in Britain and Ireland were built of timber, even when enclosed by earthern or stone ramparts. So Yeavering's influence is in no small measure a result of the technical virtuosity of Hope-Taylor's excavations, which convincingly disentangled the complex traces of superimposed wooden buildings. Hope-Taylor's drawings have become icons of the post-war tradition in medieval British archaeology. When Yeavering was being dug it was recognised as a landmark of excavation method: cropmark archaeology was in its infancy and its potential (and limitations) were not yet fully recognised. When it was published Hope-Taylor's report was hailed as a benchmark for the future, but it now rather looks like a monument to a passed heroic age of archaeology, when one man thought he could do it all and did. (The multidisciplinary collaboration happened inside Hope-Taylor's head.) For a long time the technical achievements of the excavation, supported by the superb illustrations, the bold historical identifications and the familiar narrative context, have deflected sustained critical assessment. Indeed Hope-Taylor's discoveries were so visually arresting that they have been accepted largely at face value. Yeavering almost immediately inspired work in emulation and, as others approached timber archaeology with new confidence, it has come to serve as as a paradigm for royal estates in the early middle ages.

Yeavering has generated an important empirical legacy which informs us about the architectural possibilities of the Anglo-Saxon (and possibly the British) hall and it provides some of the most compelling evidence for the adoption of Christianity in the north. The rich textual associations of the site have inspired a range of discussions on the mechanics of royal governance (*cf.* Alcock 2003), but they also place Yeavering centrally in the narrative of popular conversion. In this chapter I want to explore what can be taken from these two themes of royalty and religion and put to use in Scotland. The coming of Christianity was, as Bede makes plain, a highly politicised process and with Christianity came profound ideological changes. These changes are literally reflected in the shifting political geography of royal authority and it is in this area that I think Yeavering will have made its greatest contribution to those interested in the Early Historic north.

The interpretative perspective that Hope-Taylor brought to his reading of this amazing array of material remains and textual records appears now to belong to a tradition of romantic narrative in early medieval archaeology which had as its central objective the amplification and elucidation of Bede's account. The historical events and archaeological deposits are worked into a tidy narrative of Yeavering's rise from unremarkable, but ancient, origins to be at the heart of a significant historical transition before rapidly fading into obscurity. Such a grand narrative seems in keeping with the scale of the projects undertaken by the scholarly titans of his day, such as Kenneth Jackson (1953). This historical perspective seems increasingly unsustainable in light of the critical standards of the twenty-first century. The degree to which things have moved on can be gauged by considering recent scholarly perspectives on Caedualla, *rex Brettonum*, who occupied a significant position in the Hope-Taylor chronology. We will turn to this shortly.

There is another problem with Hope-Taylor's paradigm. Although Yeavering is a key site for understanding the conversion of the North, Hope-Taylor seems overly concerned to make his evidence correspond to the accounts of Bede and other contemporary witnesses, rather than critically evaluating it on its own terms. The lack of discussion of the unique plan of the church, building B, is the most conspicuous instance of this. Perhaps it is because Hope-Taylor followed Bede so closely that he never adequately got to grips with the site's setting and the importance of the prehistoric landscape for understanding the pagan–Christian watershed.

AD GEFRIN AND SCOTLAND

EMPIRICAL LEGACY AND INTERPRETATIVE FRAMEWORKS

The empirical legacy is pervasive, predominantly in a literal, comparative way. Initially it inspired a hunt for halls in the aerial photographic record, as systematic reconnaissance was just getting off the ground in the early 1980s (Maxwell 1983). The most spectacular result was the cautionary tale of the cropmark timber hall at Balbridie, Aberdeenshire, initially thought to be Dark Age but which upon excavation proved to be Neolithic (Reynolds 1980). Hope-Taylor himself had better luck at Doon Hill, where he excavated a hall very similar to the Yeavering-style buildings (1980) (55). Frustratingly, for anyone seeking to trace Northumbrian manifest destiny archaeologically, the excavations at Dunbar reveal an Anglian royal centre which differed from Yeavering and Doon Hill both in constructional detail (specifically the ninth-century masonry building) and in the layout of the settlement in and around the British promontory fort (Perry 2000). Perhaps Yeavering's architecture is more regionally specific than has been supposed. Ian Smith's systematic examination of the aerial photographic record for evidence of

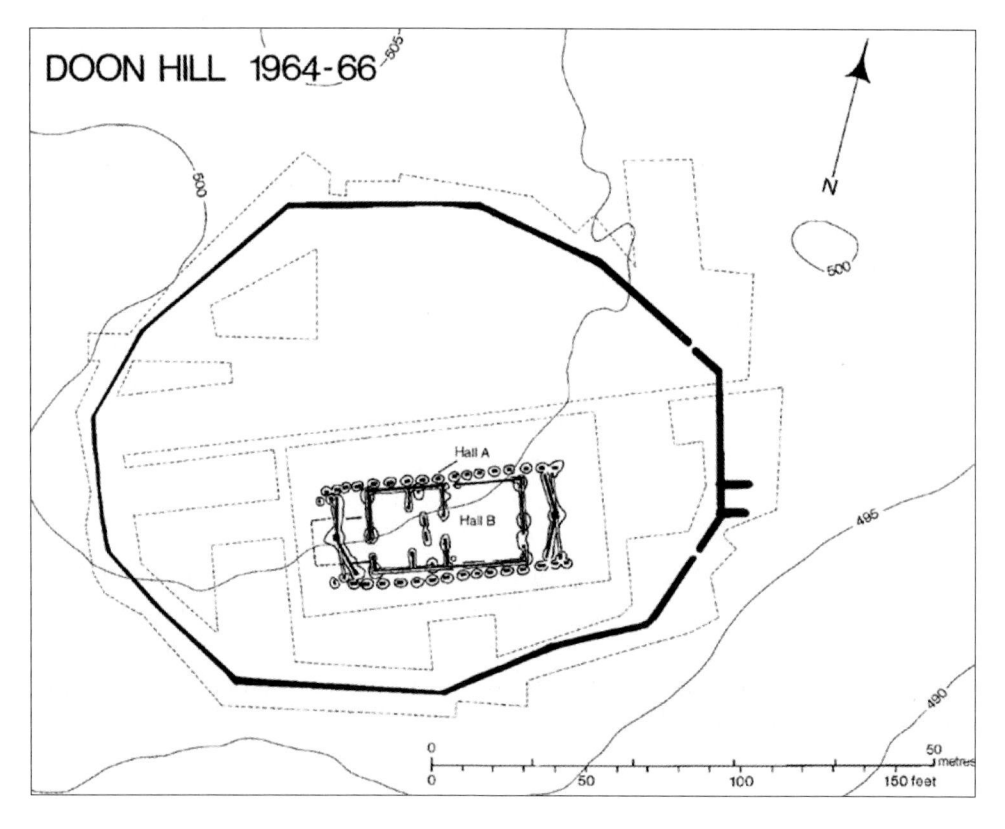

55 Plan of Doon Hill. After Reynolds. *Reproduced from Alcock 2003, figure 85*

Northumbrian settlement revealed that, at least in the Tweed Basin, there was a Yeavering building tradition, which is exemplified by the Sprouston and Milfield cropmark complexes (Smith 1991), but we are still waiting for a confirmed example of a Yeavering hall outside of greater Northumbria.

The first substantive critical response to Hope-Taylor's reading of the cultural significance of the Yeavering architectural tradition questioned the cultural attributions applied to the architectural change from the early post-and-panel structures ('British') to the later plank-built ones of the 'Anglian' *villa regia* (Scull 1991, 58-9). Scull used Hope-Taylor's lucid record to suggest an alternative chronology and argues that comparative evidence elsewhere suggests that the earliest structures were at least as likely to belong to an 'Anglo-Saxon' architectural tradition as they were to be British. At a stroke Hope-Taylor's cultural fusion model, which saw the plank-built structures as a hybrid Anglo-British design, was called into question. In this critique Chris Scull effectively challenged this comfortable, if unlikely, construct and in the process raised some disturbing questions about ethnicity – 'integration and assimilation' or 'imposition and annihilation' – which are rarely addressed by English archaeology. Building technology aside, the British component at Yeavering is not so easily dismissed: the British place name persists still and the buried population probably included a substantial British component in the early phase. Who knows what the DNA could have told us, if only the bone evidence had survived?

The second substantive critique, which draws us firmly into Scotland, was delivered by Leslie Alcock in Edinburgh at the 1989 Rhind Lectures, finally pubished in 2003. The discussions here build upon arguments which Alcock developed in the 1980s as he was constructing a new understanding of what he termed the Early Historic archaeology of Scotland (2003, 234-56). Understandably for a hillfort man, Alcock was frustrated by the limited examination of the Great Enclosure and concluded that 'it is not easy to comprehend the function of the double palisade enclosures (at Yeavering, Milfield and Sprouston) because they are peripheral to the buildings' (2003, 238). On the other hand, he thought the grandstand the most 'thought-provoking' of structures and explored the implication of its Roman antecedents in a way which complemented Hope-Taylor's own reading of the evidence.

Alcock's most important criticisms relate to the absolute chronology of the hall sequence which is notoriously unsteady, balanced as it is on two artefacts and Bede. Alcock rejects the idea that the archaeologically attested conflagration which destroyed the hall A4 should be attributed to Caedualla. First of all, Bede does not attribute the destruction to the great British warrior, which he might have been expected to do if it had been the case. Moreover, Alcock questions whether Caedualla, king of Gwynedd, can be responsible, since early medieval sources never place him east of Cheviot. The Alcock critique emphasises the problems of attributing the destruction of Yeavering to Caedualla using a close, perhaps too close, reading of Bede and the *Historia Brettonum*. However, the problem is more profound according to Alex Woolf (2004): Caedualla, slayer of Edwin, has probably been mis-identified as the ruler of Gwynedd. Caedualla *Brettonum* is more likely to have been a different person, the ruler of one of the lost kingdoms of the 'Old North' and not from Wales at all. Woolf's argument is based on a fine-grained assessment of the primary historical records of the sort which has revolutionised early British history in recent decades (*cf.* Dumville 1977; Charles-Edwards 1978; Davies 1982; Koch 1997). This new historical source criticism was just beginning at the time *Yeavering* was coming to publication. This sort of critical source analysis, while detrimental to the tidy narrative, offers in its place glimpses of a more authentic, if fragmented and unfamiliar past. In this case, it reveals the presence, amongst the genealogies of the dynasties of the Old North, of a Caedualla, who although less well-known than his Gwynedd namesake, is altogether a more plausible protagonist for the events of Bede's *Ecclesiastical History* ii. 20 and iii. 1. The point of this digression is to show how much perspectives on early medieval history have changed since Hope-Taylor embarked on his investigations. It is now clear that there are profound uncertainties within the evidence that militate against producing a satisfying narrative. Hope-Taylor was operating in a different intellectual climate and it shows: contemporary archaeologists are more cautious of adopting historical identifications in order to provide a narrative context for their evidence.

Alcock's consideration of the hall sequence independent of the Caedualla horizon allowed him to propose that the two similar great halls (A2 and A4) were Edwin's work (AD 617-33) and to suggest that a significant shift is represented by the successor hall, A3, which is markedly different in structure and layout from its predecessors. Alcock proposed to account for this as the work of the Bernician Oswald (AD 634-42). By this reading, the destruction of A4 occurred in the context of interdynastic strife, rather than as a consequence of British counter-insurgency. The rebuilding of A3 also assumes a different complexion: the building of a new hall directly on the site of the rival hall is not only a blatant gesture of conquest, but it also suggests a reverence for the enduring significance of Yeavering as a special place in the seventh century.

In Scotland these problems should be salutary, but the Alcock reading also has more specific implications for the sequences at Doon Hill and, perhaps less obviously, at Dunbar. The setting of Doon Hill, high on the shoulder of the Lammermuirs, overlooking Dunbar, contrasts with Yeavering's low position and restricted prospect. At Doon Hill the post-built Hall A within its polygonal palisade was replaced by Hall B, which compares well with Yeavering Hall A1(c).

At Dunbar the Northumbrian evidence comes from a marginal part of the site where the architectural and artefactual evidence are indicative of domestic residence and service activities (Perry 2000, 35-76). Both sites seem to point to architectural transition linked to the Northumbrians. Alcock is particularly keen on seeing the palisade as a British architectural tradition and reinforces his argument by reference to the British fort place-name element *dun-* in *Doon* Hill and *Dun*bar, which he regards as evidence of the British origins of the enclosed phases of these sites. In both of these East Lothian instances, Alcock seems content with the notion of an 'ethnic' reading for these transitions (Alcock 2003, 237), but, given the limitations of the evidence, does not stress it.

ROYAL GOVERNMENT

What is not in doubt is that Edwin and his entourage are recorded in near-contemporary sources as having made periodic visits to Yeavering. As a consequence the royal circuit has become an essential feature of the model of northern estate management. The physical manifestation of the system of landholding and estate management envisioned by G.W.S. Barrow (1973) as extending from the northern English midlands to the Moray Firth, found its most concrete archaeological expression in Yeavering. As a result Yeavering has come to have had a strong influence on discussions on the development of royal government and kingship in the North. Leslie Alcock has been the most explicit in linking the archaeology of early historic power centres to the historical discussion of royal institutions (1988). Indeed, almost all of Alcock's programme of reconnaissance excavations on early historic sites in Scotland is tied into places mentioned because they were frequented by the king and royal officials. These investigations of places associated with the 'activities of potentates' are reviewed in *Kings and Warriors Craftsmen and Priests* (2003), where Alcock attempts to fit these sites into those strands of the historical narrative as have come down to us. He links the royal circuit, with its worldly display and 'daily rejoicing through the cities, forts and villages', with the mundane practical requirements to store produce, host banquets and accommodate followers (2003, 49-50).

The Yeavering excavations may have been little known to G.W.S. Barrow when he was working out the ideas which appeared in *Pre-feudal Scotland: Thanes and Shires* (1973), which surveyed the institutional framework of lordship in the early North. Barrow was not the first to suggest that Northumbria was both essential to understanding the system and was likely to have been an instrument for the spread of some characteristic features of the system of royal officials (i.e. thanes) managing holdings of the crown and great magnates. In this respect he was

AD GEFRIN AND SCOTLAND

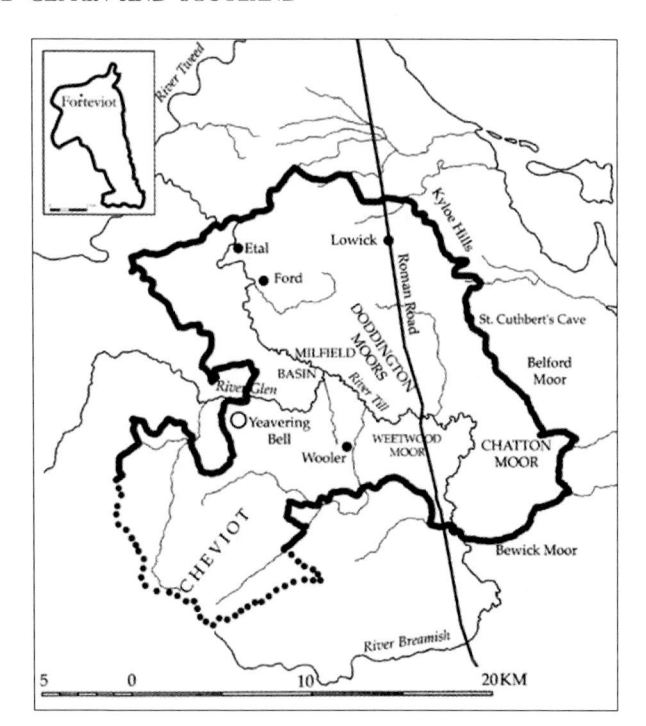

56 Conjectural extent of the thanage of Forteviot (from Driscoll 1991) compared with the extent of Gefrin (from O'Brien 2002) at the same scale

building on the tradition of scholarship mapped out by Skene (1876-80), Jolliffe (1926), Jones (1976; 1984) and others. Certainly I had Yeavering in mind when I was trying to apply these ideas to the archaeology of the thanage in Pictland (Driscoll 1991). Scholarship on the subject has continued to progress. Sandy Grant (1993) has refined Barrow's lists of thanages and proposed an alternative historical context for the dissemination of the institution of the thanage, which he links to the reign of Malcolm II (1005-34) who was both King of Scots and ruler of Northumbria. This contradicts the long established position of Barrow and others who maintained that the institutional similarities of lordship reflect shared common roots that are deep and early (i.e. British). Establishing the origins of customary obligations that underpin the social structure will probably always remain a matter of faith rather than of hard evidence. It nonetheless remains profitable to consider Northumbrian notions of lordship when trying to understand the Scottish evidence because of the manifest similarities of the Northumbrians with the Northern Britons and the Picts. The most significant advance for understanding how this might have worked at Yeavering is Colm O'Brien's analysis of the shire of *Gefrin* (2002), which suggests that the hinterlands of Yeavering were vast. These are significantly larger than any of the thanages to have been examined in Scotland hitherto (*56*), so we need to consider the validity of some aspects of the Northumbrian model for the Scottish scene.

Implicit in much of Alcock's writing is that a major reason for the royal peregrinations was to create an opportunity from the king to interact with his subjects. 'We may infer that, for both Edwin and Ecgfrith, the display and rejoicing were intended to make the physical person and the king highly visible throughout the kingdom: a very necessary act in a period of poor communications' (2003, 49). The buildings of Yeavering emerge as prominent instruments of royal authority and centres of judicial practice. That being so, it seems surprising that more attention has not been given over to thinking about Yeavering's position at the foot of Yeavering Bell. I think we should ask why such an out-of-the-way site was selected for development into a royal centre. What drew successive Northumbrian kings to establish a *villa regia* here? And then why abandon it? I think the landscape situation indicates that *Gefrin* was already a place of regional assembly by the seventh century. Hope-Taylor to his credit did see this, but he did not really pursue it, particularly not in the context of the conversion to Christianity. And who can blame him? He had ample evidence for changing religious practice: a burnt temple, the grandstand, and shifting burial rites. Moreover he was not helped by the lamentable state of Iron Age studies at the time he was working, which in the absence of radiocarbon dates and large-scale excavation were based on survey evidence that was slotted into the Roman military sequence. Discussions of hillforts in the 1950-1960s as proto-urban centres, *oppida* (with all its implications of progress and settled, civilized town life), reveal a preoccupation with the diffusion of urbanism to the exclusion of other models for explaining places of social importance where large numbers of people regularly gathered and large amounts of labour were expended on construction of ramparts (Feachem 1966). Rather than think of such places as failed towns, we would do well to reflect that *Gefrin* and Eildon Hill on the Tweed were the focus of 'tribal' gatherings for centuries.

THE CONVERSION

Given our nearly complete reliance on burial practice as an indicator of the conversion amongst society at large, one could hardly imagine a more compelling discovery than the long sequence of pagan burials with the associated temple, which was replaced by a 'church' and a Christian cemetery. Hope-Taylor can perhaps be forgiven for having been drawn too deeply into Bede's narrative to consider the wider landscape context of the conversion account. Certainly we cannot have expected him to rethink the nature of late Iron Age religion in north-eastern Britain or to think of the hillfort on Yeavering Bell in terms of a sacred tribal enclosure, one which retained an interest to post-Roman peoples

(Hope-Taylor 1977, 267; Alcock 2003, 235-6). Fortunately, the sacred quality of some of these great hillforts has been more widely recognised recently (*cf.* Frodsham 2004a, 36-8).

The general population has a shadowy presence in Hope-Taylor's reading of the conversion process. Up to 300 filled the grandstand and were awed by its Roman appearance. They buried their loved ones in large numbers, first around the pagan temple and then next to the 'church'. Above all, in Bede's narrative, they were converted in great numbers by Bishop Paulinus during 36 days of continuous preaching and alfresco baptisms (Bede, *Historia Ecclesiastica*: ii, 14). Taking the long view, it looks as though the royal complex was located at the foot of a holy mountain which served as a traditional place of assembly; in short, an ideal place to meet people of the district regularly to conduct public business and also ideal for preaching.

We must accept Hope-Taylor's suggestion that the *villa regia* was in some sense a successor to the great hillfort on Yeavering Bell (Hope-Taylor 1977, 6-9), even if he was at a loss to explain the link. Although the sacred character of Yeavering's prehistory was recognised by Hope-Taylor, it took a prehistorian, Richard Bradley (1987), to explain the logic which linked a modest stone circle and cremation cemetery to the location of the *villa regia*, particularly given that the early prehistoric monuments do not in themselves appear sufficiently impressive to account for the selection of site. Now, thanks to the work of Richard Bradley, we are beginning to understand the more general connections being made during the early Middle Ages with more ancient landscape features, which, like the place name, point to *Gefrin* being a native British creation. This observation provides powerful lesson for understanding where and why politically important sites were located in early medieval Scotland (Driscoll 1998; 2004).

DISPLAY OF ROYAL AUTHORITY

An important consequence of the Yeavering excavations is that we are more willing to allow that early medieval peoples were deliberately manipulating the landscape and the cultural resources embedded within it for political purposes (Williams 2004; FitzPatrick 2004). This is arguably the most important implication for the North to flow from the Yeavering excavations. Not least it allows us to explore the ways that power shifted with the coming of Christianity. This can be illustrated with respect to the southern Pictish kingdom of Fortriu and three historically attested sites there: Forteviot, Moncrieffe, and Scone. The interpretation which follows builds upon ideas of landscape reuse and manipulation inspired by the Yeavering sequence.

57 The arch discovered at Forteviot is interpreted by Alcock (2003, 231) as a chancel arch

According to the *Chronicles of the Kings of Scotland* Cinead mac Alpin died in 858 '*in palacium Fothiurabaichtt*' (Anderson 1980, 250; Broun 1999). Unfortunately, ninth-century palaces are so thin on the ground that we have no idea what this might have looked like. It is not difficult to imagine that it was a grand palace, perhaps built on the scale of Yeavering, but being longer-lived it eventually incorporated masonry architecture (*57*). Between the local sculpture, including the Dupplin cross (Henderson 1997), the arch and five other cross fragments, there can be little doubt that a church occupied a prominent place in the complex. However, that is not the full story and does not begin to take the wider landscape into account. In the fields immediately to the south is found one of the largest concentrations of prehistoric ritual monuments in east central Scotland. Today they exist only as cropmarks but in the early medieval period they would have been most imposing earthwork monuments (*58*). The presence of Pictish square barrows mingling with the Neolithic henges shows that the prehistoric monuments still had an appeal for the Picts. Forteviot was arguably the least successful of Alcock's reconnaissance excavations, because, as we can now appreciate, his approach of targeted small-scale excavations, was unsuited to resolving the questions presented by a sprawling monumental landscape. Without more extensive investigations around Forteviot we cannot say when in the Pictish era it emerged as a royal centre, although it is clear that the Picts sought to appropriate the Neolithic monuments.

If one were looking for a tribal assembly place in Strathearn, analogous to Yeavering Bell, one would look to Moncrieffe Hill, east of Forteviot. W.J. Watson

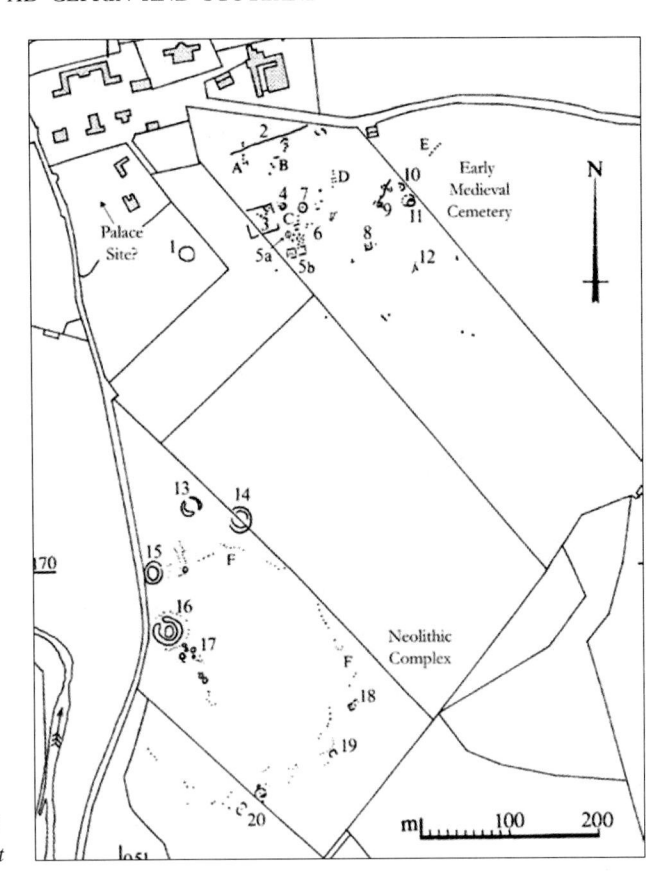

58 Transcription of the cropmarks at Forteviot by RCAHMS, showing the Neolithic complex just to the south of the modern village and site of the palace. Crown copyright

interpreted the name, *Monad Croib*, 'hill of the tree', as referring to a 'conspicuous... possibly tribal tree' (1926, 400-1), analogous to the *bile* or sacred, tribal trees which are common features at Irish royal centres (59). Although unexcavated, the main fort on Moncrieffe Hill occupies a conspicuous position and the surface remains invite comparison with the hillforts mentioned previously, while at the same time the final phase of fortification invites comparison with the great Pictish hillforts at Dunnichan (Alexander and Ralston 1999; Ralston 2004). Most revealingly, it is recorded in the Annals of Ulster as the site of a battle between two rivals for the Pictish throne in 729 (*sa* 728; Anderson 1980, 38, 177); battles between dynastic rivals at sacred sites of tribal assembly are well documented in early medieval Ireland. After 729 the site is not mentioned again.

The emergence of Scone in the early tenth century is critical to our understanding of the dynamics of the political geography of Fortriu. The ancient features in Scone's landscape have tended to obscure the fact that 906 is the first historical mention of the place, particularly as its position seems so naturally 'royal' with a commanding vista including the ancient crossing of the Tay and

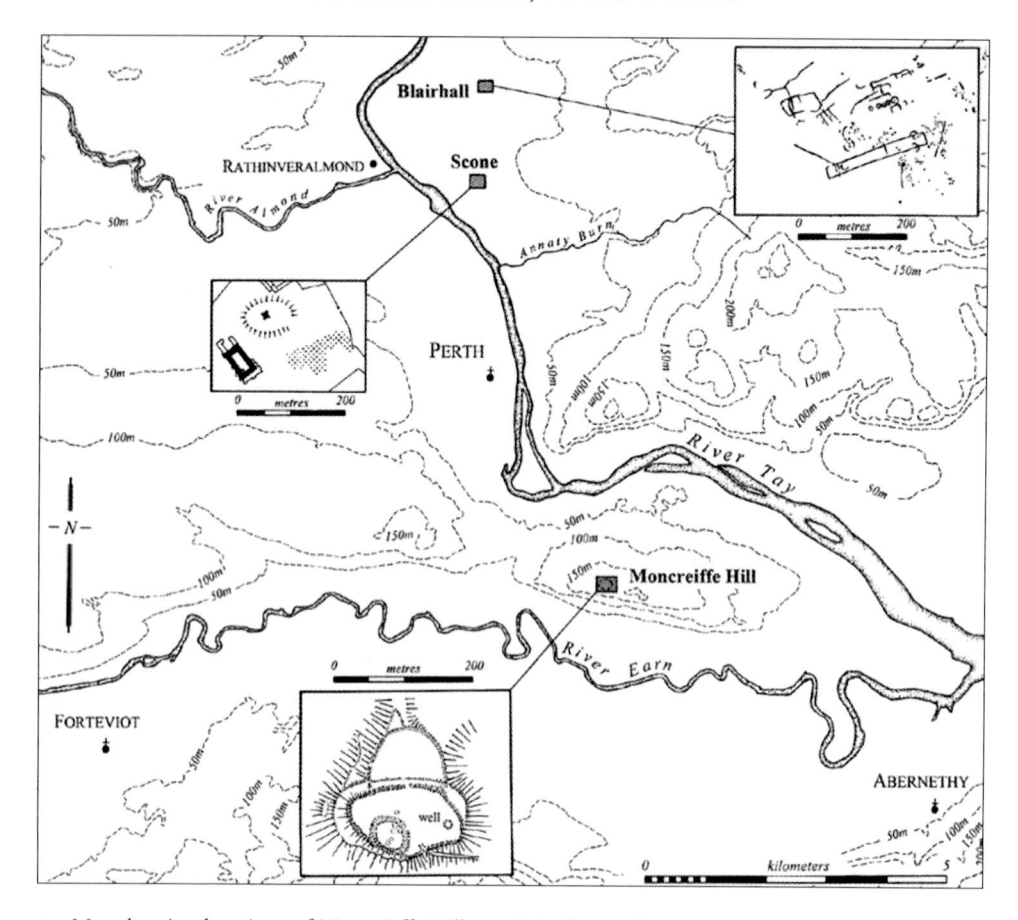

59 Map showing locations of Moncrieffe Hill etc. Driscoll 2004, figure 3.3

with its own complement of prehistoric ritual monuments every bit as impressive as those at Forteviot (Brophy, in press). I would like to suggest that, as in the case of Yeavering, the shift away from an old centre, Moncrieffe, to the new one at Scone reflects a shift in values, which was motivated by political changes, including the increasing influence of the Church. This seems to correspond with the shift from the Pictish to the Gaelic kingdom and was undertaken for ideological and political reasons (Driscoll 2004, 81-7).

The current generation of Scottish historians, conspicuously Alex Woolf and Dauvit Broun, have identified Constantine II (900-43) as the architect of the Gaelic kingdom of Alba (Broun 1999; Driscoll 2004, 74). *Landscape* architect might be more appropriate, if it was he who designed the assembly place at Scone. Not content with the ancient burials or a hillfort with a tribal tree he located his focal point near to the ancient church indicated by the phrase '*civitas scoan*. The form of the great, flat 'moot hill' echoes both Irish royal inauguration sites and the stepped-mounds which appeared at the Thing places of Viking Age Dublin and Man (FitzPatrick 2004, 45-6; Darvill 2004).

CONCLUSION

Returning to this appraisal of the long-term significance of Yeavering, we have yet to see Yeavering-style buildings north of the Forth and the early estate model also needs 'ground proofing'. It may be that its greatest legacy will have been to encourage us to think more about the wider landscape and the political potential of ancient assembly places in the way we are now able to in Ireland, although ironically this does not appear to have been in the forefront of Brian Hope-Taylor's thoughts. Ideally this fertilisation should not be one-way. We might like to reflect that if the shift from Moncrieffe to Scone is comparable to the shift from Yeavering to Milfield, we might look to the rising influence of the Northumbrian Church as having had a role in the process.

ACKNOWLEDGEMENTS

When first asked to participate in the conference I considered asking Leslie Alcock if he would like to make it a joint effort. Unfortunately I was too late; poor health had brought his scholarly career to a premature close. Yeavering always loomed large in Leslie Alcock's teaching, and his views on it influenced a generation of students in Glasgow, of which I was fortunate to be one. Of course Leslie's scholarship lives on in his work, as I have tried to emphasise here. As a way of commemorating his achievement and of building upon the Alcock contribution to Early Historic archaeology, a new research centre has been established in the University of Glasgow, based around his library and the research materials he collected. This, I hope, will be a more lasting and fitting tribute than any short paper could be. My further thanks are extended to the patient editors and to Katherine Forsyth for her editorial interventions.

9

ANGLIAN YEAVERING: A CONTINENTAL PERSPECTIVE

P.S. Barnwell

Towards the end of his monumental report of the excavations at the Bernician cult centre and royal vill of Yeavering, Brian Hope-Taylor noted that the site, 'speaks volumes ... about the work of royal hall-builders, but is silent about the portable emblems and other accompaniments of the kingship to which all its great buildings give monumental expression' (Hope-Taylor 1977, 315). He went on to make a number of suggestions about the ways in which the buildings might have been decorated, especially with wood-carving and painted plaster, but, although the veil he draws back in the penultimate thematic section of the report enriches and enlivens the excavated material, the site is presented more as an artefact than as encapsulating evidence for activity or 'process': the decoration, furnishings and objects appropriate to a periodic royal residence are discussed, but not the kinds of royal activity and ceremonial for which buildings and adornments provided the set and props. It is to a partial sketch of that activity that much of this chapter is devoted, concentrating on the unique Building E (the 'grandstand') and its platform and post (Post E). After reconsideration of the excavated evidence for the physical form of the structures, their function is examined against a context which draws on a range of evidence from late antiquity on the continent where primary written sources are more plentiful than those for early Anglo-Saxon England. This is, therefore, an essay in comparative history, the results of which are necessarily tentative, but the conclusions may point towards fuller appreciation of what manner of place Yeavering was.

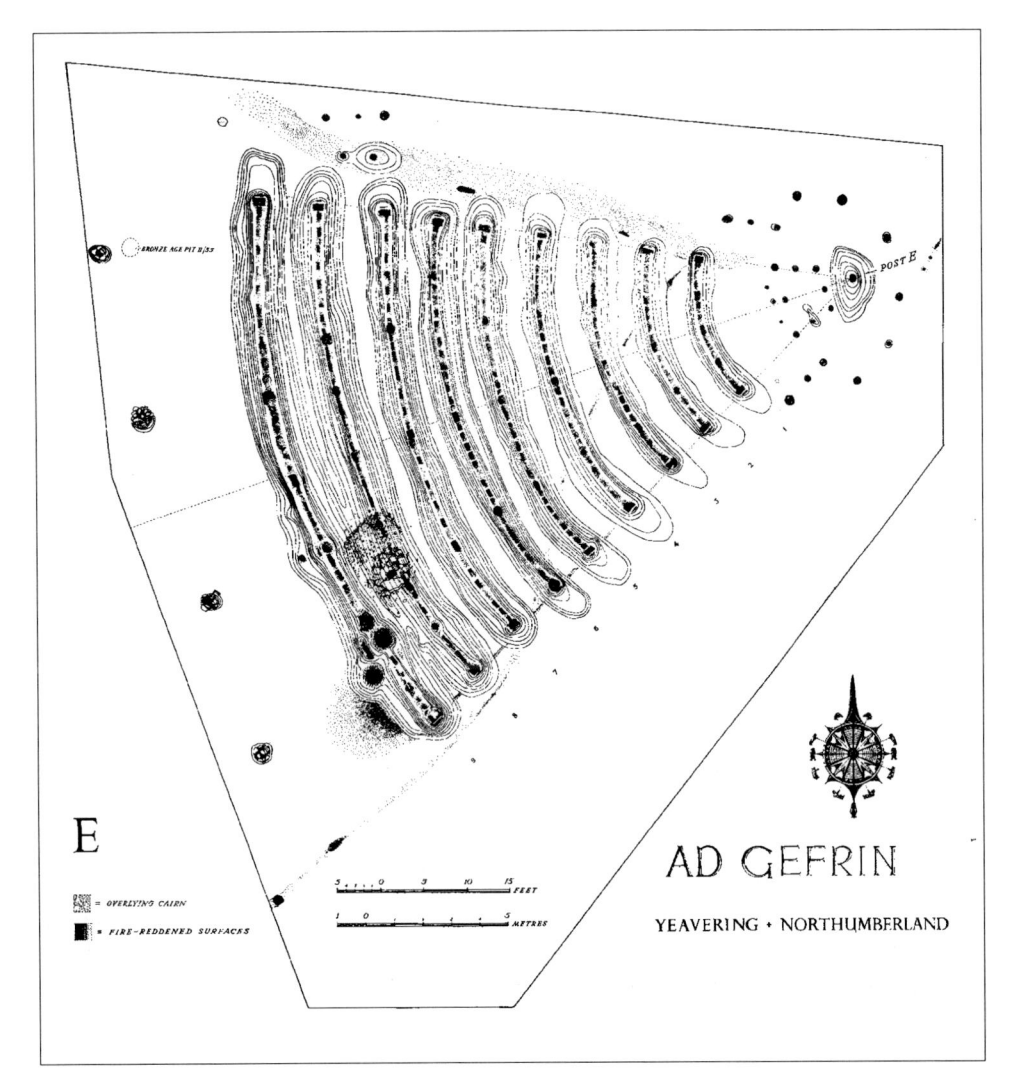

60 Plan of Building E and associated structures. Hope-Taylor 1977, figure 55. © Crown copyright – reproduced by permission of English Heritage

BUILDING E

The published evidence relating to Building E and associated structures is surprisingly summary for so unique a construction, and contains a number of inconsistencies which cannot be resolved (Hope-Taylor 1977, 119-24). Excavation revealed nine more-or-less concentric trenches forming the arcs of a structure of triangular ground plan. The trenches, which were of varying depth, held solid timber walls of substantial vertical timbers with intermittent larger posts. According to the text of the report, the trenches became progressively deeper as they became longer, with the single exception of Trench 7, which was slightly less deep than Trench 6. Hope-Taylor viewed this pattern as evidence that the structure was tiered, the deeper trenches representing walls which stood higher above ground than the shallower ones. The plan of the trenches (*60*), which contains form lines at intervals of 6in (15cm), appears to illustrate what is described in the text, but the accompanying drawing of a section through the trenches does not (*61*). If the section is correctly drawn, the differences in the depths of most of the trenches were considerably less marked than the text suggests. Further, the depths of the trenches given in the text are inconsistent with those which can be estimated from the plan, and neither matches the section, whatever level is taken as the datum.

These inconsistencies significantly weaken the specific argument that the depths of the trenches are evidence for a tiered structure. They need not, however, affect the overall interpretation of the building, for there is no structural need for the taller posts to have been buried more deeply than the shorter ones. Indeed, it would have been quite possible, using box-framing techniques, to erect a tiered structure without burying the posts at all, as the Romans appear to have done centuries earlier when they constructed timber amphitheatres. Nevertheless, one piece of evidence may demonstrate that the longer walls were indeed taller than the others: their timbers were of smaller scantling than those of the shorter walls. Hope-Taylor combined this with the fact that the longer walls were slightly less regularly curved than the shorter ones to suggest that the structure was built in two phases. An alternative is that the building was erected in a single phase, but that the timbers of the longer walls were narrower than the others on account of the nature of the construction. The three back walls, the longest of which must have stood more than 20ft (6m) above ground, required a total of about 20 posts and 130 intermediate timbers. Since the walls were solid, timbers which tapered

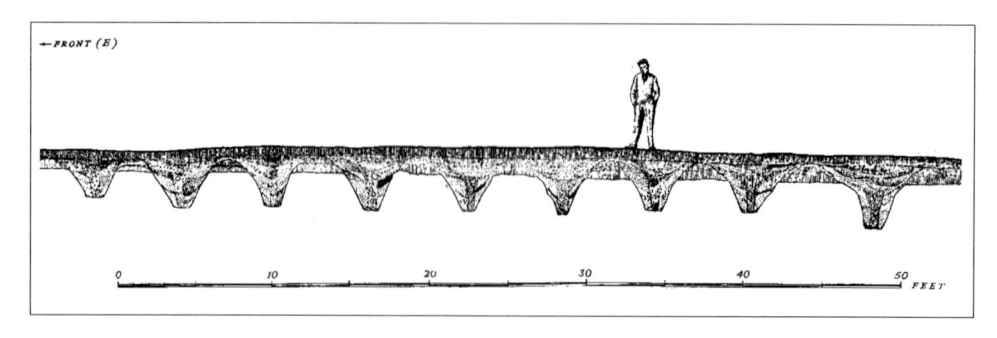

61 Section through Building E. Hope-Taylor 1977, figure 56. © Crown copyright – reproduced by permission of English Heritage

or had significant waney edges could not have been used, and it may have been impossible to find enough trees of sufficient length and girth to replicate the larger scantling used for the shorter walls.

The height of the rear wall is suggested both by the angle of the sockets for the struts behind it and by the dimensions of the rest of the structure. The sockets for the bracing struts were set some 19ft (5.8m) behind the longest wall, and can be estimated, from a photograph (plate 103) in the published report, to have been at an angle of 40 degrees or a little more. A line projected from the sockets intersects with the wall about 16ft (4.9m) above ground. This suggests that the wall would have extended rather higher, perhaps 21 or 22ft (6.5m), the most effective bracing point being two-thirds or three-quarters of the way up. Approximately the same height can be obtained from consideration of the rest of the structure, assuming that it is correctly interpreted as tiered. Comparison with surviving stone amphitheatres of the Roman period suggests that the timber walls were so spaced as to accommodate two tiers of seats between them, each about 16in (40cm) high and 3ft (0.9m) deep, sufficient for someone to sit down and leave room for the feet of the people on the tier behind. Such proportions create a rake of about 25 degrees and a rear wall a little over 21ft (6.5m) tall, perhaps with a palisade above that. Adding the length of timber buried in the ground, such a height for the main structure places its longest timbers at the upper end of what is easily obtainable from managed woodland. Although the calculations are not discussed in the published report, they appear to be broadly similar to those employed by Hope-Taylor in his reconstruction drawing (62).

Hope-Taylor's presentation and interpretation of the evidence for the platform, screens and Post E, which stood to the east of the tiered structure, is as summary as that for Building E itself, but does not contain obvious contradictions. One feature to which reference was not made in the text of the published report, however, is the set of five post-holes set in a trapezoidal pattern to the north of Trenches 6 and 7, the two nearer the body of the building being deeper than the others, one set in a large depression. Because they are nowhere discussed, it is not certain that they were coeval with Building E. If they were, they could perhaps represent foundations for some kind of stair-like access to the upper levels of the structure. Without such a contrivance, the only means of attaining the upper levels would have been to ascend from the bottom, immediately in front of the platform and Post E, which would have been inconvenient since the flanking screens restricted access to the area.

62 Reconstruction of Building E and associated structures. Hope-Taylor 1977, figure 57. © Crown copyright – reproduced by permission of English Heritage

ROMAN MODELS: THEATRES AND AMPHITHEATRES

Assuming that Building E is correctly reconstructed, one obvious inspiration for its unique form, as Hope-Taylor himself recognised, would have been the remains of the stone theatres and amphitheatres of Roman Britain. Such structures had been used in Roman times both for entertainment and for gatherings of people for other purposes. The amphitheatre at Carmarthen, for example, had a capacity greater than that required by the town, perhaps suggesting that it was a tribal gathering place (Wacher 1995, 392-3). At Gosbecks Farm near Colchester a theatre associated with a shrine may have fulfilled a similar function, administrative or political business being intimately connected with religious activity: such association of theatres and rural native shrines was commonplace in northern Gaul (Wacher 1995, 113, 127). The remains of several amphitheatres and theatres would still have been visible in the later sixth century, the Cirencester amphitheatre, for example, perhaps having become a defensible retreat for a time in the sub-Roman period.

Hope-Taylor's emphasis on Yeavering as a specifically *royal* centre might lead to a suggestion that the idea for Building E was in some way derived from the kinds of structure with concentric tiers of seats used by other early medieval rulers as settings for displays of power. The most famous is the circus at Constantinople, which was important both for chariot-racing and as a place where emperors could be seen in the midst of the people, to be acclaimed and to receive petitions (Cameron 1976, 162-3, 182-3). From what was originally opportunistic exploitation of the circus by emperors, there evolved specific imperial associations, particularly related to emperor-making ceremonies and the celebration of victories. The Germanic rulers of several of the kingdoms which were established in the former western provinces of the Empire imitated imperial ceremonies at the circus. In 550, during Justinian's attempt to take Italy back into the Empire, Totila, king of the Ostrogoths, held horse races immediately after regaining control of Rome, probably for the combined reasons of celebrating his victory and demonstrating and affirming his power (Procopius, *History of the Wars*: vii.37.4). A few years earlier, King Theodebert I of the Franks acted similarly when he acquired the former imperial capital of Arles (Procopius, *History of the Wars*: vii.33.5), and in 577 his cousin, Chilperic I, built circuses at Paris and Soissons, his principal residences, ostensibly to provide entertainment for the citizens, but perhaps to furnish himself with opportunities for displaying his power (Gregory of Tours, *Libri Historiarum*: v.17). Finally, in 604, when King Agilulf of the Lombards made his son, Adaloald, joint ruler with himself, the coronation ceremony was staged at the circus in Milan (Paul the Deacon, *Historia Langobardorum*: iv.30).

Notwithstanding these examples, a relationship between the Yeavering building and a circus is very unlikely, for the form of Building E is not that of a segment of a circus building, or even an amphitheatre. In both those types of monument the emperor or other presiding dignitary sat in a box at the top of the structure, while at Yeavering the focus is entirely on the platform and pole at the bottom. In addition, in circuses and amphitheatres the lower end of the tiered seating was raised on a podium, rather than resting on the ground, a feature precluded by the proportions of Building E. The structural affinity is, as Hope-Taylor himself recognised, with a theatre (Hope-Taylor 1977, 242). This opens up a different range of Roman associations, which are derived from the provincial administration rather than the central imperial government. Although evidence for provincial administration in much of the western Empire is slight, sources from further afield indicate that theatres were used for assemblies of citizens. Such assemblies at one time elected local magistrates, and the assembled people could make their views known by acclamation or otherwise, but the people could also be summoned to the theatre by the provincial governor so that he could read out imperial letters or transact other public business (Jones 1964, 722; Brown 1992, 85, 149; Browning 1952, 17). The choice of the theatre as the place for conducting the last kind of business may have been connected with the fact that it was built for public speaking, and its acoustics were better than those of amphitheatres and circuses. Experiments conducted by Hope-Taylor on the site of Building E suggested that its width and depth marked the maximum area in which his voice could be heard as he spoke from the platform at its base (Hope-Taylor 1977, 242). While it is not possible to determine from where the builder of Yeavering obtained the idea for Building E, it appears that at least one Roman theatre, that at Canterbury, may have continued to be used long after the Romans had left. Parts of the building are known to have stood into the eleventh century, but more significant is the fact that the streets of the city were realigned so that the main roads met at the theatre, suggesting that it was a place of some importance and may have been used for public or ceremonial purposes, perhaps including ones associated with the royal court of the early kingdom of Kent (Brooks 1984, 24-5).

EVIDENCE FROM FRANCIA

If the Roman theatre provides a possible model for the form of the seating of Building E, it does not provide an antecedent for the platform, which is too small for any significant kind of performance, or for Post E. Bearing in mind the fact that Yeavering had for centuries been a place of burial and religious cult, and the fact that similar poles were erected over two of its high-status graves (AX and BX), Hope-Taylor hesitantly suggested that Post E might have borne totemic significance (Hope-Taylor 1977, 270). While that is possible, the best analogy for the post at the base of the theatre is perhaps found in *Lex Ribuaria*, a law-code issued in the 620s for the Austrasian, or Rhineland, part of the Frankish kingdom. Several of its clauses refer to legal cases that could find resolution at the king's *staffolus*, a stone, column or post, associated with, or perhaps set upon, a podium or platform; so the king's *staffolus* designated a place of royal power (Schützeichel 1964). The word itself was known in Old English, where it contains the same range of meaning, relating to both a step and a column: hence, for example, in *Beowulf*, Hrothgar's praise of the hero for slaying Grendel was delivered from on or beside the *stapol* in Heorot (line 926), while at the end of the poem the same word describes the columns which supported the dragon's barrow (line 2718). The etymological connections of the word also lead into a wider realm of association, particularly to runes, or the sticks upon which they were carved, and their use for divining. The postulated Germanic root, **stab*, therefore contains undertones relating to fate or judgement (Green 1998, 255-6, 382-3). In the early ninth-century version of the other great Frankish law-code, *Lex Salica*, *staffolus* describes a grave-marker, perhaps reinforcing the association with fate (*Pactus*

Legis Salicae, Lex Salica Karolina 55). The *staffolus* of the king might designate a place where the king's judgement was given or men's fate became known, while the poles over the graves might mark places where those commemorated had encountered their ultimate fate.

Of the three sections of *Lex Ribuaria* which refer to the *staffolus*, the simplest (chapter 78) stipulates that anyone finding lost property should display it on three boundaries of the territory where he found it so that the owner could reclaim it; if it remained unclaimed, the finder was to exhibit it at the king's *staffolus*. The second provision in the law-code forms part of an involved series of instructions (chapter 37) for settling disputes concerning the ownership of property. Both parties to a dispute were to swear that the property was theirs. The defendant, the person accused of making an unlawful claim to the property, was then to bring forward as witness the person who gave him the property. This was to be done within 14 nights, though that was extended to 40 if the donor had to travel from outside the immediate area. If, however, the donor came from outside the Frankish kingdom, that upper limit was doubled to 80 nights, and the donor had to be presented either at the place where the assembly (*mallus*) of the defendant's tribe met, or at the king's *staffolus*. If resolution by such means proved impossible, the matter could be terminated by means of oaths sworn at the sanctuary or *harahus*, implying that both local assembly places and the king's *staffolus* were associated with a religious building. The final reference to the *staffolus* in *Lex Ribuaria* (chapter 69) concerns the resolution of cases of unspecified kind by the swearing of oaths, and comes nearest to providing a description of an actual procedure or ritual. The last in the series of clauses relates to the means of obtaining redress from someone who, supported by six witnesses, took an oath in a church casting doubt on the freedom or rightful inheritance of another. Either the claim had to be repeated at the king's *staffolus* with the support of 12 oath-helpers standing in a circle around it, or else the claimant had to pay compensation. It is not difficult to imagine a ritual of this kind being conducted round Post E at Yeavering, with the oath-takers arranged either around the post or in a semi-circle in front of the curved screen; in some kinds of case parts of the procedure might also have been conducted in the religious building which stood in an adjacent part of the site.

Association of the platform and Post E with the Frankish *staffolus* suggests that Yeavering was where the highest jurisdiction might be sought, and many kinds of legal business may have been transacted there. Perhaps the king, having taken counsel in the large hall which stood nearby and was aligned on the post, would have made a ceremonial procession from the hall to the 'theatre' where, with his advisers, he would have proclaimed his decisions to the assembled people. The 'theatre' may also have provided the setting for other kinds of royal ceremonial, including the welcoming of the king when he arrived at the site on his itinerary, in much the same way as Roman provincial governors might be welcomed at theatres in towns they visited as they made circuits of their provinces. It could also have been the setting for diplomatic activity, particularly since continental and Irish evidence suggests a strong association between assemblies and the receipt of foreign rulers or their emissaries. Even when the king was not in residence, which was most of the time, the site may have been occupied by officials who could probably administer justice in his name at the *staffolus*. Although Yeavering was but one among several royal vills in the Bernician kingdom, and was unique on account of the 'theatre', it is possible that other vills could have been furnished with platforms and/or posts for the administration of justice, but they are unlikely to be found since they would be very difficult to identify archaeologically without the associated assembly structure.

Even when they were not being used as a setting for legal, administrative or ceremonial activity, the structures at Yeavering would have impressed, not least by bearing witness to the king's ability to draw upon resources of ingenuity to obtain the design followed by those of labour and raw materials necessary to execute it. The back three walls of the 'theatre' alone required up to 150 timbers cut from trees with trunks over 20ft (6m) tall, and would perhaps have used all the mature standards from 10-12 acres (4-5ha) of woodland which had been managed over the long term. The rest of that single structure might have required at least twice that amount for the main timbers. Taking into account the other buildings in use on the site in the years on either side of 600, the amount of managed woodland required for the overall programme of building was very considerable, and the form of construction employed could be seen as a form of conspicuous consumption, designed to convey the king's opulence at least as much as the carved panels or painted decoration discussed by Hope-Taylor. In addition to display of that kind, the *staffolus* and its associated buildings would have fulfilled a powerful symbolic function, reminding native and stranger alike of the authority and presence of the ruler.

CONCLUSION

The evidence drawn upon to sketch the functions and affinities of the 'theatre' and the *staffolus* comes from what at first appear two rather different cultural worlds, that for the 'theatre' relating to Mediterranean Rome, and that for the post and platform to the Frankish Rhineland. The two are not, however, incompatible. If the *staffolus* conjures up a world of primitive Germanic forests, runes and divination, the impeccably Mediterranean Greek word *stoicheion* shares its range of meaning and association, the singular referring to a stick or pole, the plural to the controlling forces of the universe, or fate, and serves as a reminder that divination was also a prominent feature of the Classical world (Green 1998, 383).

The civic culture of Rome had always to some extent been a veneer, as were the imperial administration and much of that body of literate Roman law, Civil Law, which has survived. Beneath, particularly in the remoter provinces, there was another world, one which can only dimly be perceived through the surviving written sources of the Roman period, in which administration was often semi-private, resting in the hands of towns, estates and villages. In that world, legal procedure was less formalised and largely unwritten; judicial affairs were settled locally in semi-official ways and perhaps with the aid of rituals to assist illiterate or semi-literate participants. It is likely that it is often procedures of this kind which are reflected in the later law-codes of the Germanic kingdoms, including *Lex Ribuaria*, rather than an alien 'Germanic' law imported by the new rulers (Wood 1998; Barnwell 2000). A link between the two systems can be traced through the Frankish formularies, collections of specimen documents largely associated with the administration of legal affairs in the cities of post-Roman Gaul. Some of the kinds of legal business outlined in the formularies are very similar to those outlined in *Lex Ribuaria*, especially in relation to matters involving property. At one level, the procedures appear very different from those of the law-code, for they clearly refer to an urban culture and, unlike the laws, rely heavily upon the use of written instruments; many of the procedures outlined are clearly derived from Roman law. Yet there are also some similarities, in particular in the way in which they envisage the use of oath as a means of proof, and in the referral of some cases from the hall (*basilica*) in which they were heard, to the church (*ecclesia*), a direct equivalent of the sanctuary (*harahus*) of *Lex Ribuaria* (Wood 1986; Barnwell 2004). In the outer provinces of the Empire, the 'Roman' and 'Germanic' may always have blended into each other.

Although Yeavering stands at the remotest boundary of the Roman world, the kind of kingship it suggests is not so very different from that of other kingdoms, established in provinces closer to Rome. Like them, the Bernicians appear to have derived some of their symbols of power from Rome, still the only prestige power of the time. Also like their contemporaries in the former western provinces, the Bernicians adopted or imitated the structures with which they or their forebears came into contact, which were often provincial, rather than those of the better documented, literate and central, but more distant, imperial administration, so that their own governmental machinery was largely a fusion of the different elements (Barnwell 1992; 1997). Yeavering's specific amalgam, the result of a syncretic process, lies in an adaptation of a kind of local Roman theatre structure combined with what appears to be a Germanic *staffolus* to create a setting fitted not only for the transaction of local business but also for larger-scale royal ceremonial. Interesting though that is, it is perhaps more striking that it should have occurred in so liminal a place, at a site which, although of great significance in the prehistoric period, and of continuing religious importance, had no Roman antecedents and no ghosts of Roman power to challenge or lay to rest. It is unlikely that the Bernicians would have known that the Romans had, centuries earlier, taken over native shrines in Gaul and Britain and built theatres at them, but the nature of the unique structure they erected when they took control of the cult site at Yeavering bears testament to the continuing pervasiveness of other, more recent, Roman traditions and their continuing hold on the definition, realities and symbols of power.

10

AN HISTORICAL CONTEXT FOR HOPE-TAYLOR'S *YEAVERING*

Ian Wood

It is difficult for most of us to remember a time when Brian Hope-Taylor's Yeavering excavation was not well known. The HMSO publication only appeared in 1977, but the excavations had been completed in 1962, and rumours about what had been found were many. Thus the 1969 edition of Bede by Colgrave and Mynors knew of the excavations, indeed Colgrave mentioned them in his note on the unlocated debate in Edwin's hall (1969, 182, n 1), offering no comment on *Ad Gefrin* itself – though he did thank Hope-Taylor for information on *Maelmin*. Plummer, of course, had dealt with Yeavering largely in a note on 'Place names compounded with prepositions' (1896, II, 103-4: see also the ensuing note on 'Yeaverin'). No one reading Bede's single reference to *Ad Gefrin* before excavations started in 1953 could have guessed what was to come. Once the Yeavering publication appeared, comments came thick and fast. In the 1988 commentary that Michael Wallace-Hadrill wrote, as a companion for the Colgrave and Mynors Bede, the note on the site (1988, 74-5) includes references to work by Alcock, Campbell, Biddle, Cramp and Addyman – and is actually much fuller than the note given by Judith McClure and Roger Collins in their later commentary (1994) on the Colgrave translation.

Perhaps not surprisingly, Wallace-Hadrill's own emphasis was on the event which Bede described rather than the place itself: 'What is significant in Bede's account is that crowds flocked to Yeavering for baptism, which was thus not confined to the court circle. It occupied Paulinus for 36 days. Who but Paulinus would have reported this fact?' The event was similarly picked up by

Richard Morris in an article on baptismal places published in 1991, in which he emphasised the fact that the phase of river baptism such as those in the Glen was shortlived (for the obvious reasons of the waters being cold and dangerous): he also emphasised the link between the *villa regia* and the site of baptism.

The importance of Hope-Taylor's excavations, of course, far exceed their value for an understanding of one chapter of Bede, who in any case said that the site was abandoned soon after Paulinus' work there, with the royal centre being relocated in *Maelmin*. Among the many points which one might pick out, I think few would doubt that the themes of British and Roman influence loom large.

In many respects the first of these was the more revolutionary at the time, not least because Bede made so little of the Britons, and what he did have to say was hostile. One has to remember that the actual excavation at Yeavering preceded that at Doon Hill, which only took place in 1964-6 — even though it was this latter excavation which meant that 'the idea of a sixth-century British world able to provide rectangular timber halls, such as Yeavering's development seemed to require, was given broader and more solid probability.' (Hope-Taylor 1977, xviii).

Nowadays we are much more attuned to the matter of British survival. British place names (and *Ad Gefrin* and *Maelmin* are two) have been elucidated by Margaret Gelling (1988). The argument for considerable Romano-British influence on Anglo-Saxon secular architecture was firmly stated by Philip Dixon in the catalogue of *The Making of England* exhibition (1991, 67-70). Meanwhile, the discoveries made by Tony Wilmott at Birdoswald between 1987 and 1992 (Wilmott 1997) have provided another example of Romano-British – Anglo-Saxon continuity. I leave aside Philip Barker's Wroxeter excavations as coming from a different part of Britain, and relating to a different sort of site. Nor, it should be said, have studies of potentially relevant literary sources stood still: there has been much work (even if not total agreement) on the *Gododdin*, while Jenny Rowland's 1990 study of the Welsh *englynion* provides a further basis for looking at the Anglo-British North.

Hope-Taylor's argument about the Britishness of Yeavering fitted in to a more ambitious argument about the origins of Bernicia, which has perhaps rather fallen from view in recent years. That it should have done so is scarcely surprising. Study of Gildas, the *Gododdin*, Bede, the *Historia Brittonum* and the Anglo-Saxon Chronicle has developed in such a way that few professional historians would now play so lightly with the material – though, to be fair to Hope-Taylor, he certainly registered the dangers of using historical sources. Equally, few would be so bold as to run through the history of the La Tène style to make points about the possibility of surviving British culture – throwing in observations on the relative importance of Irish and Anglo-Saxon style in the earlier insular Gospel Books in passing.

AN HISTORICAL CONTEXT FOR HOPE-TAYLOR'S *YEAVERING*

Unless I have overlooked a particular theme in recent work on post-Roman studies (which is more than possible), Hope-Taylor's ultimate chapter on 'The Historical Significance of Yeavering', has ceased to cause much discussion.

Yet for all its technical failings, in its abuse of written sources, it makes a number of important points. Central was the argument that phase II belongs to the reign of Ida (post 547) rather than that of Æthelfrith, *c.*600. One indication that this was the case was thought to be the fact that the men of the Gododdin skirted Bernicia on their way south to *Catraeth* – though this is an argument that would carry no water if one accepted David Dumville's early date for the battle (1993, 3). More important was the general observation that an early dating for Yeavering indicates that Northumbrian Bernicia was established as a major power rather earlier than had been thought. This case has, by implication, received some support from Dumville (1993, 9), although he does not cite Hope-Taylor. He states:

> Bede's date of 547 for the beginning of Ida's reign, and (by implication) of Bernician kingship, was calculated from the regnal list. On it has been hung a picturesque story for which no early source gives warrant. Bernicia has been thought to have originated as a pirate settlement at Bamburgh rock: but we have no grounds for placing unique beginnings of Bernician settlement there. That view, and another that Bernicia achieved little or no territorial expansion in its first generation emerged from a Welsh notice in the *Historia Brittonum* that the British King Urien, with three royal allies, besieged the Bernician King Theodric (572-579) on Lindisfarne Island/Holy Island. But these are not necessarily logical deductions from evidence which is in any case hardly first rate.

Dumville's scepticism, based as it is on very cautious reading of the evidence, comes remarkably close to Hope-Taylor's overall position. Bernicia seems to have been established remarkably early. The undefended nature of the high-status buildings on the site of Yeavering do not suggest that the local authority was under much threat. We may or may not want, like Hope-Taylor, to see the origins of that authority as developing out of Saxon federate activity (though Gildas certainly does not help here). What is clear is that it seems to be at ease with a surrounding British population, and that Bernicia might well have been a kingdom with a very small Anglian elite acting in cooperation with the British. Bede would not have wanted to give such an idea much time – though one wonders whether his bloodlines would not have been British rather than Anglian, since he was the offspring of mere tenants on the Wearmouth estate. Similar suggestions have, however, been made for other parts of the Anglo-Saxon world. Hope-Taylor's general views, as opposed to his detailed arguments, look rather less controversial now than they did in 1977.

Turning to a second aspect of Hope-Taylor's interpretation, the Romanness of Yeavering, we may come to similar conclusions. Romanness has become an important theme throughout Northumbrian studies – though it is something of a hydra given the many heads that the theme has developed. Of course it has a Bedan, Christian meaning – one that feeds into study of Anglo-Saxon sculpture. It also has a political meaning, as suggested by Paul Barnwell (chapter 9). Tony Wilmott's Birdoswald has raised the matter of Roman survival, or transformation, in ways that Hope-Taylor could only have guessed at. Rome was certainly an issue for the rulers of Bernicia. Equally this may have been reflected in white plastered buildings, as Hope-Taylor emphasised. What is less convincing is the supposed theatre: the reconstruction has become a fact. Yet it has no obvious parallels, and that a segment of a circle could be thought of in the same terms as a semi-circular theatre or a completely circular amphitheatre is unconvincing – although Paul Barnwell in this volume provides as detailed an analysis of the possibilities as one can hope for.

Ultimately I would say that much needs to be revisited. Hope-Taylor's *Yeavering* was an extraordinary excavation and is an extraordinary book. It transformed our knowledge and its main premises have been integrated into scholarship, although some aspects of it have been quietly forgotten. Since the publication came out, work has been done on other sites, which have further changed views. It deserves another hard look: things that we have come to accept should perhaps be treated with a greater pinch of salt, and points or at least questions that we have forgotten were there should perhaps be given another airing.

PART IV AFTER *AD GEFRIN*

11

GEFRIN: ORGANISATION, ABANDONMENT, AFTERMATH

Colm O'Brien

The case has been made for considering *Gefrin* as a centre of local, and sometimes regional, significance from a time deep in the prehistoric past to the early medieval era. This did not continue to be so. In time, Wooler came to be the local centre and the head place of the Muschamp barony and Yeavering was held within the barony as part of a Knight Fee comprising the contiguous townships of Akeld, Coupland and Yeavering. In Church organisation, Yeavering came to be within the parish of Kirknewton.

Yet it is possible to see in these structures of the medieval era traces of earlier arrangements which enable us to establish a territorial and administrative context for Bede's *Gefrin* (O'Brien 2002). The *villa regia* can be understood as the chief place of a shire, a unit of territory within the king's demesne and under the administrative jurisdiction of a thane (Barrow 1969; 1973). Richard Lomas (1996, 22-5) has suggested that this Muschamp Knight Fee was created out of a former thanage, with the old tenure being superseded under the new feudal settlement but with the territorial estate remaining intact. If so, then we can think of a thane at *Gefrin* in the seventh century in the same terms as the *praefecti* Tydlin at *Dynbaer* (modern Dunbar) or Osfrith of *Broninis* (location uncertain) who are identified in the *Life* of Wilfrid (Eddius Stephanus, *Vita Wilfridi*: 36-38), and the thanage estate as being the unit of land which later became divided into the three townships.

The ecclesiastical parish of Kirknewton does not sit comfortably within the geography of feudal tenure, but was split between the barony of Muschamp and the Roos barony of Wark (*63*). Geoffrey Barrow (1973, 32-5) recognised that this

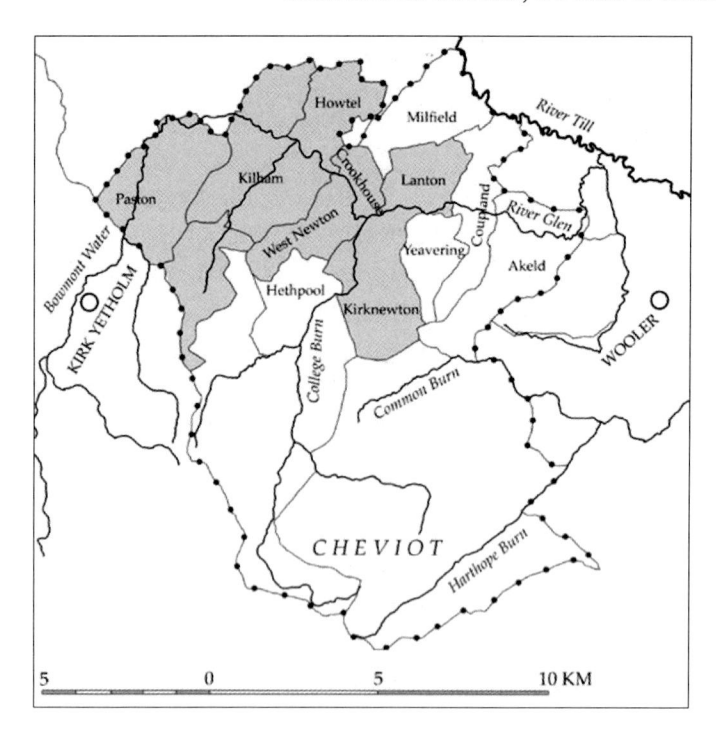

63 Townships in Kirknewton Parish – lands of the Roos barony are shaded. After O'Brien 2002, figure 1. Reproduced by kind permission of the Society of Antiquaries of Newcastle upon Tyne

division was a relic of an older administrative system. The Roos townships had been previously associated with Yetholm as elements of a shire which had been granted to St Cuthbert in the seventh century. Once the Anglo-Scottish border had come into being, this shire could no longer function as a unified entity and, with its principal church of Yetholm now in Scotland, the vills stranded on the English side of the border had to be organised within a new parochial territory which took in other land outside of the former shire of Yetholm. Again, as with the Muschamp Knight Fee, medieval feudal organisation has fossilised an element of an earlier territorial unit. Barrow's elucidation of Yetholm makes it possible to define the territory of another previously unrecognised land unit. From Kirknewton, at the east edge of the shire of Yetholm and the adjacent township to Yeavering, a clockwise circuit takes in the edge of Yetholm; and then the south and west edges of the estates of Norhamshire and Islandshire which belonged to the church of Lindisfarne and which its successor church in Durham retained into the nineteenth century; and thence around the north-west edge of a shire of Bamburgh within which the Crown retained interests into the twelfth century. This circuit delineates the bounds of a block of land which remains as the hole in the middle when the elements around the edge are in place. This, the writer has suggested (O' Brien 2002, 61-66), is the former shire of which *Gefrin* was the chief estate (*64*).

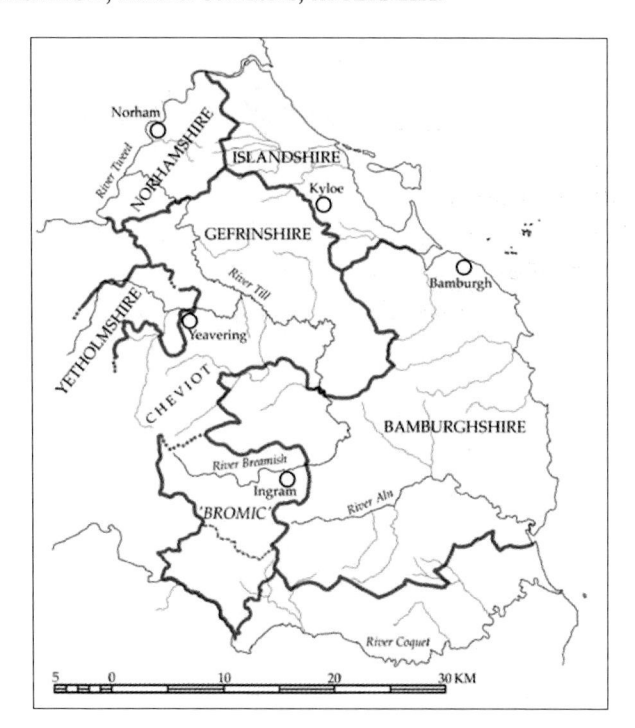

64 Possible shire of Gefrin and surrounding land units. After O'Brien 2002, figure 5. Reproduced by kind permission of the Society of Antiquaries of Newcastle upon Tyne

The *villa regia* of *Gefrin* did not survive into the eighth century. Bede records that it was abandoned in favour of *Maelmin*. He offered no explanation and, with uncharacteristic imprecision in chronology, he said no more than that this happened in the reign of kings subsequent to Edwin (Bede, *Historia Ecclesiastica*: ii, 14). This could be any time up to 100 years after AD 633. The site's excavator suggested a date around AD 685 (Hope-Taylor, 1977, 277). Why the site was abandoned is not clear. There is no evidence that it fell to hostile action: it outlived the two fire episodes which the excavator identified. It could have succumbed to a natural disaster such as disease; but that need not be identifiable in the archaeological record. The abandonment cannot be connected to any wider collapse in the territorial and administrative basis of shire organisation: that came later. To find reasons we have to look to the place itself.

Maelmin is identified as a cropmark site beside the village of Milfield, only 3.5km from *Gefrin* (Gates and O'Brien 1988). The move to *Maelmin* probably means that the administrative centre of the shire was transferred to another estate. If this was a considered, and not an enforced, decision, the reason may have been in part geographical. *Maelmin*, in the Milfield Basin, enjoys wide-open spaces of flat land along an axis of communication, factors which might have given it an advantage over *Gefrin* in the steep-sided, narrow valley of the River Glen. But a pragmatic decision of this sort may have been informed by deeper thoughts. Rosemary Cramp (1983, 275) has suggested that as the Northumbrian kings became more secure in their own identity, they had no need to refer to the traditional place of leadership and cult in support of their own position. Paul Frodsham (1999a, 204-5), reflecting on a comment of Richard Bradley, even suggests that the abandonment could be comparable to the wiping of the record of an individual from a genealogy. In an ideological sense, abandonment appears to have been a deliberate and decisive break with the past.

How long *Maelmin* remained in use is not known. There is no written record and the site has not been tested in excavation. But in time, it too became abandoned and it is not certain that Milfield had the status of a township before the late medieval era. By the time of the feudal settlement of Henry I, Wooler had emerged as the local centre: head of the barony; site of a castle; with borough status; a single-township parish. But a fragment of a pre-Conquest carved cross (Cramp 1984, 232-3) hints that this place may already have superseded *Gefrin* and *Maelmin* as the local centre before the twelfth century when the barony was established.

By the late fourteenth century, the lordship which had unified the three townships of Akeld, Coupland and Yeavering, and thus fossilised the thanage territory, had broken up. In 1443, the township of Yeavering was said to be held in socage of the manor of Wooler (Vickers 1922, 241-243), a tenure which carried the last vestiges of its former status.

Today, the modern equivalent of *Gefrin's* former social, economic and administrative functions are managed from Wooler, still the centre for Glendale life, and Berwick upon Tweed where local government resides. Yeavering, which never developed a nucleated settlement in the medieval era, now supports just one farm and a row of cottages. It enjoys no administrative status in its own right, but is absorbed into the civil parish of Kirknewton. Thus an administrative boundary which can be traced back to the seventh century is now lost.

In another sense, however, Yeavering has again, in our own time, become a prominent place; this time, for the memory of its past. We cannot know to what extent its past was remembered or forgotten in the centuries before William Camden made the connection between the place name Yeurin (as he recorded it) and Bede's *Gefrin*. But 400 years ago he followed Bede and placed Yeavering in scholarly record. The question of the precise location of the *villa regia* was opened up when George Tate (1863) rejected the designation 'King Edward's Palace' popularly applied to the late medieval defended house which survives, part-ruinous, west of the cropmark site; and this remained an open question until the discovery in 1949 of the cropmarks in the circumstances described by Tim Gates in this volume. The subsequent excavations, between 1953 and 1962, by the late Dr Brian Hope-Taylor have established Yeavering as a landmark of British archaeology.

12

AD GEFRIN TODAY AND TOMORROW

Roger Miket

In April 2002 we were considering leaving Skye after 16 years absence from Northumberland, and returning to the Wooler area. We had kept our house at Yearle Mill, but thought that perhaps a smaller property would give us more freedom for travel. In the event, we decided to keep the mill, but while we were looking for properties in Sale & Partners, the secretary, knowing of my interest in local history, mentioned that they had just received instruction to handle the sale of a 'funny bit of land at Yeavering with a history'. The site was, of course, the field in which Brian Hope Taylor's excavations had taken place; it was advertised as a field of 18 acres 'or thereabouts' and included the sand and gravel quarry at its south-western corner (*65*). Offers of over £20,000 were invited.

The oddness of the property was apparent and, in an area characterised by large farms, the size of the holding advertised was unusual. While the sale of an entire Northumbrian farm might be expected to include the occasional site of archaeological interest, the sale of smaller plots is usually an indication of an owner's wish to capitalise on an opportunity for development. Yet, as the site had long been scheduled as an ancient monument (Northumberland No 302) the designation clearly prohibited any commercial or building development. The first designation was made in 1953 and included the whole of the field north of the road. In 1978 Anthony Harding excavated the henge to the south of the road, and revealed what the aerial photographs had not, namely an extension of rectangular post-built structures across the south-eastern part of the 'whaleback', today separated from the main mass by the modern roadway. Accordingly, in 1985 the scheduling was extended south-eastwards from the quarry in a triangle to encompass the whole crest of the ridge.

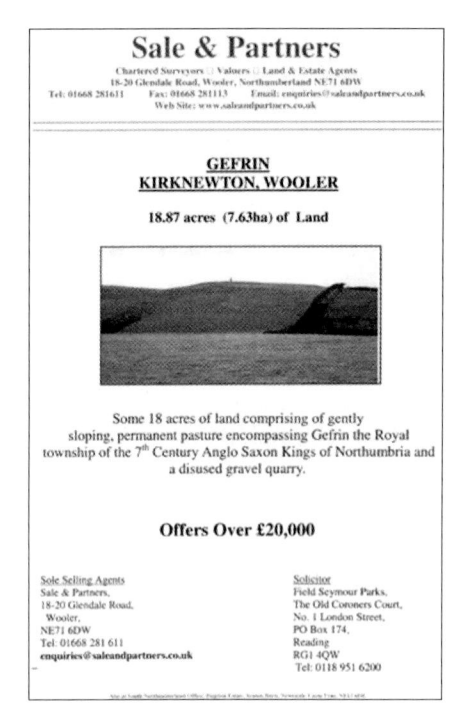

> **Sale & Partners**
> Chartered Surveyors :: Valuers :: Land & Estate Agents
> 18-20 Glendale Road, Wooler, Northumberland NE71 6DW
> Tel: 01668 281611   Fax: 01668 281113   Email: enquiries@saleandpartners.co.uk
> Web Site: www.saleandpartners.co.uk
>
> **GEFRIN**
> **KIRKNEWTON, WOOLER**
>
> 18.87 acres (7.63ha) of Land
>
> Some 18 acres of land comprising of gently sloping, permanent pasture encompassing Gefrin the Royal township of the 7th Century Anglo Saxon Kings of Northumbria and a disused gravel quarry.
>
> **Offers Over £20,000**
>
> Sole Selling Agents
> Sale & Partners,
> 18-20 Glendale Road,
> Wooler,
> NE71 6DW
> Tel: 01668 281 611
> enquiries@saleandpartners.co.uk
>
> Solicitor
> Field Seymour Parks,
> The Old Coroners Court,
> No. 1 London Street,
> PO Box 174,
> Reading
> RG1 4QW
> Tel: 0118 951 6200

65 Advertisement by Sale & Partners, April 2002

As for the quarry, extraction had ceased in the 1950s and despite offering the finest sand and gravel in the Milfield Basin, the iconic nature of the site and extent of the protected archaeology remaining would surely form a potent mix that would ensure it did not recommence. Finally, as the field had not been ploughed for a number of years the scheduling designation was able to prohibit future ploughing and the field was now under permanent pasture. Given this heady mix of designations, lapsed permissions and the relatively small size of the holding on offer, it was difficult to think of who, other than a neighbouring agricultural interest, might be interested in bidding for the site.

It would be misleading to create an impression of careful forethought at a time when our own domestic situation was far from clear. The overwhelming belief was that the field would be absorbed into a neighbouring agricultural holding and the opportunity to at last give it a voice would be missed. An immediate decision was required, and with the understanding and support of my wife, I made an offer over the asking price.

So began what proved to be only the start of a long and complicated negotiation; a journey that would take nearly two whole years to complete. As these negotiations form a part of the history of the site it seems entirely appropriate to place them on record here. Indeed, with hindsight, the tangle we were about to enter into seems utterly in keeping and consistent with the nature of all that is known about the interweaving of the thrawn human relationships at the site since Brian began excavations there in 1953 (*66*). That negotiations between the various parties during these early years did not always move easily is lightly indicated on pages xvii and 5 of his report; and indeed, since the final backfilling of his trenches in 1962, rights attached to ownership and management of the field have been fiercely disputed between the Purvis family and Barclays Bank as Trustees of the estate of the late Mr J. Purvis.

In the fullness of time we were informed by Sale & Partners that our bid for the site had been successful. With this news came two further pieces of information. The first was that there had been other bidders; these included the College Valley Estate (the anticipated 'neighbouring interest'), a second private bidder whose interest had focused upon the possibility of a wildlife development in the quarry area and, more surprisingly, an offer from Northumberland County Council, who were supported in their bid by English Heritage. We immediately contacted the private bidder to reassure them of our conservation regard for the site as a whole and also to the County Archaeologist to state our surprise that each had been unaware of the other's interest, but to give the Council an assurance that any management structure would involve their active participation.

66 Brian Hope-Taylor pointing out a feature in building D2 during his Yeavering excavations. *Crown copyright: RCAHMS. Dr Brian Hope-Taylor Collection*

At this point a discerning reader might ask, 'Why, if the sale had not yet been concluded, did you persist in your bid when clearly a good, conservation-minded offer had been made by Northumberland County Council that would have involved public money rather than your own personal expenditure?' The reasons remain as valid today as they did then, and that was a belief that the success of the venture would not be best served through ownership by any one body. By their nature, large organisations rarely ever fully commit themselves to an open-hearted engagement with other groups unless it serves their interests; rights of ownership would always cast a shadow over any decision-making and threaten any partnership. As quite plainly the interests of the site had to be put at the very forefront, no one body could then be its owner yet all had to be given an equal stake in its future. A purchaser on the outside who could then effect a transfer into truly democratic ownership seemed to offer the best hopes for the venture's success.

The second piece of news was from the vendor, Barclays Bank, to say that a complication had arisen in the sale. An agreement apparently existed that required them to offer Mr Purvis' son, John, the option to buy at the successful bid price. This would take a month to resolve; we waited.

Two months later we contacted them again, only to be informed that there was now a dispute between Barclays as Trustees of the estate and John Purvis, in which the latter claimed (rightly as the documentation showed) that he had tenancy rights to the field. The Agents had not been advised of this when setting the sale price, and it clearly affected their valuation. The months thereafter involved fruitless negotiation with Barclays to try and ascertain exactly what was being offered, and to try and secure any documentation that might reveal if any other obligations unmentioned by the vendor existed. Eventually, in frustration we contacted the late Mr J. Purvis' grandson, Michael (who we heard was currently exercising his father's grazing rights), with a view to speaking directly to his father. Finally we spoke directly to John Purvis, who could not have been more helpful and refreshingly open. The upshot was that we agreed to revise our offer to Barclays in the light of the tenancy claim and separately agreed that we would 'buy out' all the claims of the Purvis family at the price that represented the difference between what was eventually paid to Barclays and the original offer. The Grazing Tenancy would be replaced by a new Farm Business Tenancy (to run for 10 years) that gave Michael grazing rights, and would also include clauses that allowed for archaeological conservation and management, including public access. Barclays accepted the revised offer and almost two years to the day since the original offer, the sale was concluded.

We were certainly determined and never doubted that only through persistence would a way be found through the convoluted negotiations to secure proper archaeological control of a site which 'provided a context for the public and political life of that period in Anglo-Saxon England' (Cramp, this volume).

It is certainly true that in seeking to grasp the historical significance of an epoch, there is nothing so illuminating as the direct experience of buildings and objects made in that time. Here, however, was only an empty field with no structures visible to inspire a sense of historical awe. The potency of the site, as is widely recognised, is derived from a more subtle interweaving; a combination of Bede's powerful narrative, the physical appearance of the settlement resurrected through skilful elucidation by a master craftsman, the point of time it represents within a kingdom then at the height of its powers and, of course, that power of the place itself. It is this mix that distinguishes regard for *Ad Gefrin* from that which we accord to its successor, *Maelmin*, at Milfield; the latter remains an unread document, awaiting its own 'Hope-Taylor'.

Progressing the sale with Barclays was rather like trying to run uphill in a treacle factory, but as the months passed we had the opportunity to consider with more leisure the sort of structure that might best be suited to its future care. There had never been an idea as to how the site might find its public voice, and indeed such questions had appeared presumptuous. It was clear from the outset that if the sale succeeded and archaeological management were to supplant that of agriculture as the dominant driver, then any private ownership would have to be of short duration and very circumscribed in action.

One of the most prominent of sites was deserving of the best of management and the consensus from consultation with colleagues, to whom I am most grateful, was for a management committee comprised of the local community and main archaeological interests. Professor Rosemary Cramp, (who stole me from the Romanists while yet a schoolboy for willing conversion to an Anglo-Saxonist) very kindly agreed to chair a small committee, comprising representatives from English Heritage (Kate Wilson), Northumberland National Park Authority (Paul Frodsham), Northumberland County Council (Sarah Rushton/Dr Chris Burgess) and the Glendale Gateway Trust (Tom Johnson). To this has been added Dr Chris Gerrard of the Archaeology Department, Durham University. Currently I am acting secretary. In December 2004 The Gefrin Trust was established as a Company limited by guarantee, with the above as its Trustees (67). It is awaiting news of an application for charitable status.

Once the sale was concluded some early ownership decisions were unavoidable. These were only made with the agreement of the Management Committee of the nascent Gefrin Trust. The first of these was to conclude the arrangement with John Purvis by which all family claims were dropped and to enter into a Farm Business Tenancy with his son, Michael. By doing this the Trust secured rights of public access to the field at all times, the right to remove areas from pasture for whatever period necessary for conservation and research, and to introduce whatever interpretive material the Trust considered appropriate.

67 Some of the Trustees inspecting the new kissing-gates at Ad Gefrin, May 2005. From left: Paul Frodsham (Northumberland National Park Authority), Dr Chris Burgess (Northumberland County Council), Professor Emeritus Rosemary Cramp (University of Durham) and Dr Chris Gerrard (University of Durham)

At the same time we entered into a 10-year partnership agreement with Defra (Department for Environment, Food and Rural Affairs) under the Countryside Stewardship Scheme. This secured grant aid for much of the remedial work required to put the property into good heart, such as sheep-proofing the quarry to reduce erosion, rebuilding the stone wall along the roadway and replacing the farm gates. Three kissing-gates were included in the plan that would permit access for all, as were temporary information panels to provide the visitor with a little more information about the history of the site than that offered by the brisk inscription on the familiar stone monument (*colour plate 13*). A programme of regeneration within the quarry to create a wildlife habitat is in hand.

To date (July 2005) the fencing has now been renewed; half of the wall line has been repaired with the remaining half to be rebuilt in autumn 2006. Two new field-gates have been introduced and a footpath is being built from the Yeavering cottages road-end, along the side of the quarry to a kissing-gate giving access to the field.

The decoration upon the kissing-gates and the field-gates was specially commissioned from Eddie Robb, of Whitehall, College Valley (*68*). By his

AD GEFRIN TODAY AND TOMORROW

68 Cheviot feral goat inspecting the carving on the gate at Ad Gefrin (carved by Eddie Robb)

skill, the presentation of the site is enriched and establishes a standard we are committed to maintaining. Information panels are being put in place and a web site (www.thegefrintrust.com) now exists. Most recently, resistivity survey has been carried out on the site for the first time, the results to be posted on the website.

Currently the Trust holds a 999-year lease for the site and all management decisions regarding the field in which the major buildings lie now rests entirely in the hands of its trustees. The Trust's outright ownership of the site is assured well before expiry of the lease. It is our hope that at some future date, the part of the settlement lying to the south of the present roadway might be reunited in ownership with that to the north, whereupon conservation would require that it too pass out of arable cultivation and into an entirely pastoral regime.

The hope of securing the site and passing it in good heart to a Trust that will give it a future has now been realised. For the Trust this is just the start of a longer journey. The bareness of the site is both a limitation and an opportunity for innovation and creativity. For a place that has a *genius loci* that will certainly flee if disturbed too severely, balance is all.

ACKNOWLEDGEMENTS

My thanks to all the Trustees for their guidance at every turn. To Defra for their support for the project through the Countryside Stewardship Scheme; English Heritage for permission to prospect with the resistivity meter. To the College Valley Estates and especially its Chairman Charles Baker-Cresswell and Secretary, Colin Matheson. To the Northumberland National Park Authority and the North Eastern and Cumbrian Cooperative Society for grant aid towards the pathway; to Glendale Opportunities for Local Development (GOLD) for grant aid in setting up the company. To the following individuals who have certainly given of their time and expertise to ensure we progress in the right manner, and at the same time have proved the pleasantest of people to work with: Edward Brown, Else Nicol, Ingo Schüder, Eddie Robb, Steven Rickett and Lynne Neil.

PART V 'AN UNLOCKING OF WORD-HOARDS.' REFLECTIONS ON BRIAN HOPE-TAYLOR

The coastguard's challenge to Beowulf to give an account of himself prompted in reply an 'unlocking of word-hoards', an expression which Brian Hope-Taylor, himself a master of English prose style and with an ear for a good phrase, borrowed for a book review. The work in question, he suggested, would lead to an unlocking of word-hoards. *Yeavering* is Hope-Taylor's great word-hoard and it is evident from the papers in this volume that to delve into it is to come face to face with its wordsmith. His words have, rightly, been subject in these pages to critical review as part of the continuing study of the site and the ideas which he opened up. But so strongly is his presence felt even now, more than 40 years after he left the site, that we wanted, both at the conference and in these pages, to reflect on the man himself. And so we invited some of those who knew him to speak and write from personal knowledge beyond the confines of academic assessment of his work. This section is a word-hoard about Brian Hope-Taylor. Forbes Taylor, Philip Rahtz, Rosemary Cramp and Diana Murray all write in the first person: they knew him. Laura Sole came to know him indirectly through preparing an exhibition of his work.

Others have written elsewhere on Brian Hope-Taylor. Of particular note are the obituaries which were published after his death on 12 January 2001. They are listed here for reference:

James Graham Campbell, Obituary: Brian Hope-Taylor, *The Independent*, 10 Febuary 2001
Ian Ralston, 'Brian Hope-Taylor, 1923-2001', *Scottish Archaeological News* **36** (2001), 3
Ian Ralston, Obituary: Brian Hope-Taylor, *The Times*, 2 March 2001
Ian Ralston, Obituary: Brian Hope-Taylor, *The Scotsman*, 13 February 2001

13

MY FRIENDSHIP WITH BRIAN HOPE-TAYLOR

Forbes Taylor

In 1964 I was Head of Films at Anglia Television. Because of its responsibility to represent the character of its region, which included Cambridge, Anglia had a member of the university, the archaeologist Dr Glyn Daniel, on its board of directors. He proposed a major series about the origins and culture of the 'Ancient Britons' and it was accepted for national broadcasting by one of the network companies. One of its producers, a current affairs specialist, was appointed to supply the script and oversee the series. I was asked to direct. The presenter was to be Dr Brian Hope-Taylor, a popular archaeology lecturer at Cambridge. I went to meet him in Cambridge and the London producer introduced us over a drink in a pub.

I immediately liked Hope-Taylor and we embarked on one of the seemingly endless exchanges of ideas, anecdotes and jokes that was to become a feature of our relationship. After an hour or so, our London producer pleaded more important matters to attend to and left. Brian then confided that he could not stand the man. It was an early indication of another of Brian's characteristics, a total unwillingness to suffer people with whom he could not relate. (I must add that he was sometimes – perhaps often – unfair or unsympathetic in these judgements, though his background goes a long way to account for them.)

A month or two later we embarked on the filming of *Who Were The British?* At first the scripting was not my concern. It was a time of The Three Ages, pot typology and diffusionism. I had only the haziest understanding of such topics, but some of the script as supplied by the London producer seemed to me a bit glib and hard for ordinary people to swallow. There seemed not to be much theme, either. Eventually Brian went on strike and a row developed, into which I was drawn. Brian suspected that the producer was cynical about archaeology. We also guessed that, as he was a current affairs specialist, his real interests lay elsewhere. We devised ways of relieving him of the necessity of being present when we were filming, and he was only too happy to be left do his other things in London while Brian and I got on with what *we* thought should go into the programmes. We widened them from an examination of the 'Ancient Britons' *per se* to an account of what the ancient Romans thought and wrote about them. This necessitated going to Rome to film, where we had the Colosseum, the Imperial Forum, Ostia Antiqua and much else put at our disposal. It was before the world's great places had become inundated with television crews and we had all of it free.

The first bit of filming I did with Brian was in the Colosseum. We perched him up in the top terrace with a spectacular vista behind his head. 'This is the Wembley, the White City, the Madison Square Garden of ancient Rome...', he told the camera. I felt I had a star on my hands. This was confirmed later on Hadrian's Wall, when Brian became an actor, using the voice of a legionary on patrol to suggest his thoughts. His *tour de force* was on the beach at Deal, when he made us *see* the Roman galleys lined up on the horizon ready for the invasion.

Brian gave me a lightning course in current archaeology. Needless to say it was enormously pleasurable. By now I had got to know him on a personal level. It was knowledge, as I found out much later, that was carefully bounded. He became a close member of my family, staying with us on many occasions and taking a great interest in my two sons, both of whom were inspired by him to study archaeology at Cambridge. Yet although he displayed a knowledge and enjoyment of old-time music hall artistes, and gave hilarious impersonations of the likes of Harry Tate and Rob Wilton, he never told me his mother had been on the stage, even though my wife was an actress. He kept everyone away from his parents, with whom he lived until their deaths, even having me wait on his doorstep when I picked him up.

There were things about his life that he *did* confide that I found odd, inconsistent and even contradictory. He told me the story about his PhD thesis having been stolen when he put down his briefcase to buy a ticket on a Hamburg railway station. I shared his passion for Lawrence of Arabia's *Seven Pillars of Wisdom*, and it seemed to me a remarkable coincidence that Lawrence should have lost his manuscript at Oxford station.

Thanks to the success of *Who Were The British?* (some may say surprising, given that it was on commercial television rather than the BBC), it was planned that a sequel should be produced. Before that, however, Brian and I had another project to collaborate on. The Dean and Chapter of York Minster invited him to look at the foundations of the Minster as they might have to undergo strengthening work which would disturb an area under the lantern tower. Brian had suggested it might be the site of a wooden chapel established by the Anglian king Edwin, whose town of Yeavering he had discovered. The trial excavation revealed that the Minster was in imminent danger of collapsing. I was among the first few to be allowed to see the horrifying sight and I was able to persuade Anglia that we must make a film record of the work of rescue. This helped to raise the £2 million needed to carry out the work. Brian did a workmanlike job of presenting the programme, which involved his interviewing the Archbishop of Canterbury, Dr Ramsay. He was becoming an assured television personality.

Clouds were gathering, however. Brian admitted me to more of his personal life by confiding that he had received a severe dressing-down from Mortimer Wheeler over his failure to publish *Yeavering* after so many years had passed. Brian was deeply upset and I trace the beginning of his decline from that time. I was to come to the conclusion that Brian had an awful writer's block, through which his perfectionism prevented him from getting past the first page or two of a piece of writing. It was never quite good enough to satisfy him.

In early 1967 Anglia gave us the go-ahead to begin work on the sequel to *Who Were The British?* At first we thought of *Who Were The English?* in recognition of Brian's speciality in Anglo-Saxon archaeology. But then we decided to widen the theme, as we had with the former series. It would be fascinating to set the Anglo-Saxons and Danes in a European, and perhaps world, context: to make a series about the Dark Ages, in fact.

Brian was fearful of air travel, so we set off on a journey by rail and ship to visit sites and rough out a concept. It was idyllic. We were almost the only passengers on a luxury Yugoslav cruise liner from Venice to Athens, writing the outline and talking all the time. In Greece I was able to show Brian around a country I knew well from military service during the civil war. We went on a coach tour to the Peloponese sites. At Mycenae the Greek guide told us we had not enough time to visit the acropolis. 'Nonsense' said Brian, and he and I climbed to the top. When we returned to the coach, which had been delayed by our action, the guide was fuming. 'I hate blonde people!', she shrieked. Brian, of course, was very blonde in those days.

Despite a warning by the Foreign Office, we went to Syria so that we could visit Palmyra. A mysterious explosion during the previous night in Beirut did not augur well, but we could not know that it was the beginning of what became the Six Day War. When we arrived in Damascus it was to find that no aircraft would take to the air to convey us to Palmyra. It looked like disaster until someone suggested taking a taxi – a journey of 200 miles via Homs, largely across virgin desert. Of course, we did so. The first few minutes set the tone. We pulled into a group of huts and our ancient American limousine was jacked up beneath us. A new tyre was needed, we were told by our young driver, whose English was very limited. As we sat there I noticed a group of what looked like nomads gathering nearby. A lengthy negotiation took place concerning a young goat one of them was carrying. A knife was produced, and I said to Brian, 'I think we are in the butcher's shop.' 'Oh God,' he groaned. I was right – the animal was despatched, someone speedily disembowelled it and, as the Bard said, *exeunt*. A moment later a scraggy puppy appeared and gobbled up the entrails. A triumph of optimism over ability – they were too fresh and went down in a contiguous mass. The inevitable happened, and they reappeared.

Thankfully, by this time our tyre was on and we went on our way. We got to Palmyra all right, and lunched at the celebrated Zenobia hotel while our driver had another of our threadbare tyres replaced by one hardly less dilapidated. Then we set off for home. We had gone only a few miles when another tyre blew. We went for a stroll in the desert while the driver replaced it with the spare. By now the light was beginning to fail. Off we went again. An hour later yet another tyre gave up the ghost. Now we had no spare to fall back on. We sat immobilised for several hours while the stars came out and the desert cold penetrated our tropical clothes. A lone Bedouin put in an appearance, sized up the situation and sloped off. Eventually lights appeared in the distance and a lorry pulled up alongside us. A deal was done and we were jacked up again, the rear wheels taken off and loaded into the lorry. We were now without even wheels. I thought it bad taste to tell Brian what was going through my mind. We were helpless, lost, in a hostile country. If we were never heard of again we should merely be statistics. I am sure Brian's thoughts were not dissimilar. And so we sat, for another few hours. But the lorry did appear again. Only one of the tyres had been replaced but we had a chance. The last tyre went just as we reached Damascus.

It was while we were there that I again encountered another of Brian's oddities – his propensity to fantasise. He went out for a walk alone and returned to tell me, rather breathlessly, that an Arab had stopped him in the street and called him 'El Aurens' – the name Arabs called Lawrence of Arabia. Brian fancied he looked a bit like Lawrence. I could not confirm the truth or otherwise of this story, of course, but it seemed rather far-fetched – Lawrence had been dead for over 30 years and I did not think it likely that anyone who knew him would expect to meet him walking around Damascus.

The following year, 1968, we filmed the series, which was eventually titled *The Lost Centuries*. It created many difficulties for Brian, who was beginning to come under fire at the university, for absenting himself, it was said, from supervisions and lectures. I heard rumours but did not know the details. The production did not go as smoothly as before. Brian's troubles led him to neglect some of the research and there were some howlers in the script. All in all, he was far from happy at the time – and it showed. However, we journeyed as far as the Middle East again and were in Amman, Jordan, when the Israelis launched a tank incursion across the River Jordan. As we were the only film unit in the area and all communications had been cut off, I was asked by the British Embassy if I would send a despatch to ITN. I took the unit to the battle zone and Brian invited himself along for the adventure. It was a side of him that I had not seen before.

The Lost Centuries was a success despite the lack of confidence on the part of the network, which consigned it to the 'God slot' on Sundays at teatime. Nevertheless, Brian had become an established television performer, and looking back, I think he may well have been advised to consider making it his main activity. (Again looking back, it may surprise people to know that archaeology was far from popular material for mass entertainment in those days.)

Although Brian and I maintained our friendship on a personal level, it was two or three years before we had the opportunity to work together again. I filmed what became his last excavation, on the Devil's Dyke in Cambridgeshire. The dig failed to produce the exciting results it had promised, and the television programme did not provide him with opportunities for his extraordinary histrionics. It was, as they say, worthy but rather dull.

I then became drawn into the sad business at the university. Brian's parents both died, no doubt of old age, leaving him alone. He had an apparent breakdown and went into Addenbrooks for a rest. I visited him on a number of occasions. His superior in the Department, the Disney Professor, was now none other than his lifetime patron, Glyn Daniel. Daniel was also a close personal friend of mine and he asked my opinion on Brian's condition. All I was able to offer was my view, formed from long association with Brian, that he seemed to have an inferiority complex based on a feeling of inadequacy due to his lack of formal education. It was a tragedy, I thought, that Brian should be ashamed of the very thing about which he might have been most proud. I believe that Glyn Daniel shared my opinion. Brian was unable to resume his duties at the university and was pensioned off.

My last close contact with him was in 1977, when he came to stay for a night at my home to attend my farewell party when I left Anglia Television. After that, my only contact for some years was through annual Christmas greetings, when he reaffirmed his affection for me and my family. I last saw him when we ran into each other in the street in Cambridge. He looked very unwell and did not want to talk.

Brian was, I feel, the closest thing to a genius that I have met in my life. He was so talented in many differing ways. Our association was very strange, when I think back on it. We were uncannily similar in our ideas and tastes.

He used to say that we were symbiotic. Under me, he became a consummate television practitioner and under him I became a bit of an archaeologist. He was unforgettable, and for me he will always be the blonde, good-looking – utterly charming – *persuasive* enthusiast who brought archaeology to millions of viewers to whom it was entirely new. Tony Robinson and Michael Wood have much to thank him for. Brian's television achievements were, in the nature of things, ephemeral. The importance of his work in archaeology will, I am sure, endure.

14

YEAVERING REVISITED

Philip Rahtz

Brian Hope-Taylor's report on Yeavering is now a quarter of a century old; archaeology has changed considerably since then, not least in reconsideration of and new thinking on Yeavering itself and on other sites in the area.

I wrote a glowing review of the report in 1980 (Rahtz 1980) soon after I moved to the new Department of Archaeology at York. I had some advanced knowledge of the publication some years before; this was by way of notes taken by Kate Pretty from Brian Hope-Taylor's lectures and thesis in Cambridge in the 1960s. Yeavering had been dug in the 1950s when, it should be remembered, there was extremely little post-Roman archaeology going on, apart from its architectural and art-historical aspects. I was especially interested in Yeavering when I began work on the later palace complex at Cheddar in 1961. I wrote to Brian in those years to keep him informed about our discoveries. I was wondering at the time whether some of our very large post-holes, as they were appearing, might be part of another 'grandstand'; Brian firmly but kindly explained why this was very unlikely!

I met Brian personally for the first time when, in 1963, the BBC made a film of the Cheddar dig for schools. Although I was the actual person in charge of the work, I was not asked to participate, being, I was told 'not known to the headmistresses to whom the film was recommended'; while by then Brian Hope-Taylor was at the time better known as a TV personality. The photographs at the conference exhibition showed how dapper he looked in those years. Thus he was the 'front man', who was filmed showing the Cheddar dig and talking to camera. While I was somewhat miffed at this, it was for me very useful to have him seeing the excavations at Cheddar in their final stages, and to discuss with him the structural features and interpretation.

I met him again in 1964 at Yeavering, when he gave a very good exposition to the Prehistoric Society's annual conference, which was being held that year at Wooler. There was nothing visible by this time except the remarkable monument by the roadside designed by him, indicating through its aperture the area where the buildings had been. I had little to do with him in the following years, but when my review article came out in 1980, he wrote, in his elegant handwriting, a very pleasant letter of appreciation.

The last letter I received from him was much later, in 1988. I had been commissioned, as one of the few people he might reply to, to enquire about progress on the Old Windsor report. Brian's reply was a diatribe on English Heritage's role in the post-excavation process; *inter alia* that (I quote) 'they allowed the truly immense body of small finds and samples to be flooded, de-labelled and de-boxed.' Brian added some description of his ill-health from cardiovascular troubles. He concluded 'Old Windsor is very close to my heart'.

Rereading my review, I considered whether I would write in similar vein today: the answer is YES! I still believe (a view shared by Martin Carver, my successor at York) that not only was the excavation one of the highest skill and originality, but that the monograph is a milestone in archaeological publications of the later twentieth century.

Technically, the excavation was carried out with a very few people in conditions of soil and climate of *appalling* difficulty, in which features of 'a pale yellowish-grey' could be distinguished from a subsoil of 'very pale, greyish-yellow' (Hope-Taylor, 1977, 29) for very short periods, in drying after rain; or by subtle changes in texture and *sound* of the trowel; changes drawn and photographed sometimes after several hours of watching from a tower. The site had to be dug in the cold Northumbrian winters to be damp enough to observe the tenuous structural features and disturbances such as graves. Daylight hours were short, and the sun, when it came out, was usually occluded by the bulk of Yeavering Bell.

Brian used in excavation a combination of horizontal 'planum' definition and vertical section and dissection. It is interesting that in retrospect he would have preferred to rely wholly on horizontal definition, as made famous by the much-missed Philip Barker.

The staff of the dig was minimal – a few workmen from Alnwick; to quote Brian: who remained loyal and dedicated 'under the lash of sand-laden winds' (Hope-Taylor 1977, 31); also Paul Savage as assistant director and a few volunteers. Brian was personally closely involved in the excavation and recording, but it was he alone who was responsible for the subsequent analysis and drawing in the years that followed for the monograph, despite losing the only text at one stage on Hamburg station and having to begin again.

As with many archaeological reports, the most valuable part is the data: they remain highly relevant, as with those of Pitt-Rivers, while the Discussion section, which is initially what many people want to read, gradually becomes out-of-date, while (especially in this case) remaining a statement of importance in the history of archaeological thinking. Yet even the data were insufficient for some people. I have a letter of 1982 (I won' t reveal who wrote it); I quote: 'I find Yeavering much the most unsatisfactory report I have ever consulted and Hope-Taylor's treatment of the buildings is confused and confusing'.

The witty and elegant text is still worth studying in conjunction with the excellent hand-drawings and photographs. Interpretation must be approached with a critical mind – has one been taken, as I wrote, on a journey of confidence: we are persuaded to find a hypothesis plausible; then to accept it as reasonable; then it becomes difficult to refute, and finally it is presented as a fact (a sequence common to many reports). Finally one finds oneself saying 'but, wait a moment, how did the hypothesis become fact?' Yet one can see this as being challenged to examine the data more carefully, which must be a good thing.

Since the pioneering days of Hope-Taylor, many people have reconsidered Yeavering, some critically and increasingly sceptically. It is perhaps the historical interpretations which have attracted most criticism of the report (i.e. the archaeology is regarded as first rate), and it is in the ill-defined manner of the understanding, both historically and archaeologically, of the post-Roman centuries that the trouble comes.

In the 1950s and 1960s, post-Roman archaeology was very much guided by available written sources, notably in this case Bede and *Beowulf*. Both have been subject to massive discussions in recent decades, but both are still fundamental to the rethinking about Yeavering. In the light of current understanding, some arguments now seem rather dated. But this must not be allowed to obscure the superlative excavations, the compilation of such a text, and the furthering of understanding of this difficult area in a difficult period of time.

Finally, we should re-emphasise the qualities for which we are honouring Brian Hope-Taylor. Firstly, the courage that he had to embark on what he must have realised would be a very difficult excavation; secondly, the skills he used in dissection, learnt in the course of the work, and methods developed to suit the site data, in hostile conditions; thirdly, the brilliance with which he made a dramatic and convincing story in the process of post-excavation analysis, again in spite of formidable personal difficulties; and, finally, the way in which he translated analysis into a report that should still be necessary reading for all archaeology students, interpreted in the light of the historical sources as they were understood in the 1970s.

In conclusion it would be superfluous to comment on Brian's brilliant drawings, as this was a main aspect of the exhibition designed to complement the 2003 Yeavering conference (see chapter 17). One point, though: when I sent in my review to *Medieval Archaeology*, part of it was rejected – a collage of drawings that I had greatly enjoyed; each one was designed to be appropriate to the plan – *the north points*!

15

BRIAN HOPE-TAYLOR: A PERSONAL REMINISCENCE

Rosemary Cramp

When I came to work in Durham in 1955, the archaeological scene in the north had been dominated for years by long-established research and excavation on Roman military sites, and the quietly persistent exploration of native sites by George Jobey. Our students mainly did their training at the Corbridge training course (which I had myself attended as an undergraduate, like many others from universities elsewhere). There was excavation also at High Medieval monastic sites. As a newly appointed lecturer in the post quaintly entitled Anglo-Saxon Antiquities and Archaeology, I was anxious to find evidence for the Anglo-Saxon presence in the north, although my own experience had all been on Roman or prehistoric sites under the dour tutelage of Richard Atkinson.

It was therefore very exciting to hear of this amazing person who was excavating an Anglo-Saxon palace in Northumberland. I suppose it was in 1956 or 1957 that I visited the site, by some sequences of public transport which I cannot now remember. It was the first time I had seen a large open area excavation, and it was a revelation. From the top of Brian's photographic tower the foundation trenches and post pits of the great timber buildings stretched out below as he vividly described their construction, and how a huge forest would have had to be cut down to effect their building. I was ready to be impressed, and he was a compulsive mentor. He liked to work with a few workmen, trained to clean surfaces in the meticulous way he did, so that the least variation of soil colour would stand out. His other helpers were all volunteers who were not necessarily archaeologists. I do not think that Brian liked other archaeological professionals on his digs, but he enjoyed instructing the less informed on the methodology of excavation and recording, and he had wonderful powers of observation. He lived and breathed a site when he was working on it and although he later lodged in Wooler, at that time he was living in a caravan on site and enjoyed telling one of the rigours of this. The site could be a huge wind tunnel and both his photographic tower and his caravans had been blown over, not to mention the catrastrophic drying of the wind on his soil features at a site which was impossible to water.

His archaeological techniques were in advance of his time, and it is a tragedy, because his work at Yeavering took so long to appear in print, that a whole succeeding generation of archaeologists had to rediscover these. He did lecture extensively on his sites, however, and in this, and his subsequent television appearances, he could fascinate and captivate an audience. He had been a child actor and he always had something of the actor in him. He was not a very tall person but with his good looks, bright fair hair and blue eyes he stood out in a crowd. I think that when he was digging Yeavering he was at the height of his powers, and both freer and happier than he was in later life. The site made his name widely known and provided an entry into the academic life, but in return, by revealing it as he did, he provided a context for the public and political life of that period in Anglo-Saxon England, which was a revelation at the time and has remained of pivotal importance ever since.

16

BRIAN HOPE-TAYLOR: A PERSONAL REFLECTION ON HIS LIFE AND HIS ARCHIVE

Diana Murray

In January 2001, I received a phone call from Professor Ian Ralston telling me that Dr Brian Hope-Taylor had died in his house in Cambridge. We were both aware of the implications of this, not only the loss of a friend and mentor, but also the potential destruction of a life's work contained in the papers that we knew must have been in his possession. That work covered 50 years of mostly unpublished archaeological research and excavation, illustration, teaching and work with the media to bring archaeology to a wider audience.

THE ARCHIVE

Although the original intention of the Royal Commission on the Ancient and Historical Monuments of Scotland (RCAHMS) had been to retrieve only the Scottish material and to alert colleagues in England to the remaining material, what we found on arrival was an inextricable mass of documents and artefacts in extremely poor condition and in no logical order. This had been made considerably worse by the activities of a house-clearing gang before we arrived. As a former pupil of Brian's myself, I was only too well aware of the potential importance of the material and was concerned that as much as possible was salvaged. It was impossible to sort or even to evaluate the material on site and, as there was some capacity in RCAHMS and the National Monuments Record of Scotland (NMRS) has considerable experience in dealing with material of this nature, it was decided to transport the collection to Scotland. In total, 156 boxes were removed to the offices of the RCAHMS in Edinburgh.

Two initial reports were funded by Historic Scotland; one on the requirements for remedial conservation undertaken for the artefacts by AOC Archaeology Group; one for the paper and photographic material undertaken by a paper conservator to establish the work that would be required to stabilise the material. The reports indicated that 49 per cent of the paper and photographic archive was in an unacceptable condition, largely due to mould damage, which is hazardous to health, and 34 per cent of the material was in poor condition and could not be handled without stabilisation. The artefacts were in a similarly poor state having suffered abrasion, chemical damage and biological attack from mould and insects. Each artefact required to be repackaged appropriately, metal objects x-rayed and mould and infestation treated.

English Heritage agreed to fund a stabilisation and listing project to rehouse the paper and photographic items in appropriate archive materials, sorting it into a logical order and producing a consolidated catalogue in digital form. A project curator, Catherine Sweeney, was appointed in July 2002 for six months to undertake the sorting and preliminary listing of the documentary archive in collaboration with a consultant conservator, Audrey Wilson.

The documentary archive was stabilised by the removal of mouldy packaging, rehousing in archive materials, and some basic conservation treatment, which allowed most of the collection to be handled for general listing purposes. However, from a conservation point of view, much still requires surface cleaning before it can be made available for more detailed cataloguing or for research purposes. Some of the photographic material will require skilled conservation treatment before it can be used, for example to unroll tightly bound strips of negatives prior to printing or digitising. Some of the material most badly affected by mould was frozen pending detailed treatment.

Following this basic stabilisation, the collection was sorted into broad categories for listing and evaluation. The categories covered not only the excavation archive but also material relating to Brian's career as an illustrator and artist, his teaching and his media career. A list was made of the items in each category and a report has been written summarising this phase of the work. The documentary archive consists of over 30,000 items of which over 20,000 are photographs or negatives. Half of the items relate to archaeological sites and half to non site-specific material.

The report of this work has provided a limited guide to the contents of the collection as a preliminary to the research necessary to fully identify each item and ensure correct site attributions. Further work is necessary to ensure that all items are properly identified so that those doing research on the collection can be sure that all items are fully accounted for. It is clear that some of the excavation material is incomplete and that other related items may be deposited elsewhere or are missing. Some work is under way to try to identify relevant material held elsewhere, but as some clearance took place in the house before we arrived, material may well have been lost. Some of the correspondence will also assist in the understanding of items in the collection and it is also necessary to establish the relationships between the documentary material and the artefacts where possible.

Undoubtedly, the photography could be one of the most significant elements to shed light on unpublished excavations, as it was certainly one of Brian's primary methods of recording. One of the highest priorities therefore, is to unroll the negatives in conservation conditions and to print up or digitise them for matching with labelled prints and other material in the collection.

Unusually for a collection of this kind, there has been a stream of requests from individuals, societies and organisations expressing an interest in gaining access to the material and I am grateful to all those who have written in support of the project. This is not just because there is unpublished information, but because of the significance to Anglo-Saxon studies of the sites he worked on and the potential quality of the material recovered.

The report of this first phase of work was completed by December 2002 (RCAHMS 2002) and has been used to prepare a number of applications for further funding which have met with limited success.

Application was made in partnership with the University of Edinburgh to the AHRB Resource Enhancement Scheme in May 2003 to fund a three-year programme of cataloguing and conservation of the archive, and research into the life and work of Hope-Taylor. The applicants received notification that they were unsuccessful in November 2003 but were invited to resubmit the application in 2004. A reworked application was resubmitted in May 2004 and was unsuccessful in November 2004.

A number of smaller projects have been successful:

SCRAN funded the production and cataloguing of 250 captioned digital images (available at www.scran.ac.uk) (Jan-Mar 2003)
York Minster Archives funded the cataloguing and digitisation of 440 records relating to excavations at York Minster (June 2003)
Historic Scotland funded an assessment of the publication potential of Doon Hill and Mote of Urr excavations (Sept-Oct 2004) and are currently funding the digitisation and cataloguing of 1800 items that comprise the sites' excavation records (March 2005)
The Corporation of London (Apr 2005) funded the cataloguing and digitisation of the Farthing Down excavation archive

Of the 31,000 items of archive, approximately 3750 will have been catalogued by May 2005, leaving some 27,250 uncatalogued items. Funding is also still being sought for the basic treatment of the artefacts, although they are now in stable storage conditions. There are over 3000 artefacts of which over 1000 are unprovenanced. Some require conservation treatment before they can be placed in long-term storage or are suitable for handling for analysis.

A new initiative is being set up which will seek to raise the funds necessary to:

Provide a catalogue of the entire collection, which will be accessible online
Digitise more than 50 per cent of the paper and photographic archive to make available online
Provide conservation treatment of the 3,050 items identified in the English Heritage commissioned Report (2002) for mould
Flatten rolled negatives
Remove pressure sensitive tape and repair tears

The estimated time required for this work is three years at a cost of £200,000.

Somehow, obtaining funding for archives of this kind is proving extremely difficult. Most modern excavation archives are well-documented according to well-ordered procedures. The amount of information and insight that can be retrieved from all the elements of material held in collections of this kind is perhaps undervalued and certainly requires more dedicated research on the part of the user. The archaeological world tends to regard archives as site specific rather than as a corpus of work as I believe this collection should be seen. While it is perhaps more relevant to scholars rather than the general user, it also appears that there is not sufficient interest, as yet, in the historical relevance of an archaeological figure whose main work spans the 1960-70s. It might therefore be worth sketching out what we already know of the life and work of Dr Brian Hope-Taylor.

BRIAN HOPE-TAYLOR: LIFE AND WORK

Professors James Graham Campbell and Ian Ralston have worked together to build up a biographical profile and bibliography which has been of immense assistance as we worked on sorting the archive and I am grateful to them for letting me incorporate some of their work into this paper.

Kenneth Brian Hope-Taylor (*69*) was born in 1923, the only child of Herbert and Rita Taylor. His mother was the daughter of a well-known Croydon artist, William Henry Hope. A collection of his grandfather's paintings as well as his own has now been taken into the collection of his Cambridge college – Wolfson.

69 Photograph of Brian Hope-Taylor standing next to his paint brushes. *Crown copyright: RCAHMS. Dr Brian Hope-Taylor Collection*

He was known as Brian from an early age, but changed his name officially to Brian Kenneth Hope-Taylor in 1948.

As early as 1933, when he was nine, he embarked on his media career, starring in a film *The Night Watchman's Story* (a history of Cadbury's), and there is other evidence of his childhood talent. 'A future in the films is prophesied for Brian Taylor, who is the British answer to the American favourite, Jackie Cooper, whom he resembles quite a lot. Look out for him.' (*Picture Show* magazine June 3 1933). Later, his skills in presentation were used to good effect in his work for television, which included a programme for BBC Children's TV on the Anglo-Saxons in 1958, acting as consultant and anchorman for BBC schools' programme *Men in History* in 1964, and his work for Anglia TV with Forbes Taylor, with whom he had a long and successful collaboration and which has recently been documented by Forbes in an article published in *Antiquity* (2001) and in this volume. This series included *Who were the British?* and *The Lost Centuries*. I was present as a student excavating at the filming of his last production, recording the excavations at the Devil's Dyke in Cambridgeshire in 1973.

Although TV presenters earned less than they do today, it is clear that Brian received far more remuneration from his media appearances than he did from his teaching. Brian was awarded his PhD in Cambridge in 1961 for his thesis on Yeavering and was appointed University Assistant Lecturer in Archaeology in the same year and in 1967 was elected as a fellow of University College Cambridge, now Wolfson College. As with his television work, the 1960s and '70s saw the best of his academic achievements including the publication of a number of papers, including The *'Boat shaped' houses in Northern Europe* (1962), two articles in *Antiquity* on draughtsmanship (1966a; 1967) and culminating in the publication of *Yeavering* in 1977. However, by 1975, he had become very unwell and he resigned from the university in 1976. Like his television performances, his lectures were always magnificently well researched and delivered and his tutorials were always passionate for the topic under discussion, be it Celtic Art or the distribution of hog-backed stones or the typology of Anglo-Saxon metalwork. As a student at Cambridge studying archaeology from 1971-4, I remember Brian taking us round the collections in the Downing Street museum explaining the art on Anglo-Saxon brooches, and leading us on memorable field trips including one to Northumberland which took us from Yeavering and Lindisfarne, to Bamburgh, Roughting Linn and Durham, getting the coach stuck more than once in the narrow lanes in his enthusiasm to get us to a particular spot.

But excavation was his real passion and he took great pride in the techniques that he had developed, principally at Yeavering which he records in detail in the publication (70). He could combine all his skills, careful measurement and recording, teasing out the very last ounce of information from watching a site in all weather conditions, recording meticulously through his photography and drawing skills and explaining and presenting the results in a clear and well-informed way.

As a young man in Sanderstead near Croydon, he became friends with Shepherd Frere who was his first archaeological mentor. He joined the Surrey Archaeological Society in 1942 and discovered and surveyed the earthworks of a Celtic field system on Farthing Down during periods of leave from war service, carrying out excavations in 1944 and 1945 (Hope-Taylor 1950). After the war he continued to excavate regularly on a number of sites in the Croydon area and undertook what was probably his first major site in 1949 at Abinger motte in Surrey (Hope-Taylor 1952; 1956). In 1951, he commenced excavation at the Mote of Urr in Dumfries and Galloway (Hope-Taylor 1951) and started the fieldwork and examination of aerial photography that was to identify Yeavering as the site of *Ad Gefrin*. Excavations then took place at Yeavering (Hope-Taylor 1977), Old Windsor (Hope-Taylor 1958a), Preston Manor (Hope-Taylor 1953), and Lowe Hill in Wakefield (Hope-Taylor 1958b). Funding for these was supplied by the Ministry of Works and various societies, including the Society of Antiquaries of Scotland. In the 1960s there were further excavations at Yeavering, Bamburgh (with funding from Durham University) (Hope-Taylor 1960), and Doon Hill in East Lothian (Hope-Taylor 1966b), York Minster (Hope-Taylor 1971) and

70 Photograph of Brian Hope-Taylor, during his excavations at Yeavering (1953-1962), spraying water on soil marks to highlight them for photography. Crown copyright: RCAHMS. Dr Brian Hope-Taylor Collection

Lindisfarne. Finally, in 1973, he excavated at the Devil's Dyke in Cambridgeshire (Hope-Taylor and Hill 1977). Excavations at this time were always substantially under-funded, labour was voluntary or hired workmen (as at Yeavering and described in the publication), there was little or no payment for post-excavation work and Brian undertook all the illustration himself.

Illustration was, however, at the heart of his work. As a schoolboy, he had studied wood engraving with George Mackley, and this remained a major influence on him (*71*). He was a great admirer of the work of Eric Gill whose lettering styles were adopted by Brian in his illustration labelling, and he certainly corresponded with Henry Moore. During the war he worked at RAF Medmenham in the model-making section and on photographic interpretation, in common with other archaeologists of the time such as Glyn Daniel, Stuart Piggott and Richard Atkinson. His model-making skills were later used to produce a large-scale model of Yeavering that was positioned in his room in the top of the turret in the Cambridge department, now apparently lost. There is also evidence of other modelling among the photographic material in the collection though none of

Greetings from Brian Hope-Taylor, War Coppice, Caterham, Surrey

71 A Christmas card of a mole with quill on the Uffington horse, printed from a wood block designed by Brian Hope-Taylor. *Crown copyright: RCAHMS. Dr Brian Hope-Taylor Collection*

the actual objects appear to survive. Much of his reconstruction drawing has, to my mind, a modelling style. From 1949-51, he worked as a graphic artist in London where he was part of an artistic circle that included Dylan Thomas, and, in 1951, he designed and executed mural panels for the private site museum at Abinger. His artwork includes, most famously, the cover for the *Ordnance Survey map of Southern Britain in the Iron Age* (Ordnance Survey 1962), and the Stonehenge logo for *Antiquity*, but also a detailed drawing of the Mold collar (Hope-Taylor 1954). The dust jacket of Yeavering is his own work and he drew some very skilled portraits including Glyn Daniel and Nora Chadwick. We have also discovered work for advertisements and magazine illustrations, including the *Radio Times* and several of his wooden and metal engraving blocks.

He took considerable pride in his archaeological illustration (72) as he explains in the two articles for *Antiquity*. It is perhaps symptomatic of the time that it was possible to write two articles on draughtsmanship using only one illustration and that relating to line thickness. He concludes 'If the drawings to be made are to be of any lasting importance, extra expense (for good quality materials) is abundantly justified. It is to be hoped, after all, that there will one day be a

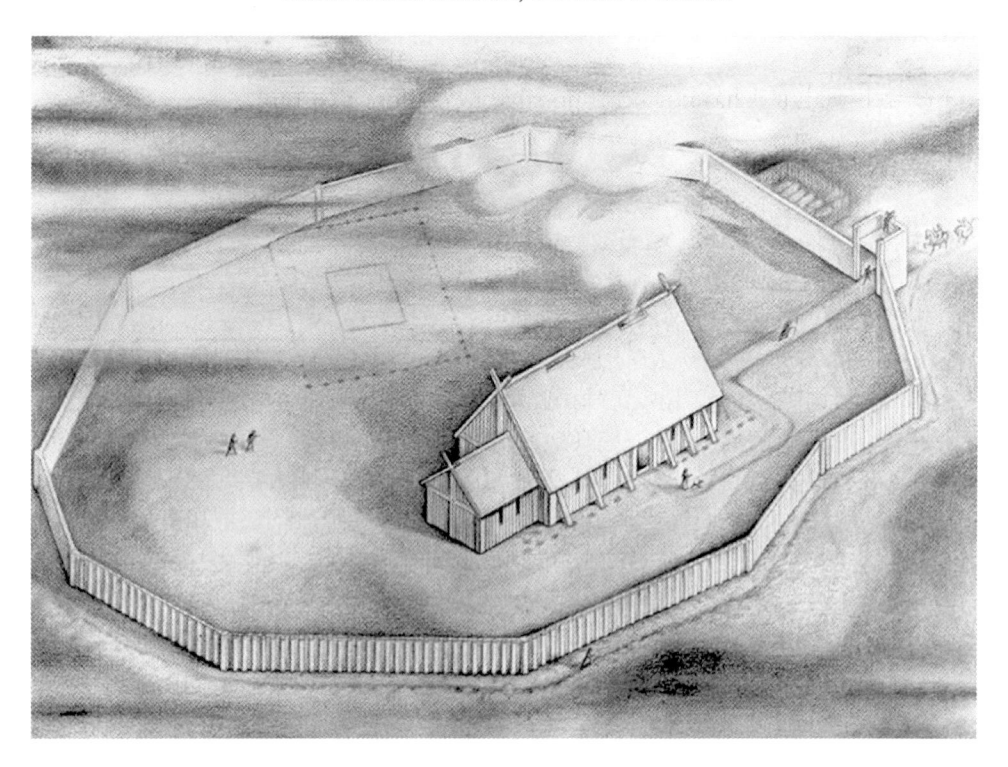

72 Reconstruction drawing of the timber hall and palisaded enclosure at Doon Hill, East Lothian, by Brian Hope-Taylor. Crown copyright: RCAHMS. Dr Brian Hope-Taylor Collection

central archive of archaeological records – and one part of it will be in effect a National Gallery of Archaeological Draughtsmanship' (1966a, 113).

In 2001 three archaeologists who had a profound influence on my own approach to archaeology died. They were Brian Hope-Taylor, Philip Barker and Peter Reynolds. All taught me to observe, to excavate, to draw and to evaluate. They and others of their time influenced a whole generation of archaeologists in the period of the 1950s to the 1970s when the profession was growing rapidly and maturing.

That generation of archaeologists was groundbreaking, and it was exciting to be part of it. Those that I have mentioned, including Brian, regarded the techniques of excavation, and what you could recover from the ground and what inferences you could make from that information, as paramount. Their approach was intuitive as well as carefully observed and they were exploring a methodology that taught us much about our approach to the recovery of information. As students at the time, we were privileged to share in the growing research and ideas given stage by stage in Cambridge lectures and supervisions as described in the preface to *Yeavering*. I much regret that in a rash moment of tidying out I threw out my lecture notes which I had kept for over 20 years. We think that there are lecture notes, however, in the archive, but it has not been possible to explore them fully.

Recording techniques and the importance of post-excavation work (recognised by proper funding) has moved on. The preparation and presentation of archaeology so that it can be appreciated more widely is on our televisions two or three times a week – or so it seems. Much of what Brian's generation was struggling to achieve is now the norm and taken for granted by the present generation.

What we recovered from Brian's house in Cambridge is, to some extent, a time capsule epitomising the style of archaeology practised at the time, the limitations (such as lack of funding), his methods and skill of illustration, his career with the media and, importantly, his correspondence with other influential figures of the day. It is unique because it was not self-selected, so contains much of what most people would normally throw out as being irrelevant – lists of site equipment, bills for supplies, newscuttings etc.

When the collection is catalogued, it will be possible to research not only more about Brian's work, but also the history of this period of archaeology. We are almost too close to it to appreciate its importance and I am probably only aware of it because of my work in RCAHMS, an archaeological archive in which we hold collections of personalia for a number of key figures in archaeology, Gordon Childe, O.G.S. Crawford, A.O. Curle, J.K. St Joseph, Jack Scott and others … none of which have attracted significant funding for cataloguing and therefore remain largely unexplored. I would like to think that the value of these collections will be better recognised in future, but of these, the Brian Hope-Taylor collection offers perhaps the most complete and a unique opportunity that I very much hope will be recognised.

17

A PROCESS OF DISCOVERY. EXHIBITING THE WORK OF BRIAN HOPE-TAYLOR

Laura M. Sole

Brian Hope-Taylor (1923-2001) was an exceptionally talented man. His contribution to the study of Anglo-Saxon archaeology and his development of innovative archaeological techniques through his work at Yeavering have been widely applauded. However, Brian Hope-Taylor was not simply an archaeologist; his exceptional work at Yeavering represented a culmination of skills honed through experiences in other areas of life: as professional artist and illustrator; as air-photograph interpreter and model-maker in the RAF through World War II, as Diana Murray has discussed in this volume. His talent for engaging public communication, first seen in his career as child actor, applied at Yeavering in his ability to train a largely unskilled labour force, would later become apparent through his teaching and media careers.

One of the remarkable elements of Hope-Taylor's work at Yeavering did not emerge until the publication of *Yeavering: an Anglo-British centre of early Northumbria* in 1977. This was the precision with which his illustrations captured the archaeological features he had examined. The subtle soil-stains which enabled Hope-Taylor to detect the post-holes of the timber buildings which once stood at *Ad Gefrin*, and the complex intersections of building phases which Hope-Taylor had unpicked, were laid out with absolute clarity in his drawings. As the majority of Hope-Taylor's original drawings for publication had fortunately been deposited in the Museum of Antiquities of Newcastle upon Tyne, the opportunity arose to create a temporary display featuring some of them during the *Yeavering: Context, Continuity, Kingship* conference.

A PROCESS OF DISCOVERY. EXHIBITING THE WORK OF BRIAN HOPE-TAYLOR

Placing Hope-Taylor's Yeavering illustrations at the centre of an exhibition about his life and work seemed appropriate since Hope-Taylor himself clearly viewed the role of illustration as an integral part of the archaeological investigation process, not merely a record-keeping exercise, as he stated more than once in one of his two contributions to the series on archaeological draughtsmanship commissioned by *Antiquity* (1966a, 109):

> It would be a mistake to suppose that archaeological draughtsmanship is, so to speak, a public activity that begins only at the end of an investigation and is confined to the inking in of measured plans and sections. It is actually from first to last the natural medium for exploration of archaeological material and ideas. There is no other activity that brings the characteristics of a site or an object so sharply into focus, that so concentrates all the faculties of the investigator on his subject. It is essentially a process of discovery, of revelation; and the archaeologist who delegates his work of draughtsmanship to others is denying both to himself and to posterity a chance of new insight.

Hope-Taylor's description of the process of archaeological draughtsmanship as 'a process of discovery' provided the title for the exhibition, and by accident provided an apt description for the rapid process of research which followed, as contacts with a variety of Hope-Taylor's former friends and colleagues enabled the assembly of a collection of exhibits which allowed the interpretation of his work at Yeavering in the context of his other skills, achievements and experiences. *A Process of Discovery* brought together for the first and probably only time exhibits from a variety of lenders to illustrate Hope-Taylor's career, displaying not only his varied talents, but also his firm commitment to preserving information about the past, understanding it, and communicating it to a wide public audience.

Funding for the exhibition was supplied predominantly through the Aggregates Levy Sustainability Fund. This was because Hope-Taylor's initial excavation at Yeavering had been driven by the need to rescue the site – which he had already identified through air photographs as potentially that of Bede's *Ad Gefrin* – saving it from threatened destruction by the extension of an adjacent sand quarry which had already removed traces of buildings at the edge of the site (1977, xvii-xix, 5 and figure 12) (*colour plates 1 & 12*). Consequently, an element of the exhibition played an educative role, questioning the conflicting need to extract aggregates from the land with that of understanding and preserving the historic environment. This was supplemented by a special curriculum-linked visit for school groups, *Beneath the Feet of Kings*, which ran alongside the exhibition, dealing not only with looking at archaeological evidence, but also linking the

73 Inscription from the front cover of Hope-Taylor's 'Outline of a Campaign of Archaeological Propaganda'. Reproduced courtesy of the Council for British Archaeology. Photograph: Laura Sole

questions raised when balancing the need for aggregate extraction with the need to preserve the past to the Citizenship strand of the National Curriculum.

This educative agenda would, I believe, have received Hope-Taylor's full endorsement, as it echoed themes he himself raised in another set of exhibits provided by the Council for British Archaeology. After the Second World War, Hope-Taylor was one of a small group of archaeologists who came together through a shared concern for the damage being done to the historic environment by the rapid construction of houses and roads. Hope-Taylor had by that time established a career for himself as a commercial graphic artist, and had also carried out some archaeological investigations in Surrey, where he was brought up. This combination of artistic ability and archaeological commitment resulted in a proposal by Hope-Taylor that he offer his services as a commercial artist, free of charge, to establish a campaign of 'Archaeological Propaganda', the title itself evocative of the then still recent wartime Government-led public information campaigns.

The proposal for the campaign of 'Archaeological Propaganda' survives in its entirety having been preserved in the archives of the Council for British Archaeology in York. It consists of a foolscap sugar-paper scrapbook with Hope-Taylor's calligraphic hand-lettering on the front inscribing: 'Outline of a Campaign of Archaeological Propaganda' (*73*). The entire folder was wrapped in a War Office map of Norway dated 1940, presumably obtained by Hope-Taylor when he was undertaking his wartime duties at RAF Medmenham. Inside, Hope-Taylor presented his outline for the campaign. First, in three pages of typescript he set out the proposal for his scheme, couched in rather strong language, with the introductory words:

A PROCESS OF DISCOVERY. EXHIBITING THE WORK OF BRIAN HOPE-TAYLOR

Public apathy is the pernicious anaemia of British archaeology; it deprives research of the data and financial support which constitute its bloodstream.

There is no cure for the malady, other than enlightened education: this is a long-term treatment, and in the meantime the symptoms must be relieved. As was noticed above, an enormous amount of material has undoubtedly been destroyed through non-recognition by an ignorant and indifferent public: post-war expansion on a large scale, of buildings and industry, threatens to destroy a great deal more if public sympathy is not encouraged and enlisted.

There is one means, and one means only, of relieving the situation: intelligent propaganda. A publicity campaign on as large a scale as economically possible will give immediate results: the poster, in particular, is unequalled in its ability to arouse the public's interest and curiosity. It is significant that in America, where museums have given sensible publicity to archaeological research, funds are forthcoming with corresponding ease; the difficulty (and of course the necessity!) of obtaining funds from the public of this country is an index of the disaffection that exists. This would have been avoided had good relations between the public and the archaeologist been cultivated.

Hope-Taylor's concern was twofold: firstly, the rate of unrecorded destruction of the archaeological record, and, secondly, the need to secure adequate funds to provide for its investigation and record. His vision was that a series of leaflets and posters, displayed in public libraries, post offices and schools, would encourage members of the public to recognise chance archaeological finds and report them to a specialist. He included three poster designs, one featuring a charismatic drawing of Father Time alongside the text 'Father Time has buried a jigsaw...' (*colour plate 16*), and a second with a bearded, bespectacled Professor character, 'the archaeologist' (*colour plate 17*), challenging the reader: 'Do you know what these are?' and holding a large drawing depicting various archaeological artefacts. A third contained more drawings of archaeological artefacts with a pointing hand and the question 'What are these?' with a smaller 'archaeologist' caricature informing the reader 'They are stone tools made by Prehistoric Man...'. The rather over-authoritative style of communication embodied in these poster designs, which now seems out of place but which was very much of its time, continued in the accompanying three pages of typescript carrying Hope-Taylor's draft leaflet text for his campaign 'The Future of the Past' (*74*). The leaflet, subtitled 'THE ARCHAEOLOGIST SPEAKS TO THE PUBLIC' alongside a pencil-drawn caricature of 'the archaeologist' as featured on the poster, informed the reader:

...the second, and more dangerous, factor [contributing to the 'unprecedented rate' of destruction of 'precious relics of the past'] is the inability of the general public to recognise such remains when they are accidentally revealed by building or industrial working.

74 The draft leaflet design for 'Future of the Past'. *Reproduced courtesy of the Council for British Archaeology. Photograph: Laura Sole*

…Thus, the weapons and instruments used by ancient man, his pottery, dwelling places, defensive works and burial sites, have survived, almost miraculously, for thousands of years: a legacy well-nigh forgotten until the present day. It is OUR duty, archaeologists and the public alike, to ensure that we do not wantonly destroy that legacy: if we do not preserve our national antiquities we shall deserve the name 'vandal'; and that name our descendents will certainly give us if we fail through ignorance or irresponsibility. That is why the Archaeologist asks you, the Public, for your interest and help.

The top of the leaflet carried a pencil sketch of the design which appears to emerge as the signature for this draft campaign as it is the only element retained in its eventual realisation: a collection of artefacts. This was presumably selected by Hope-Taylor deliberately to expose the public as much as possible to images of archaeological artefacts in order that they might recognise any chance finds. The leaflet text then went on to give very clear and informative instructions, detailing the places in which archaeological material might appear, describing in more detail the types of artefact which might be found (incorporating a series of pencil sketches illustrating the process of flint-knapping to enable members of the public to recognise worked flint), and then instructing what the finder should do with any such material, including under what circumstances and how the material should be moved, and to whom it should be taken. The level of detailed information in publicity material intended for the general public more than 50 years ago appears much greater than what might be provided today, an interesting reflection on the modern assumption of the level of intelligence of the general public, mirroring a similar comparison of past archaeological television broadcasting to that of today expressed by Forbes Taylor (2001) in the context of Brian Hope-Taylor's media work. Despite the quality of the idea and its execution, however, the practicalities of putting into place the network of 'local archaeological advisors' in touch with a range of national specialists envisaged by Hope-Taylor, together with the costs involved in producing and distributing nationally a sufficient quantity of leaflets and posters, presumably proved two stumbling blocks of mammoth proportion, so the original 'Future of the Past' campaign never happened.

However, 'Future of the Past' did sow a germ of an idea that eventually became the Council for British Archaeology's 'History from the Ground' poster, which realised Hope-Taylor's concept of a poster campaign to encourage members of the public to report archaeological finds. These posters were also designed by Brian Hope-Taylor and featured the signature collection of artefacts, against a background of dug soil and sky against which two heads contrast 'early man' with 'modern man'; 'the archaeologist' presumably represented a more authoritative style of communication which seemed out of place by the time the 'History from the Ground' campaign was launched as neither he nor Father Time featured. The archives of the Council for British Archaeology hold both Hope-Taylor's original draft for this poster and the final design and both were displayed in *A Process of Discovery* (*colour plate 18*) alongside all the original drafts and typescripts for the 'Future of the Past' campaign.

The concept behind the campaign – a network of specialists to whom archaeological finds can be reported – has only recently come to fruition through the Portable Antiquities Scheme whereby a network of Liaison Officers and Finds Specialists are funded to fulfil the role of the 'specialist' to whom finds should be reported, and the internet has provided the technology to record the finds speedily in a systematic way that is readily available to the general public and to researchers. Hope-Taylor's initial idea may have taken half a century to come fully to fruition, but the fact that he conceived it, taken with his appreciation that a public awareness-raising campaign was an appropriate vehicle to produce academic results, demonstrates the breadth of his achievement in archaeology: as expert, advocate and public communicator. Many were drawn into archaeology as a result of the evocative poster.

Hope-Taylor's passion for the communication of archaeology to the general public eventually translated into a career in what was, in the 1960s, a newly emerging field, that of television archaeology (discussed elsewhere and in this volume by his director Forbes Taylor). Here he showed exceptional creative flair in combining his archaeological knowledge and enthusiasm with a very personable presenting style and an imaginative approach to communicating archaeological information to a general audience. He made two major series with Forbes Taylor for Anglia Television: *Who were the British?* (1965) and *The*

Lost Centuries (1968) as well as two feature-length programmes on excavation projects he was involved in at York Minster and Devil's Dyke, Cambridgeshire.

The Lost Centuries programme five 'A Golden Age' allowed him to return to Yeavering. This programme was shown in full in *A Process of Discovery*, owing to its inspired approach in providing context for a site where there is currently nothing to see on the ground other than a field, the River Glen and a large inscribed stone marking the place of *Ad Gefrin*. The opening sequence of the programme is dramatic, and deserves description in full. The camera opens on a black Rolls Royce, being towed with ropes pulled by men in dark suits into a newly-dug area of earth in a field. Inside the car, on the back seat, sits a very well-dressed gentleman in a bowler hat, obviously dead. With no sound other than funerary music, a select group of mourners dressed in stylish contemporary black pass objects one by one into the interior of the car. These are the trappings of a rich lifestyle: two filled crystal decanters with glasses on a silver tray, sporting trophies, guns, golf clubs and a large gilt-framed oil-painting of a horse. The mourners close the car doors and step out of the newly-dug hole, and a tractor arrives and begins to bury the Rolls Royce. The camera then pans back onto Brian Hope-Taylor, standing some distance away, and as the 'Rolls Royce burial' continues in the background he speaks to camera: 'I know you'll think this is just a piece of off-beat fantasy, but no, in a way it is true. Something very like this actually happened thirteen hundred years ago…'. This leads him on to Sutton Hoo, by an analogy which in an instant transports viewers from the material culture of status in the 1960s to that of the early middle ages. Developing the theme of early kingship, Hope-Taylor goes on to lead the viewer to Yeavering – quite literally, by driving north in a very smart, red Lotus sports car – where some stunning aerial footage combined with reconstruction drawings and Hope-Taylor's own model reconstructing Yeavering were used to illustrate his commentary on the site; the theme of kingship was further developed through extracts from *Beowulf* and visiting Bamburgh, where Hope-Taylor was also excavating at that time. Although the production lacked the finish of today's computer-generated reconstructions and animations, advanced photographic technologies, and costumed re-enactors, the quality of Hope-Taylor's content, with its imaginative structure, and his likeable style of presentation resulted in a programme which can hold the twenty-first-century viewers' interest and far surpasses much of the television archaeology which has more recently been on our screens.

Given Hope-Taylor's background as artist and model-maker and his passion for the visual and dramatic approach of communicating archaeology to the public via television, the manner in which his work was presented in *A Process of Discovery* required attention not only to exhibits and text but also to exhibition design. A design was developed with MKW Design Partnership which drew on the concept of Hope-Taylor as archaeologist and artist. A large dark-green canvas

A PROCESS OF DISCOVERY. EXHIBITING THE WORK OF BRIAN HOPE-TAYLOR

75 *A Process of Discovery* used a canvas tent and wooden easels to evoke the period in which Hope-Taylor was work working. Photograph: MKW Design

tent occupied the centre of the exhibition space in which visitors could sit to watch 'A Golden Age' (*75*); this was designed to be evocative of the tents available during the 1950s and 1960s when Hope-Taylor was excavating at Yeavering, although his descriptions (1977, 30-1) of the 'persistent west to south-westerly winds, often strong and sometimes ferocious' alongside rain, frost and snow during the autumn and winter seasons of excavation on site make the actual use of such a tent rather unlikely! The artwork displayed was mounted on large wooden easels (*76*), and the interpretative text panels used enlarged versions of Hope-Taylor's playful compass points which appear throughout *Yeavering* (*77*; *colour plate 19*) as a design theme.

Alongside a selection of Hope-Taylor's original drawings for *Yeavering* – most of which are extremely large, include his own hand-lettering, and demonstrate the principles of preparing drawings for print which he described so eloquently in *Antiquity* (1967) – and the artwork for 'The Future of the Past' and 'History from the Ground', we were fortunate enough to be able to show some of his other artwork. This included framed copies of the four paintings demonstrating the construction of Stonehenge, commissioned for *The National Geographic* (Egerton and Hope-Taylor 1960) and on loan from Panos Antoniou, the owner of a Greek restaurant in Cambridge who had helped to look after Hope-Taylor during his ill health in

76 Original artwork for Yeavering *was displayed in wooden frames on large wooden easels in* A Process of Discovery. *Photograph: MKW Design*

his final years, and to whom Hope-Taylor had left the pictures in thanks. Wolfson College, Cambridge, formerly University College where Hope-Taylor had been a fellow, lent three original works of art which demonstrated the diversity of Hope-Taylor's illustrative range: 'The Church in the Trees. Sanderstead Church, Surrey', 'Sir Ralph Richardson as Cyrano de Bergerac', and 'The Sanctuary of the Leaf-God'. We also borrowed for display a selection of six wood engravings produced as personal and Christmas cards, four from Professor James Graham-Campbell and two from the Brian Hope-Taylor Archive held at the Royal Commission for Ancient and Historic Monuments of Scotland. The Archive also added a personal element to the exhibition by lending his trowel, monogrammed wooden slide box and pair of compasses, alongside his business card and a sheet of headed note-paper, also printed from a wood engraving. The style of the cards and notepaper would be instantly recognisable to those familiar with the *Antiquity* logo which Hope-Taylor also designed, and his designs incorporated elements of the historic environment: ruined stone walls, tombstones, hillforts; alongside stylised plants, animals and landscapes. A design which he used both on his headed notepaper and some of his cards symbolised himself: a mole, carrying an over-sized feather quill pen, riding on a white horse of the kind carved on hillsides in prehistory (*71*).

Interactive exhibits were used to encourage visitors to follow Hope-

A PROCESS OF DISCOVERY. EXHIBITING THE WORK OF BRIAN HOPE-TAYLOR

77 A compass point from *Yeavering*. Extract from Hope-Taylor 1977, figure 39. © Crown copyright – reproduced by permission of English Heritage

Taylor's instruction in archaeological draughtsmanship, in particular his advice (1966a, 111) that potential draughtsmen should practice through doodling and tracing the work of experienced draughtsmen. A tracing table reproduced additional drawings from *Yeavering* alongside Hope-Taylor's instructions, and his comment:

> 'First I have a think and then I draw a line around my think.' These words, which were said by a child, offer the key to draughtsmanship. That key is usually lost during the business of growing up, and has to be rediscovered (1966a, 107).

As exhibition curator, I came to Brian Hope-Taylor having known him only as a name on the spine of an archaeological publication, and was struck by the way in which the range of exhibits illustrated the breadth of his talents: not just as archaeologist, but as accomplished artist and illustrator, advocate for the historic environment, and engaging television presenter. I was also touched by the way in which the generosity of the contributions of Hope-Taylor's friends, colleagues and former students, many of whom are now leaders in the archaeological arena, reflected the impact of his work and personality. The interesting thing that emerged for me at the exhibition opening was how private Hope-Taylor had been and how compartmentalised he had kept elements of his life, so that even for many of those present who knew him well, the exhibition was indeed *A Process of Discovery*.

ACKNOWLEDGEMENTS

A Process of Discovery benefited immensely from the contributions of a number of people and organisations, many with personal connections to Hope-Taylor. It would not have been possible without Colm O' Brien and Richard K. Morris whose knowledge of Hope-Taylor-related material in the Museum of Antiquities of Newcastle upon Tyne and the Council for British Archaeology formed the core of the original idea, and both of whom contributed to much of the background research from which interesting supplementary material was drawn. I am extremely grateful to Dr Peter Addyman, Colm O' Brien, Tim Gates, Richard K. Morris and Forbes Taylor, all of whom contributed to the exhibition text. I am also grateful to Lindsay Allason-Jones and the Museum of Antiquities of Newcastle upon Tyne, Dr Mike Heyworth and the Council for British Archaeology, Diana Murray and the Royal Commission of Ancient and Historical Monuments of Scotland, Dr Peter Addyman, David Sherlock, Panos Antoniou, Professor James Graham Campbell and Professor Rosemary Cramp, Dr Gordon Johnson and the Fellows of Wolfson College, University of Cambridge, all of whom either loaned material for the exhibition or put me in touch with relevant lenders. Granada-Anglia plc. gave kind permission to display archive footage from *The Lost Centuries* (1968). Exhibition design was by MKW Design Partnership. *A Process of Discovery* was made possible thanks to funding from the Aggregates Levy Sustainability Fund administered by English Heritage and Defra, and from the Society of Antiquaries of Newcastle upon Tyne. I am also extremely grateful to Diana Murray and the Brian Hope-Taylor Archive at the Royal Commission for Ancient and Historical Monuments of Scotland for making available to me the short biography and bibliography of Brian Hope-Taylor prepared by Professor James Graham Campbell and Professor Ian Ralston in 'The Brian Hope-Taylor Archaeological and Personal Papers Collection, Phase 3: detailed listing and prioritisation, report for 1 July 2002 – 31 December 2002' (RCAHMS, 2003, available at http://www.rcahms.gov.uk/bhtreport.pdf [2005]), pp. 28-33.

APPENDIX

After careful consideration, the editors opted to include the following letter in this volume for two reasons. Firstly, it includes first-hand information from Brian Hope-Taylor about aspects of his work at Yeavering that is not available elsewhere. Second, it demonstrates that a little more than a year before his death, and in spite of his failing health from which he must have known he was unlikely to recover, Brian was generous in offering support for a new programme of research and interpretation at Yeavering which the Northumberland National Park Authority was (and still is) keen to progress.

The letter (in Brian's immaculate handwriting) was in response to a list of questions relating specifically to the excavations on Yeavering Bell, though the unfortunate flooding of the 'storage-place' (known to be a cellar in Wooler) presumably also resulted in the loss of much material from the palace site.

Dr. Brian Hope-Taylor, F.S.A.
The Studio
158 Hills Road
CAMBRIDGE
CB2 2PB

4th October 1999

Dear Paul,

YEAVERING BELL

Many thanks for your letter of 20 September, and for your kind and most welcome enclosures.

I too must now apologize for delay. Alas I cannot report any improvement in my illness – in fact a crucial piece of surgery has been postponed yet again because I am still not fit enough to withstand it. Meanwhile, I am ordered further rest and medication, and am in a rather weak state.

Although most of my replies are inescapably negative, I will respond below to each of your numbered questions:-

1) Certainly there is no surviving archive-material from my excavations on Yeavering Bell. My notebooks, with all their detailed drawings, plus the master-plan, are known to have been destroyed by flooding of their storage-place. Nothing could be salvaged by laboratory-work from the disintegrating and water-blackened fragments that survived.

2) The finds also were lost in the muddy and trampled chaos of the storage-place. It may be of interest to note that the Samian-ware and the two <u>minimi</u> were examined both by Sir Ian Richmond and by George Jobey, but as both Richmond and Jobey have since died, no further information can be forthcoming. With the notebooks gone, my one clear memory is that these 5 particular finds all came from huts on the north-facing slope of the fortification's interior, on or close to the Bell's 'saddle'.

3) Your Figure 7* seems to show most of the cuttings that I dug, but omits the exposure of the rectangular hut shown in my Plate 11. <u>All</u> my excavational activities on the Bell were confined to the summer of 1958 – <u>after</u>, not during, my long investigation of the Anglo-Saxon township.

4) Within the palisade, small interstitial patches of reddened clay (flecked with charcoal) appeared possibly to be survivals from a more extensive deposit (severe erosion of all the highest areas within the Bell's fortifications had reduced most of the 'native' pottery to little seams and blobs of crumbled fragments). I suspected, on insufficient evidence, the possibility of a very large hearth – or even a beacon site – at the centre of the palisade enclosure, and certainly regarded the palisade-enclosure as a very late (if not final) feature of the Bell's structural history.

5) Yes, I tried to locate the George Tate finds and archives, but fruitlessly. Nobody was able to provide any clues (Jobey baffled too, he told me).

I am so very sorry that my wretched health still does not allow me to meet you in Northumberland or in Cambridge, but still hope that medical science will make such things possible again in the next few years!

Meanwhile, thanks again and <u>every</u> good wish with all your truly important work – building now so impressively.

Yours sincerely,

Brian

Paul Frodsham
Northumberland National Park Authority
Eastburn, South Park, Hexham NE46 1BS

---

* The 'Figure 7' referred to here is the plan on page 22 of the RCHME Yeavering Bell survey report (Pearson 1998) which shows the location of Hope-Taylor's excavation trenches based on aerial photographs taken by St Joseph during the excavations in July 1958 (see figures 11 and 34, this volume).

NOTES

CHAPTER 2: YEAVERING AND AIR PHOTOGRAPHY: DISCOVERY AND INTERPRETATION

1. Negative numbers DN 49-56.
2. Figures for potential soil moisture deficit were calculated using rainfall data for Acklington airfield supplied by the Ministry of Defence.
3. A copy of St Joseph's type-written letter to Richmond exists in the archive of Christianbury Trust papers held in the Museum of Antiquities, University of Newcastle-upon-Tyne. His description is evidently based on contemporary notes contained in his 'Photographic Log Book' covering flights made between 29 June and 10 July 1949 (1949, Book 2). I am grateful to Mrs Rose Desmond at the Unit for Landscape Modelling at Cambridge University for drawing my attention to this logbook.
4. The quotation and sketch from this letter, dated 10 August 1949, are used by kind permission of the literary executor of the estate of the late Professor J.K.S. St Joseph.
5. George Tate's reference to Old Yeavering provides a likely contemporary source for the Ordnance Survey's attribution (Tate 1863, 433).
6. In other contexts the same toponym may denote barrows or cairns. Here it is not clear if it was originally applied to the 'camp' or to now vanished mounds or burials.
7. In an unpublished report for the Northumberland National Park, Peter Ryder has convincingly argued that the building traditionally known as 'King Edwin's Palace' dates back to the mid-sixteenth century AD and can best be described as an aberrant type of defended farmhouse or 'pele' (Ryder 1991).
8. Letter from Hogg to O.G.S. Crawford, dated 6 April 1942 – 'I still manage an occasional furtive survey of a small site in the Northumbrian wilds, but I haven't much time to spare, and one has to keep a watch for Home Guards all the time! I have only been arrested once though....' Crawford MS 6/64, Bodleian Library, Oxford.
9. After an adjustment for changes in the retail price index, the sum provided by Sir Walter would be the equivalent of almost £112,000 in 2003.
10. Christianbury papers in the Museum of Antiquities, University of Newcastle upon Tyne.
11. Letter from St Joseph to O.G.S. Crawford dated 12 Ocotober 1938. Crawford MS 85/5-8,

Bodleian Library, Oxford. Again, this quotation is used by kind permission of the literary executor of the estate of the late Professor J.K.S. St Joseph. Although we do not know precisely what air photographs St Joseph is referring to, there are some verticals now in the NMR in Swindon that were taken by the RAF in or before 1930 and which cover parts of the College Valley and Doddington Moor. As these once belonged to Crawford they may well be the photographs that were lent to St Joseph. What is certain, however, is that it was these same photographs of the College Valley which were later used by A.H.A. Hogg in connection with his own fieldwork.

12 According to his Photographic Log Book (1949, Book 2), St Joseph had been intending to photograph Margaret Piggott's excavation at Hayhope Knowe but failed to identify the site probably because she and her team had already packed up and left. After photographing a more conspicuous hillfort on the summit of Great Hetha he was heading NE towards Coupland when the cropmarks at Yeavering caught his eye.

13 Letter to Ian Richmond dated 8 September 1945. Richmond archive, Sackler Library, Oxford. Correspondence file 'S'.

14 For example, ice-wedge casts at *c*.NT 934 303 and 940 302 were mapped in 2002 by Rog Palmer as part of a wider study of cropmarks in the area of the Milfield Plain (forthcoming).

15 See references cited in J.G. Evans (1972).

16 *cf.* for example ice-wedge casts excavated at Broome Heath in Norfolk and at other sites discussed by J G Evans (1972).

17 Negative numbers DN 49 and TU 41, taken respectively on 9 July 1949 and 2 August 1951.

18 I am indebted to Lindsay Allason-Jones for information concerning the glass beads. So far as is known, both beads were lost before the remaining finds were deposited in the Museum of Antiquities at Newcastle University.

19 This site can dimly be seen on four photographs taken by St Joseph in July 1962 (AGG 59-62) but shows more clearly on photographs taken in July 1970 (BDB 67-70). The photograph reproduced by Hope-Taylor as Plate 6 in his report was one of the former (AAG 59).

20 MacLauchlan's original pencil sketch of the site, dated June 1860, is preserved in the Alnwick Castle copy of 'Notes not included….' (Charlton and Day, 1984). Another copy of the same volume belonging to the Newcastle Society of Antiquaries contains extracts from the 1866 OS six-inch map that have been annotated in MacLauchlan's own hand. One such extract, inserted between pages 22 and 23, depicts the site at 'Burrowses' as a double pecked circle accompanied by the legend 'Faint traces of Camp'.

21 Even if the innermost ditch could be proved to be a *later* addition, reversing the sequence suggested here, the point about longevity still stands.

22 In conversation, both Lindsay-Allason Jones and Alastair Oswald have raised a further possibility, namely that the enclosure could represent a Roman signal station similar to the one discovered on Eildon Hill North (RCAHMS, 1956, ii, 306f). While this suggestion is attractive in several respects, the form of the monument (unless unfinished ?) seems too irregular for a Roman military work.

23 Negative number AAG 59, 20 July 1962.

24 A similar displacement occurs at West Heslerton in North Yorkshire where *Grubenhäuser* are concentrated in a 'Craft Zone' lying to one side of a 'Housing Zone' (Powlesland 1999, figure 4.2).

NOTES

CHAPTER 5: EARLY MEDIEVAL BURIAL AT YEAVERING: A RETROSPECTIVE

1 The one object that Hope-Taylor saw as 'unambiguously Germanic' – the inlaid buckle loop found stratified in demolition fills of the Great Enclosure – has been identified as a Frankish import, dating to between 570-80 and 630-40 (Welch 1984).
2 There is one aspect to his interpretation that jars, however: that is the reliance on skeletal height to infer ethnicity. Confirmation of the Anglo-Saxon identity of the individual in Grave BZ is seen as supported by this being the tallest individual recognised, whereas the burials with knives in the Western Ring-ditch complex are seen as less likely to be so, given their lack of stature (Hope-Taylor 1977, 246). In addition, the occupants of the string-graves are said to be of short stature; therefore 'there can be no doubt that these graves were made by and for the natives of the district' (1977, 252).
3 I am grateful to Graeme Young and Philip Wood of the Bamburgh Research Project, and Sarah Groves of the Department of Archaeology, University of Durham, for the information supplied here.
4 As Alcock (1988, 8) has already pointed out, the entirety of the Yeavering chronology rests on Hope-Taylor's association of the two burning episodes at the ends of Phase IIIC and IV with Bede's record of destructive activity by Penda of Mercia in the region in 633 and before 651.

CHAPTER 7: THE SOCIAL USE OF SPACE AT *GEFRIN*

1 It should be noted that Hope-Taylor (1977, 200-203) considered this to be a surveyor's *groma* and rejected the interpretation which I favour.

BIBLIOGRAPHY

Abbreviations conform to those of the British and Irish Archaeological Bibliography (see www.biab.ac.uk).

Ainsworth, S., Oswald, A.W.P. and Pearson, T. 2002 *An Iron Age hillfort on Staw Hill, Northumberland*. English Heritage: Archaeological Investigation Report Series AI/17/2002

Aldhouse-Green, S. and Pettitt, P., 1998 Paviland Cave: contextualizing the 'Red Lady', *Antiquity*, **72**, 756-772

Alexander, D.L. and Ralston, I.B.M., 1999 Survey work on Turin Hill, Angus, *Tayside Fife Archaeol Journal*, **5**, 36-49

Alcock, E., 1992 Burials and Cemeteries in Scotland, in N. Edwards and A. Lane (eds) 1992, 125-9

Alcock, L., 1981 Quantity or quality: the Anglian graves of Bernicia, in V.I. Evison (ed) *Angles, Saxons, and Jutes – Essays presented to J N L Myres*. Oxford: Clarendon Press, 168-186

Alcock, L., 1988 *Bede, Eddius and the Forts of the North Britons* Jarrow: Jarrow Lecture

Alcock, L., 2003 *Kings and Warriors, Craftsmen and Priests in Northern Britain AD 550-850*, Soc Antiq Scotl Monogr Ser, **24**. Edinburgh: Society of Antiquaries of Scotland

Alcock, L. and Alcock, E., 1987 Reconnaissance excavations on early historic fortifications and other royal sites in Scotland 1974–84: 2, Excavations at Dunollie Castle, Oban, Argyll, 1978, *Proc Soc Antiq Scotl*, **117**, 119-47

Alcock, L. and Alcock, E., 1992 Reconnaissance excavations on early historic fortifications and other royal sites in Scotland 1974-84; 5: A, Excavations and other fieldwork at Forteviot, Perthshire, 1981; B, Excavations at Urquhart Castle, Inverness-shire, 1983; C, Excavations at Dunnottar, Kincardineshire, 1984, *Proc Soc Antiq Scotl*, **122**, 215-87

Alcock, L., Alcock, E. and Foster, S.M., 1986 Reconnaissance excavations on Early Historic fortifications and other royal sites in Scotland 1976-82: 1, Excavations near St Abb's Head, Berwickshire, 1980, *Proc Soc Antiq Scotl*, **116**, 255-79

Anderson, M.O., 1980 *Kings and Kingship in Early Scotland*. Edinburgh: Scottish Academic Press

Archer, D., 1992 *Land of Singing Waters Rivers and Great Floods of Northumbria*. Stocksfield, Northumberland: Spredden Press

BIBLIOGRAPHY

Armstrong, A., 1769 *Map of the County of Northumberland*. Northumberland County Record Office Ref: ZBK sheet 2

Ashmore, W. and Knapp, A.B., 1999 *Archaeologies of Landscape: Contemporary Perspectives*. Oxford: Blackwell

Barnwell, P.S., 1992 *Emperor, Prefects and Kings: The Roman West 395-565*. London: Duckworth

Barnwell, P.S., 1997 *Kings, Courtiers and Imperium: The Barbarian West 565-725*. London: Duckworth

Barnwell, P.S., 2000 Emperors, Jurists and Kings: Law and Custom on the Late Roman and Early Medieval West, *Past and Present*, **168**, 2-29

Barnwell, P.S., 2004 The Early Frankish *Mallus*: Its Nature, Participants and Practices, in A. Pantos and S. Semple (eds) 2004, 233-46

Barrett, J.C., 1999 The Mythical Landscapes of the British Iron Age, in W. Ashmore and A.B. Knapp (eds) 1999, 253-265

Barrow, G.W.S., 1969 Northern English Society in the twelfth and thirteenth centuries, *Northern Hist*, **4**, 1-28

Barrow, G.W.S., 1973 Pre-Feudal Scotland: Shires and Thanes, in *The Kingdom of the Scots: government, church and society from the eleventh to the fourteenth century*. London: Edward Arnold, 1-68

Bede, *Historia Ecclesiastica de Gentis Anglorum*. ed and trans B. Colgrave and R. Mynors, 1969 *Bede's Ecclesiastical History*. Oxford: Clarendon Press

Beowulf, C.L. Wrenn (ed.), 1953 *Beowulf with the Finnesburgh Fragment*. London: Harrap; trans S. Heaney, 1999 *Beowulf: a new translation*. London: Faber and Faber

Bersu, G., 1940 Excavations at Little Woodbury, Wiltshire: the settlement as revealed by excavation, *Proc Prehist Soc*, **6**, 30-111

Blair, J., 1995 Anglo-Saxon Pagan Shrines and their Prototypes, *Anglo-Saxon Stud Archaeol Hist*, **8**, 1-28

Bourdieu, P., 1970 The Berber House, in M. Douglas (ed), *Rules and Meanings: The Anthropology of Everyday Knowledge*. Harmondsworth: Penguin, 98-110

Bowden, M. and McOmish, D.S., 1987 The required barrier, *Scott Archaeol Rev*, **4**, 76-84

Bowden, M. and McOmish, D.S., 1989 Little boxes: more about hillforts, *Scott Archaeol Rev*, **6**, 12-16

Bradley, R., 1987 Time Regained: the Creation of Continuity, *J Brit Archaeol Assoc*, **140**, 1-17

Bradley, R., 1993 *Altering the Earth: The origins of Monuments in Britain and Continental Europe*. Edinburgh: Society of Antiquaries of Scotland

Bradley, R., 1998 *The Significance of Monuments*. London: Routledge

Bradley, R., 2000 *An Archaeology of Natural Places*. London: Routledge

Bradley, R., 2002 *The Past in Prehistoric Societies*. London: Routledge

Bradley, R., 2005 *Ritual and Domestic Life in Prehistoric Europe*. London: Routledge

Breeze, A., 2001 The Name of *Maelmin*, near Yeavering, *Archaeol Aeliana*[5], **29**, 31-32

Brooks, N.P., 1984 *The Early History of the Church at Canterbury: Christ Church from 597 to 1066*. Leicester: Leicester University Press

Brophy, K., in press *The Neolithic Cursus Monuments of Scotland*. Edinburgh: RCAHMS

Broun, D., 1999 *The Irish Identity of the Kingdom of the Scots in the Twelfth and Thirteenth Centuries*. Woodbridge: Boydell Press

Brown, P., 1992 *Power and Persuasion in Late Antiquity: Towards a Christian Empire*. Madison: Wisconsin University Press

Browning, R., 1952 The Riot of AD 387 in Antioch: The Role of the Theatre Claques in the Later Roman Empire, *J Roman Stud*, **42**, 13-20

Brück, J., 1999 Houses, Lifecycles and Deposition on Middle Bronze Age Settlements in Southern England, *Proc Prehist Soc*, **65**, 145-166

Budd, P., Millard, A., Chenery, C., Lucy, S. and Roberts, C., 2004 Investigating population movement by stable isotope analysis: a report from Britain, *Antiquity*, **78**, 127-41

Bulleid, A. and Gray, H. St George, 1911 *The Glastonbury lake village: a full description of the excavations and the relics discovered, 1892-1907*, Volume 1. Glastonbury: Glastonbury Antiquarian Society

Bulleid, A. and Gray, H. St George, 1917 *The Glastonbury lake village: a full description of the excavations and the relics discovered, 1892-1907*, Volume 2. Glastonbury: Glastonbury Antiquarian Society

Burgess, C.B., 1972 Goatscrag, A Bronze Age rock shelter cemetery in North Northumberland, *Archaeol Aeliana[4]*, **50**, 15-69

Burgess, C.B., 1984 The Prehistoric Settlement of Northumberland: A Speculative Survey, in C.B. Burgess and R. Miket (eds) *Between and Beyond the Walls: Essays on the Prehistory and History of North Britain in Honour of George Jobey*. Edinburgh: John Donald, 126-75

Burgess, C.B., 1995 Bronze Age Settlements and Domestic Pottery in Northern Britain: some suggestions, in I. Kinnes and G. Varndell (eds) *Unbaked Urns of Rudeley Shape. Essays on British and Irish Pottery for Ian Longworth*. Oxford: Oxbow, 145-158

Butler, G.G., 1907 Address delivered to the Berwickshire Naturalists' Club at Berwick, 13th October 1904, *Hist Berwickshire Natur Club*, **19**, 97-107

Camden, W., 1637 *Britain, or a chorographical description of the most flourishing kingdomes, England, Scotland, and Ireland, and the islands adjoyning, out of the depth of antiquitie*. London: William Aspley

Cameron, A., 1976 *Circus Factions: Blues and Greens at Rome and Byzantium*. Oxford: Clarendon Press

Carmichael, D.L., Hubert, J., Reeves, B. and Schanche, A., (eds) *Sacred Sites, Sacred Places. One World Archaeology*, **23**, Routledge: London

Chapman, J.C. and Mytum, H.C., (eds) *Settlement in North Britain 1000 BC - 1000 AD*. BAR Brit Ser **118**, 103-48. Oxford: British Archaeological Reports

Charles-Edwards, T., 1978 The Authenticity of the Gododdin: an historian's view, in R. Bromwich and R. Brinley Jones (eds) *Astudiathau ar y Hengerrod: Studies in Old Welsh Poetry*. Cardiff: University of Wales Press, 44-71

Charlton, B. and Day, J., 1985 The Archaeological Field-Sketches of Henry MacLauchlan, Draftsman and Surveyor (1792-1882), *Archaeol Aeliana[5]*, **13**, 147-161

Clapperton, C.M., 1970 The Evidence for a Cheviot Ice Cap, *Inst British Geographers Trans*, **50**, 115-127

Clapperton, C.M., 1971 The pattern of deglaciation in north Northumberland, *Inst British Geographers Trans*, **53**, 67-78

Close-Brooks, J., 1984 Pictish and Other Burials, in J.G.P. Freill and W.G. Watson (eds) *Pictish Studies: settlement, Burial and Art in Dark Age Northern Britain*. BAR Brit Ser **125**, 87-111. Oxford: British Archaeological Reports

Colgrave, B. and Mynors, R., 1969 *Bede's Ecclesiastical History*. Oxford: Clarendon Press

Cramp, R., 1957 Beowulf and Archaeology, *Medieval Archaeol*, **1**, 55-77

Cramp, R., 1980 Review – Yeavering: an Anglo-British centre of early Northumbria, *Antiquity*, **54**, 63-65

BIBLIOGRAPHY

Cramp, R., 1983 Anglo-Saxon Settlement, in J.C. Chapman and H.C. Mytum (eds) 1983, 263-97

Cramp, R., 1984 *Corpus of Anglo-Saxon Carved Stone Sculpture in England: Vol 1 County Durham and Northumberland.* London: British Academy

Cunnington, M.E., 1929 *Woodhenge.* Devizes: Simpson

Dalland, M., 1992 Long cist burials at Four Winds, Longniddry, East Lothian, *Proc Soc Antiq Scotl*, **122**, 197-206

Darvill, T., 2004 Tynwald Hill and 'things' of power, in A. Pantos and S. Semple (eds) 2004, 217-232

Davies, W., 1982 *Wales in the Early Middle Ages.* Leicester: Leicester University Press

Dixon, P.W., 1982 How Saxon is the Saxon house? in P.J. Drury (ed) *Structural Reconstruction.* BAR Brit Ser **110**, 275-88. Oxford: British Archaeological Reports

Dixon, P.W., 1991 Secular Architecture, in L. Webster and J. Backhouse (eds) *The Making of England: Anglo-Saxon art and culture AD600-900.* London: British Museum Press, 67-70

Driscoll, S.T., 1991 The archaeology of state formation in Scotland, in W.S. Hanson and E.A. Slater (eds) *Scottish Archaeology: New Perceptions.* Aberdeen: Aberdeen University Press, 81-111

Driscoll, S.T., 1998 Picts and Prehistory: cultural resource management in early medieval Scotland, *World Archaeol*, **30 (1)**, 142-58

Driscoll, S.T., 2004 The Archaeological Context of Assembly in Early Medieval Scotland – Scone and its Comparanda, in A. Pantos and S. Semple (eds) 2004, 73-94

Dumville, D., 1977 Sub-Roman Britain in History and Legend, *History*, **62**, 173-92

Dumville, D.N., 1993 *Britons and Anglo-Saxons in the early middle ages.* Aldershot: Ashgate

Eddius Stephanus, *Vita Wilfridi.* ed and trans B. Colgrave, 1927 *The Life of Bishop Wilfrid by Eddius Stephanus.* Cambridge: Cambridge University Press

Edwards, N. and Lane, A., (eds) 1992 *The Early Church in Wales and the West.* Monograph **16**, Oxford: Oxbow

Egerton, H.E. and Hope-Taylor, B.K., 1960 Stonehenge – new light on an old riddle, *National Geographic*, **117 (6)**, 846-866

Ekwall, E., 1977 *Concise Oxford Dictionary of English Place-Names* (4th edition). Oxford: Clarendon Press

Ellis Davidson, H.R., 1969 *Scandinavian Mythology.* London: Hamlyn

Erdrich, M., Giannotta K.M. and Hanson, W.S., 2000 Traprain Law: native and Roman on the northern frontier, *Proc Soc Antiqs Scot*, **130(2)**, 441-56

Evans, C., 1989 Archaeology and modern times: Bersu's Woodbury 1938 & 1939, *Antiquity*, **63**, 436-60

Evans, J.G., 1972 Ice-wedge casts at Broome Heath, Norfolk, *Proc Prehist Soc*, **38**, 77-86

Feacham, R., 1966, Hill-forts of Northern Britain, in A.L.F. Rivet (ed.) *The Iron Age in Northern Britain.* Edinburgh: Edinburgh University Press, 59-87

Feachem, R., 1977 *Guide to Prehistoric Scotland.* London: Batsford

Ferrell, G., 1990 A Reassessment of the Prehistoric Pottery From the 1952-62 Excavations at Yeavering, *Archaeol Aeliana⁵*, **18**, 29-49

Ferrell, G., 1997 Space and society in the Iron Age of north-east England, in A. Gwilt and C. Haselgrove (eds) 1997, 228-38

FitzPatrick, E., 2004 *Royal Inauguration in Gaelic Ireland c 1100-1600: a cultural landscape study.* Woodbridge: Boydell Press

Flood, J., 1983 *Archaeology of the Dreamtime: The Story of Prehistoric Australia and Her People.* Honolulu: University of Hawaii Press

Foster, S., 1998 Before Alba: Pictish and Dál Riata power centres from the fifth to late ninth centuries AD, in S. Foster, A. Macinnes and R. MacInnes (eds) *Scottish Power Centres from the Early Middle Ages to the Twentieth Century*. Glasgow: Cruithne Press, 1-31

Foster, S., 2004 *Picts, Gaels and Scots*. London: Batsford/Historic Scotland

Frodsham, P., 1999a Forgetting *Gefrin*: Elements of the Past in the Past at Yeavering, in P. Frodsham, P. Topping and D. Cowley (eds) 1999, 191-205

Frodsham, P., 1999b Discovering our Hillfort Heritage, in *Archaeology in Northumberland 1998-9*. Morpeth: Northumberland County Council, 18-19

Frodsham, P., 2004a Long ago in the land of the far horizons... An Introduction to the Archaeology of Northumberland National Park, in P. Frodsham 2004b, 1-152

Frodsham, P., 2004b *Archaeology in Northumberland National Park*. Research Report **136**, York: CBA

Frodsham, P., Topping, P. and Cowley, D., (eds) 1999 *'We were always chasing time.' Papers presented to Keith Blood. Northern Archaeol*, **17/18** (special edition)

Garrow, D., Lucy, S. and Gibson, D., forthcoming Excavations at Kilverstone, Norfolk, *East Anglian Archaeol*

Gates, T., 1983 Unenclosed settlements in Northumberland, in J.C. Chapman and H.C. Mytum (eds) 1983, 103-48

Gates, T. and O'Brien, C., 1988 Cropmarks at Milfield and New Bewick and the Recognition of Grubenhäuser in Northumberland, *Archaeol Aeliana*[5], **16**, 1-10

Geake, H., 1997 *The Use of Grave-Goods in Conversion Period England, c 600-800*. BAR Brit Ser **261**, Oxford: British Archaeological Reports

Gelling, M., 1988 *Signposts to the Past*. Chichester: Phillimore

Gibson, A., 2002 A matter of pegs and labels: a review of some of the prehistoric pottery from the Milfield basin, *Archaeol Aeliana*[5], **30**, 175-180

Grant, A., 1993 Thanes and Thanages, from the Eleventh to the Fourteenth Centuries, in A. Grant and K.J. Stringer (eds) *Medieval Scotland Crown, Lordship and Community*. Edinburgh: Edinburgh University Press, 39-81

Green, D.H., 1998 *Language and History in the Early Germanic World*. Cambridge: Cambridge University Press

Green, M.J., 1992 *Dictionary of Celtic Myth and Legend*. London: Thames and Hudson

Greenwell, W. and Rolleston, G., 1877 *British Barrows*. Oxford: Clarendon Press

Greenwood, C. and Greenwood, J., 1828 *Map of the County of Northumberland*. Northumberland County Record Office Ref: ZCR PLANS 42, sheet 1

Gregory of Tours, *Libri Historiarum*, ed. B. Krusch and W. Levison, 1937-51 *Monumenta Gernamiae Historica, Scriptores Rerum Merovingicarum*, vol 1 part 1 Hanover: Hahn; trans L. Thorpe, 1974 *Gregory of Tours: The History of the Franks*. Harmondsworth: Penguin

Guido, M., 1978 *The Glass Beads of the Prehistoric and Roman Periods in Britain and Ireland*. London: Society of Antiquaries of London

Gwilt, A. and Haselgrove, C., (eds) 1997 *Reconstructing Iron Age Societies*. Oxbow Monograph **71**, Oxford: Oxbow

Hamerow, H., 2002 *Early Medieval Settlements: the archaeology of rural communities in Northwest Europe 400-900*. Oxford: Oxford University Press

Harding, A.F., 1981 Excavations in the Prehistoric Ritual Complex near Milfield, Northumberland, *Proc Prehist Soc*, **47**, 87-135

Harding, A.F., 2000 Henge monuments and landscape features in Northern England: monumentality and nature, in A. Ritchie (ed.) *Neolithic Orkney in its European Context*.

Cambridge: McDonald Institute for Archaeological Research, 267-274

Harding, A.F. and Lee, G.E., 1987 *Henge Monuments and Related Sites of Great Britain Air Photographic Evidence and Catalogue*. BAR Brit Ser **175**, Oxford: British Archaeological Reports

Harding, D.W., (ed.) 1982 *Later Prehistoric Settlement in South-East Scotland*. Edinburgh: University of Edinburgh, Department of Archaeology

Harding, J., 2000 Later Neolithic ceremonial centres, ritual and pilgirmage: the monument complex of Thornborough, North Yorkshire, in A.Ritchie (ed.) *Neolithic Orkney in its European Context*. Cambridge: McDonald Institute for Archaeological Research, 31-46

Hardy, J., 1895 *The Denham Tracts. A Collection of Folklore by Michael Aislabie Denham, reprinted from the original tracts and pamphlets printed by Mr. Denham between 1846 and 1859*. London: David Nutt

Hartridge, R., 1978 Excavations at the prehistoric and Romano-British site on Slonk Hill, Shoreham, Sussex, *Sussex Archaeological Collections*, **116**, 69-41

Hawkes, C.F.C., 1931 Hill-Forts. *Antiquity*, **5**, 60-97

Hawkes, J. and Mills, S., (eds) 1999 *Northumbria's Golden Age*. Stroud: Alan Sutton

Hawkes, S.C. and Gray, M., 1969 Preliminary Note on the Early Anglo-Saxon Settlement at New Wintles Farm, Eynsham, *Oxoniensia*, **34**, 1-4

Heaney, S., 1999 *Beowulf*. London: Faber and Faber

Henderson, I., 1999 The Dupplin Cross, in J. Hawkes and S. Mills (eds) 1999, 161-177

Higham, N.J., 1986 *The Northern Counties to AD 1000*. London: Longman

Hill, J., 1995 *The Cultural World in Beowulf*. London: University of Toronto Press

Hill, J.D., 1995 How should we understand Iron Age societies and hillforts? A contextual study from southern Britain, in J.D. Hill and C.G. Cumberpatch (eds) *Different Iron Ages: Studies on the Iron Age in Temperate Europe*. BAR Internat Ser **602**, 45-66. Oxford: British Archaeological Reports

Hill, J.D., 1996 Hill-forts and the Iron Age of Wessex in T.C. Champion and J.R. Collis (eds) *The Iron Age in Britain and Ireland: Recent Trends*. 95-116. Sheffield: University of Sheffield

Hill, P.H., 1982a Settlement and chronology, in D.W. Harding (ed.) 1982, 4-43

Hill, P.H., 1982b Broxmouth hillfort excavations, 1977-78: an interim report in D.W. Harding (ed.) 1982, 141-88

Hill, P.H., 1987 Traprain Law: the Votadini and the Romans, *Scott Archaeol Rev*, **4**, 85-91

Hills, C., 2003 *Origins of the English*. London: Duckworth

Hingley, R., 1997 Iron, iron-working and regeneration: a study of the symbolic meaning of metalworking in Iron Age Britain, in A. Gwilt and C. Haselgrove (eds) 1997, 9-18

Hinton, D.A., 1990 *Archaeology, Economy and Society England from the fifth to the fifteenth century*. London: Seaby

Hirsch, E. and O'Hanlon, M., (eds) 1995 *The Anthropology of Landscape: perspectives on place and space*. Oxford: Clarendon Press

Hogg, A.H.A., 1947 A New List of Native Sites in Northumberland, *Proc Soc Antiq Ncl*[4], **11**, 140-179

Holtorf, C.J., 1997 Christian Landscapes of Pagan Monuments, A Radical Constructivist Perspective, in G Nash (ed) *Semiotics of Landscape: Archaeology of Mind*. BAR Internat Ser **661**. Oxford: British Archaeological Reports, 80-88

Hope-Taylor, B.K., 1950 Excavations on Farthing Down, Coulsdon, Surrey, *Archaeol Newsletter*, **2:10**, 170

Hope-Taylor, B.K., 1951 Excavations at Mote of Urr – interim report: 1951 season, *Trans Dumfriesshire Galloway Natur Hist Antiq Soc*, **29**, 167-72

Hope-Taylor, B.K., 1952 The excavation of a motte at Abinger in Surrey, *Archaeol J*, **107**, 15-43

Hope-Taylor, B.K., 1953 The discovery of Preston Manor, Tadworth, *Banstead District Gazette*, **5:1**, 23-30

Hope-Taylor, B.K., 1954 'Report' and 'reconstructional drawing' in T.G.E. Powell, The gold ornament from Mold, Flintshire, North Wales, *Proc Prehist Soc*, **7**, 161-78

Hope-Taylor, B.K., 1956 The Norman motte at Abinger, Surrey, and its wooden castle, in R.L.S. Bruce-Mitford (ed.) *Recent Archaeological Excavations in Britain*. 223-49

Hope-Taylor, B.K., 1958a Old Windsor, *Medieval Archaeol*, **2**, 183-5

Hope-Taylor, B.K., 1958b *Report on the Excavations at Lowe Hill, Wakefield, Yorkshire.* Wakefield: Wakefield Historical Society, nd

Hope-Taylor, B.K., 1960 Bamburgh, *University of Durham Gazette*, new series, **8(2)**, 11-12

Hope-Taylor, B.K., 1962 The 'boat-shaped' house in Northern Europe, *Proc Cambridge Antiq Soc*, **55**, 16-22

Hope-Taylor, B.K., 1966a Archaeological draughtsmanship: principles and practice Part II: ends and means, *Antiquity*, **40**, 107-13

Hope-Taylor, B.K., 1966b Doon Hill, Dunbar, *Medieval Archaeol*, **10**, 175-6

Hope-Taylor, B.K., 1967 Archaeological draughtsmanship: principles and practice Part III: lines of communication, *Antiquity*, **41**, 181-9

Hope-Taylor, B.K., 1971 *Under York Minster; archaeological discoveries, 1966-71.* York

Hope-Taylor, B.K., 1977 *Yeavering: An Anglo-British Centre of Early Northumbria*. London: HMSO

Hope-Taylor, B.K., 1980 Balbridie and Doon Hill, *Current Archaeol*, **72**, 18-9

Hope-Taylor, B.K. and Hill, D., 1977 The Cambridgeshire Dykes, *Proc Cambridge Antiq Soc*, **66**, 123-8

Horsley J., nd *Inedited contributions towards the history of Northumberland*. Newcastle. Privately printed for John Hodgson-Hinde by Stevensen and Dryden

Hume, K., 1974 The Concept of the Hall in Old English Poetry, *Anglo-Saxon Engl*, **3**, 51-62

Hunter Blair, P., 1954 The Bernicians and their Northern Frontier, in H.M. Chadwick, N.K. Chadwick, K. Jackson, R. Bromwich, P. Hunter Blair and O. Chadwick (eds) *Studies in Early British History*. Cambridge: Cambridge University Press, 137-72

Hutchinson, W., 1778 *A View of Northumberland*. Newcastle: W. Charnley and Messrs Vesey and Whitfield

Jackson, K.H., 1953 *Language and History in Early Britain*. Edinburgh: Edinburgh University Press

James, H., 1992 Early Medieval Cemeteries in Wales, in N Edwards and A Lane (eds) 1992, 90-103

James, S., Marshall, A. and Millett, M., 1984 An Early Medieval Building Tradition, *Archaeol J*, **141**, 207-12

Jobey, G., 1962 An Iron Age Homestead at West Brandon, Durham – Appendix II : Palisaded Works in Northumberland and Durham, *Archaeol Aeliana*[4], **40**, 31-34

Jobey, G., 1964 Enclosed Stone Built Settlements in North Northumberland, *Archaeol Aeliana*[4], **42**, 41-64

Jobey, G., 1965 Hillforts and settlements in Northumberland, *Archaeol Aeliana*[4], **43**, 21-64

Jobey, G., 1966 A field survey in Northumberland, in A..L.F. Rivet (ed.) *The Iron Age in Northern Britain*. Edinburgh: University Press, 89-109

Jobey, G., 1971 Excavations at Brough Law and Ingram Hill, *Archaeol Aeliana*[4], **49**, 71-93

Jobey, G., 1978 Iron Age and Romano-British Settlements on Kennel Hall Knowe, North Tynedale, Northumberland, *Archaeol Aeliana⁵*, **6**, 1-28

Jobey, G., 1981 Green Knowe unenclosed platform settlement and Harehope cairn, Peebleshire, *Proc Soc Antiq Scotl*, **110**, 72-113

Jobey, G., 1983 Excavation of an unenclosed settlement on Standrop Rigg, and some problems related to similar settlements between Tyne and Forth, *Archaeol Aeliana⁵*, **11**, 1-21

Jobey, G., 1985 The unenclosed settlements of Tyne-Forth: a summary, in D. Spratt and C.B. Burgess (eds) *Upland Settlement in Britain. The Second Millennium BC and after*. BAR Brit Ser, **143**, 177-94. Oxford: British Archaeological Reports

Jobey, I. and Jobey G., 1987 Prehistoric, Romano-British and Later Remains on Murton High Crags, Northumberland, *Archaeol Aeliana⁴*, **15**, 151-198

Jobey, G. and Tait, J., 1966 Excavations on Palisaded Settlements and Cairnfields at Alnham, Northumberland, *Archaeol Aeliana⁵*, **44**, 5-48

Jolliffe, J.E.A., 1926 Northumbrian Institutions, *English Historical Review*, **41**, 1-42

Jones, A.H.M., 1964 *The Later Roman Empire 284-602: A Social, Economic and Administrative Survey*. 3 vols. Oxford: Blackwell

Jones, G.R.J., 1976 Multiple Estates and Early Settlement, in P.H. Sawyer (ed.) *Medieval Settlement: continuity and change*. London: Edward Arnold, 15-40

Jones, G.R.J., 1984 The Multiple Estate: a Model for Tracing the Interrelationships of Society, Economy and Habitat in K. Biddick (ed.) *Archaeological Approaches to Medieval Europe*. Kalamazoo, Michigan: University of Michigan Press, 9-42

Keeney, G.S., 1935 Anglo-Saxon Burials at Galewood, within Ewart, near Milfield, *Proc Soc Antiq Ncl⁴*, **7**, 15-17

Keeney, G.S., 1939 A Pagan Anglian Cemetery at Howick, Northumberland, *Archaeol Aeliana⁴*, **16**, 120-8

Knapp, A.B. and Ashmore, W., 1999 Archaeological landscapes: Constructed, Conceptualised, Ideational, in W. Ashmore and A.B. Knapp (eds) 1999, 1-30

Knowles, D. and St Joseph, J.K.S., 1952 *Monastic Sites from the Air*. Cambridge: Cambridge University Press

Koch, J., 1997 *The Gododdin of Aneirin: text and context from Dark Age North Britain*. Cardiff: University of Wales Press

Larsson, L., 1989 Late Mesolithic settlement and cemeteries at Skateholm, southern Sweden, in C. Bonsall (ed.) *The Mesolithic in Europe: Papers Presented at the Third International Symposium, Edinburgh 1985*. Edinburgh: John Donald, 367-378

Lex Ribuaria, F. Beyerle and R. Buchner (eds), 1954 *Monumenta Germaniae Historica, Leges*, section 1, vol 3 part 2. Hanover: Hahn; trans T.J. Rivers, 1986, *Laws of the Salian and Ripuarian Franks*. New York: AMS

Lomas, R., 1996 *County of Conflict: Northumberland from Conquest to Civil War*. East Linton: Tuckwell Press

Long, B., 1967 *Castles of Northumberland*. Newcastle upon Tyne: Harold Hill

Loveday, R., 1998 Double Entrance Henges – Routes to the Past? In A. Gibson and D. Simpson (ed.) *Prehistoric Ritual and Religion*. Stroud: Sutton, 14-31

Lowenthal, D., 1985 *The Past is a Foreign Country*. Cambridge: Cambridge University Press

Lucy, S.J., 1998 *The Early Anglo-Saxon Cemeteries of East Yorkshire: an analysis and reinterpretation*. BAR Brit Ser **272**, Oxford: British Archaeological Reports

Lucy, S.J., 2000 *The Anglo-Saxon Way of Death*. Stroud: Sutton

McClure, J. and Collins, R., (eds) 1994 *Bede: the ecclesiastical history of the English people*. Oxford: Oxford University Press

McCord, N. and Jobey, G., 1971 Notes on Air Reconnaissance in Northumberland and Durham – II, *Archaeol Aeliana⁴*, **49**, 119-130

Mackenzie, E., 1825 *An Historical, Topographical, and Descriptive View of the County of Northumberland* (2nd edition). Newcastle upon Tyne:Mackenzie & Dent

MacLauchlan, H., 1867a *Notes not included in the memoirs already published on Roman Roads in Northumberland*. Privately Printed

MacLauchlan, H., 1867b *Additional Notes to the memoir on Roman Roads and Other Remains in Northumberland*. Original manuscript held in the private collection of the Duke of Northumberland

McOmish, D.S., 1989 Non-hillfort settlement and its implications in M. Bowden, D. Mackay and P. Topping (eds) *From Cornwall to Caithness: Some Aspects of British Field Archaeology. Papers Presented to Norman V Quinnell*. BAR Brit Ser **209**, 99-110. Oxford: British Archaeological Reports

McOmish, D.S., 1999 Wether Hill and Cheviots Hillforts, in P. Frodsham, P. Topping and D. Cowley (eds) 1999, 191-207

Marsden, J., 1992 *Northanhymbre Saga: The History of the Anglo-Saxon Kings of Northumbria*. London: Kyle Cathie

Marshall, A. and Marshall, G., 1993 Differentiation, Change and Continuity in Anglo-Saxon Buildings, *Archaeol J*, **150**, 366-402

Maxwell, G.S., 1983 Recent Aerial Survey in Scotland in G.S. Maxwell (ed) *The Impact of Aerial Reconnaissiance on Archaeology*, CBA Res Rep **49**. London: Council for British Archaeology, 27-40

Miket, R., 1976 The evidence for Neolithic activity in the Milfield Basin, Northumberland, in C.B. Burgess and R. Miket (eds) *Settlement and Economy in the Third and Second Millennia BC*. BAR Brit Ser **33**, Oxford: British Archaeological Reports, 278-88

Miket, R., 1980 A Restatement of Evidence from Bernician Anglo-Saxon Burials, in P. Rahtz, T. Dickenson and L. Watts (eds) *Anglo-Saxon Cemeteries, 1979*. BAR Brit Ser **82**, 289-305. Oxford: British Archaeological Reports

Miket, R., 1981 Pit Alignments in the Milfield Basin, and the Excavation of Ewart 1, *Proc Prehist Soc*, **47**, 137-146

Miket, R., 1985 Ritual Enclosures at Whitton Hill, Northumberland, *Proc Prehist Soc,* **51**, 137-148

Miket, R., 1987 *The Milfield Basin, Northumberland 4000 BC - AD 800*. MLitt Thesis (unpublished), University of Newcastle upon Tyne

Millett, M., 1983 Excavations at Cowdery's Down, Basingstoke, Hants 1978–81, *Archaeol J*, **141**, 182–215

Monaghan, J., 1994 An unenclosed Bronze Age House Site at Lookout Plantation, Northumberland, *Archaeol Aeliana⁵*, **22**, 29-41

Morris, R.K., 1991 Baptismal Places: 600-800, in I. Wood and N. Lund (eds) *People and Places in Northern Europe, 500-1600: Essays in honour of Peter Hayes Sawyer*. Woodbridge: Boydell, 15-24

Muir, R., 1982 *The Lost Villages of Britain*. London: Michael Joseph

Nennius, *Historia Brittonum*, ed. and trans J. Morris, 1980 *Nennius, British History and Welsh Annals*. Arthurian Sources vol 8. London and Chichester: Phillimore

Newbigin, N., 1935 Neolithic 'A' pottery from Ford, Northumberland, *Archaeol Aeliana⁴*, **12**, 148-157

BIBLIOGRAPHY

O'Brien, C., 2000 Thirlings Building C: a pagan shrine? *Archaeol Aeliana*[5], **28**, 47-9

O'Brien, C., 2002 The Early Medieval Shires of Yeavering, Bamburgh and Breamish *Archaeol Aeliana*[5], **30**, 53-73.

O'Brien, C. and Miket, R., 1991 The early medieval settlement of Thirlings, *Durham Archaeol J*, **7**, 57-91

Ordnance Survey, 1866 *First Edition 6-inch scale map*, sheet XIX

Ordnance Survey, 1897 *First Edition 25-inch scale map,* sheet XIX.2

Ordnance Survey, 1924 *25-inch scale map*, sheet XIX.2

Ordnance Survey, 1962 *Map of Southern Britain in the Iron Age*

Oswald, A.W.P., 1997a A doorway on the past: practical and mystic concerns in the orientation of roundhouse doorways, in A. Gwilt and C. Haselgrove (eds) 1997, 87-95

Oswald, A.W.P., 1997b *Hambledon Hill, Dorset.* RCHME Field Survey Report held in the National Monuments Record, ref: AI/5/1997

Oswald, A.W.P., 2004 An Iron Age hillfort in an evolving landscape. Analytical field survey on West Hill, Kirknewton, in P. Frodsham 2004, 202-12

Oswald, A.W.P., Jecock, M. and Ainsworth, S., 2000 *An Iron Age hillfort and its environs on West Hill, Kirknewton*. English Heritage: Archaeological Investigation Report Series AI/12/2000

Oswald, A.W.P. and McOmish, D., 2002 *An Iron Age hillfort and its environs on St Gregory's Hill, Northumberland*. English Heritage: Archaeological Investigation Report Series AI/1/2002

Oswald, A.W.P., Pearson, T. and Ainsworth, S., 2002 *Ring Chesters, Northumberland: an Iron Age hillfort and its environs*. English Heritage Archaeological Investigation Report Series AI/1/2002

Owen, O.A., 1992 Eildon Hill North, in Rideout, J.S., Owen, O.A. and Halpin, E., (eds) 1992, 21-71

Pactus Legis Salicae, K.A. Eckhardt (ed.), 1962 *Monumenta Germaniae Historica, Leges*, section I, vol 4 part 1 Hanover: Hahn; trans K.F. Drew, 1991 *The Laws of the Salian Franks*. Philadelphia: University of Pennsylvania Press

Pantos, A. and Semple, S., (eds) 2004 *Assembly Places and Practices in Medieval Europe*. Dublin: Four Courts Press

Passmore, D.G., Waddington, C. and Houghton, S.J., 2002 Geoarchaeology of the Milfield Basin, northern England; towards an integrated archaeological prospection, research and management framework, *Archaeol Prospection*, **9**, 71-91

Paul the Deacon, *Historia Langobardorum*, G. Waitz (ed.), 1878 *Monumenta Germaniae Historica, Scriptores Rerum Germanicarum in usum scholarum separatim editi* Hanover: Hahn; trans W.D. Foulke, 1974, *Paul the Deacon: History of the Lombards*. Philadelphia: University of Pennsylvania Press

Payton, R.W., 1980 The Soils of the Milfield Plain, Northumberland, North of England, *Soil Discussion Group Proceedings*, **16**, 1-52

Payton, R.W., 1992 Fragipan formation in argillic brown earths (Fragiudalfs) of the Milfield Plain, north-east England: Evidence for a periglacial stage of development, *Jnl Soil Science*, **43**, 621-644

Pearson, T., 1998 *Yeavering Bell hillfort, Northumberland*. English Heritage: Archaeological Investigation Report Series AI/24/1998

Pearson, T., 2002 *Norham Castle, Northumberland*. English Heritage: Archaeological Investigation Report Series AI/25/2002

Pearson, T. and Lax, A., 2001 *An Iron Age hillfort on Great Hetha, Northumberland*. English Heritage: Archaeological Investigation Report Series AI/3/2001

Perry, D., 2000 *Castle Park Dunbar: Two thousand years of a fortified headland*, Soc Antiq Scotl Monogr Ser **13**. Edinburgh: Society of Antiquaries of Scotland

Piddocke, M.M., 1935 President's reminiscences: prehistoric relics in a border parish, *Hist Berwickshire Natur Club*, **29.1**, 2-9

Piggott C.M., 1950 The excavations at Hownam Rings, Roxburghshire, 1948, *Proc Soc Antiq Scotl*, **82**, 193-225

Piggott, S., 1958 Native economies and the Roman occupation of North Britain, in I.A. Richmond (ed.) *Roman and Native in North Britain*. Edinburgh: Nelson, 1-27

Plummer, C., 1896 *Venerabilis Baedae Historiam ecclesiasticam gentis anglorum, Vols 1 and 2*. Oxford: Clarendon Press

Powlesland, D., 1999 The Anglo-Saxon settlement at West Heslerton, North Yorkshire, in J. Hawkes and S. Mills (eds) 1999, 55-65

Procopius, *History of the Wars*, ed and trans H.B. Dewing, 1913-28, 5 vols, Loeb Classical Library. London and Cambridge MA: Heinemann

Proudfoot, E., 1996 Excavations at the Long Cist Cemetery on Hallow Hill, St Andrews, Fife, 1975-9, *Proc Soc Antiq Scotl*, **126**, 387-454

Rahtz, P., 1980 Review – Yeavering: an Anglo-British centre of early Northumbria, *Medieval Archaeol*, **24**, 265-70

Ralston, I.B.M., 2004 *The Hill-forts of Pictland since the 'Problem of the Picts'*. Rosemarkie: Groam House Museum

Rapoport, A., 1990 Systems of activities and systems of settings, in S. Kent (ed.) *Domestic Architecture and the Use of Space*. Cambridge: Cambridge University Press, 9-21

RCAHMS, 2002 *The Brian Hope-Taylor Archaeological and Personal Papers Collection Phase 3: Detailed listing and prioritisation Report for Period 1 July 2002-31 December 2002*. Available: http://www.rcahms.gov.uk/bhtreport.pdf

RCHME, 1986 *Yeavering Estate Survey archives*, National Monuments Record, collections ref: 1031529

Rees, A.R., 2002 A First Millennium AD Cemetery, Rectangular Bronze Age Structure and Late Prehistoric Settlement at Thorneybank, Midlothian, *Proc Soc Antiq Scotl*, **132**, 313-55

Reynolds, N.B., 1980 Dark Age Timber Halls and the Background to the Excavations at Balbridie, *Scott Archaeol Forum*, **10**, 41-60

Richards, C. and Thomas, J., 1984 Ritual activity and structured deposition in Later Neolithic Wessex, in R. Bradley and J. Gardiner (eds) *Neolithic Studies A Review of Some Current Research*. BAR Brit Ser, **133**. Oxford: British Archaeological Reports, 189-218

Rideout, J.S. and Owen, O.A., 1992 Discussion, in J.S. Rideout, O.A. Owen and E. Halpin (eds) 1992, 139-143

Rideout, J.S., Owen, O.A. and Halpin, E., (eds) 1992 *Hillforts of southern Scotland*. AOC Monograph 1. Dundee: AOC (Scotland) Ltd

Rowland, J., 1990 *Early Welsh saga poetry: a study and edition of the Englynion*. Cambridge: D.S. Brewer

Ryder, P., 1991 *King Edwin's Palace: Old Yeavering Structural and Historical Assessment*. Unpublished report for the Northumberland National Park Authority

St Joseph, J.K.S., 1934 Roman Camps near High Rochester from the Air, *Proc Soc Antiq Ncl*[4], **6**, 238-243

St Joseph, J.K.S., 1958 Oblique aerial photographs of Yeavering Bell held in the Cambridge University collection, refs: XG 35-47

Schama, S., 1995 *Landscape and Memory*. London: Harper Collins

BIBLIOGRAPHY

Schützeichel, R., 1964 Staffolus Regis Zum Zeugnis der Lex Ribuaria für die zweite Lautverschiebung, *Rhienische Vierteljahrsblätter*, **29**, 138-67

Scull, C.J,. 1991 Post-Roman Phase I at Yeavering: a reconsideration, *Medieval Archaeol*, **35**, 51-63

Scull, C.J., 1993 Archaeology, Anglo-Saxon Society and the Origins of the Anglo-Saxon Kingdoms, *Anglo-Saxon Stud Archaeol Hist*, **6**, 65-82

Scull, C.J. and Harding, A.F., 1990 Two Early Medieval Cemeteries at Milfield, Northumberland, *Durham Archaeol J*, **6**, 1-29

Semple, S., 1998 A Fear of the Past: the place of the prehistoric burial mound in the ideology of middle and later Anglo-Saxon England, *World Archaeol*, **30(1)**, 109-126

Simpson, D.D.A. and Scott-Elliott, J., 1964 Excavations at Camp Hill, Trohoughton, Dumfries, *Trans Dumfriesshire Galloway Natur Hist Antiq Soc*, **41**, 125-34

Skene, W.F., 1876-80 *Celtic Scotland*. Edinburgh: D. Douglas

Smith, I.M., 1991 Sprouston, Roxburghshire: an Early Anglian Centre of the Eastern Tweed Basin, *Proc Soc Antiq Scotl*, **121**, 261-94

Speed, J., 1610 *Map of the County of Northumberland*. Northumberland County Record Office Ref: ZAN M16 B21

Stenton, F.M., 1971 *Anglo-Saxon England*. Oxford: Clarendon Press

Tait, J., 1965 *Beakers from Northumberland*. Newcastle upon Tyne: Oriel Press

Tate, G., 1863 The Antiquities of Yevering Bell and Three Stone Burn, among the Cheviots in Northumberland, with an account of Excavations made into Celtic Forts, Hut dwellings, Barrows and Stone Circle, *Hist Berwickshire Natur Club*, **4**, 431-53

Taylor, F., 2001 Not entirely what it could be; historical perspectives on modern archaeology TV programmes, *Antiquity*, **75**, 468-478

Thomas, J., 1996 *Time, Culture and Identity: An Interpretative Archaeology*. London: Routledge

Tilley, C., 1994 *A Phenomenology of Landscape: Places, Paths and Monuments*. Oxford: Berg

Tilley, C., 2004 *The Materiality of Stone Explorations in Landscape Phenomenology*. Oxford: Berg

Tilley, C., 2005 Phenomenological archaeology, in C. Renfrew and P. Bahn (eds) *Archaeology: The Key Concepts*. London: Routledge

Tinniswood, A. and Harding, A.F., 1991 Anglo-Saxon Occupation and Industrial Features in the Henge Monument at Yeavering, Northumberland, *Durham Archaeol J*, **7**, 93-108

Topping, P., 1989 Early cultivation in Northumberland and the Borders, *Proc Prehist Soc*, **55**, 161-79

Topping, P., 2004 Hillforts, farms and fields. Excavations on Wether Hill, Ingram, 1993-2002, in P. Frodsham 2004, 190-201.

van Hoek, M. and Smith, C., 1988 Rock Carvings at Goatscrag Rock Shelters, Northumberland, *Archaeol Aeliana*[5], **16**, 29-35

Vickers, K.A., 1922 *A History of Northumberland, vol 11*. Newcastle upon Tyne: Northumberland County History Committee

Wacher, J.S., 1995 *The Towns of Roman Britain*. London: Routledge

Waddington, C., 1997 A review of 'pit alignments' and a tentative interpretation of the Milfield complex, *Durham Archaeol J*, **13**, 21-33

Waddington, C., 1999 *A Landscape Archaeological Study of the Mesolithic-Neolithic in the Milfield Basin, Northumberland*. BAR Brit Ser, **291**. Oxford: British Archaeological Reports

Waddington, C., 2000 Neolithic pottery from Woodbridge Farm, The Old Airfield, Milfield, *Archaeol Aeliana*[5], **28**, 1-9

Waddington, C., Bailey, G., Bayliss, A., Boomer, I., Milner, N.J., Pedersen, K., Shiel, R. and Stevenson, T., 2003 A Mesolithic settlement site at Howick, Northumberland: a preliminary report, *Archaeol Aeliana*[5], **32**, 1-12

Waddington, C. and Davies, J., 2002 Excavation of a Neolithic settlement and late Bronze Age burial cairn near Bolam Lake, Northumberland, *Archaeol Aeliana*[5], **30**, 1-47

Wallace-Hadrill, J.M., 1988 *Bede's Ecclesiastical history of the English people: a historical commentary*. Oxford: Clarendon Press

Wallis, J., 1769 *The Natural History and Antiquities of Northumberland and so much of the County of Durham as lies between the Rivers Tyne and Tweed*. (2 volumes). Newcastle: privately printed

Warburton, J., 1716 *Map of the County of Northumberland*

Waterson, R., 1997 *The Living House: An Anthropology of Architecture in South-East Asia*. London: Thames and Hudson

Watson, W.J., 1926 *Celtic Place-names of Scotland*. Edinburgh and London: W. Blackwood and Sons

Welch, M., 1984 The Dating and Significance of the Inlaid Buckle Loop from Yeavering, Northumberland, *Anglo-Saxon Stud Archaeol Hist*, **3**, 77-8

Welfare, H., 1992 Yeavering Bell, in J. Grundy, G. McCombie, P. Ryder, H. Welfare and N. Pevsner, *The Buildings of England: Northumberland* (2nd edition). Harmondsworth: Penguin, 638-9

Williams, H., 1998 Monuments and the past in early Anglo-Saxon England, *World Archaeol*, **30 (1)**, 90-108

Williams, H., 2004 Assembling the Dead in Anglo-Saxon England, in A. Pantos and S. Semple (eds) 2004, 109-134

Wilmott, T., 1997 *Birdoswald: excavations of a Roman fort on Hadrian's Wall and its successor settlements, 1987-92*. Archaeological Report **14**. London: English Heritage

Wood, I.N., 1986 Disputes in Late Fifth- and Sixth-Century Gaul: Some Problems, in W. Davies and P. Fouracre (eds) *The Settlement of Disputes in Early Medieval Europe*. Cambridge: Cambridge University Press, 7-22

Wood, I.N., 1998 Jural Relations amongst the Franks and Alamanni, in I.N. Wood (ed.) *Franks and Alamanni in the Merovingian Period: An Ethnographic Perspective*, Studies in Historical Archaeoethnology **3**. Woodbridge: Boydell, 213-26

Woolf, A., 2004 Caedualla *Rex Brettonum* and the Passing of the Old North, *Northern Hist*, **41**, 5-24

Young, R., 2004 Peat, pollen and people. Palaeoenvironmental reconstruction in Northumberland National Park, in P. Frodsham 2004, 156-170

Youngs, S. and Clark, J., 1982 Medieval Britain in 1981, *Medieval Archaeol*, **26**, 164-227

INDEX

A Process of Discovery, exhibition 9, 126, 224–5, 227, 229, 230–4
Acklington 67, 237
Ad Gefrin 14, 17–8, 21–2, 24–7, 29–31, 34–5, 38–41, 44, 46–7, 50–4, 56–7, 60–2, 65, 68, 70, 76, 84, 98, 118, 131, 161–184, 185–6, 189, 193, 197–9, 219, 224–5, 230, **1, 8, 9, 10, 11, 12, 13**
Aethelfrith, king 25, 145, 152, 187
Agilulf, king of the Lombards 179
Akeld 23, 36, 71, 82, 189, 192
Alba 172, 244
Anglian palace (see *Ad Gefrin*)
Ardwall Isle, Kirkcudbrightshire 142
Arthur, king 33, 248

Balbridie, Aberdeenshire 163, 250
Bamburgh 10, 135, 137–9, 144–5, 152, 187, 190, 219, 230, 239, 246, 249
Barrasford 137
Battle Stone 18, 32, 57, **3**
Bebba, queen 152
Bede 9–10, 12–3, 24–5, 27, 41, 55–7, 60, 68, 71, 98, 138–9, 145, 148, 152, 154, 160, 162, 164–5, 168–9, 185–7, 189, 191–2, 197, 210, 225, 239, 240–2, 248
Benwell 137
Beowulf 38–9, 50–2, 54, 154, 180, 201, 210, 230, 241, 242, 245
Bernicia 24–5, 51, 53, 96, 137, 143, 145, 152, 165, 174, 182–4, 186–8, 240, 246, 248
Berwick Upon Tweed 192
Birdoswald 137, 186, 188

Bolam Lake 91
Breamish, river 85, 117, 121
Broomridge 92
Brough Law 121–2, 246
Burrowses 68, 76–8, 80, 238

Cadwallon 25, 148, 158
Caedualla, king of Gwynedd 162, 164–5
Cambridge 69–70, 137, 202–3, 206, 208, 214, 217–20, 222–3, 231–2, 234, 236
Camphill, Dumfriesshire 142
Canterbury 180
Capel Meulog, Radnor 139
Carmarthen 178
Carrock Fell, Cumbria 44
Castle Park, Dunbar 142, 250
Celtic cowboys idea 106, 113
Cheviot Hills 14, 17, 19–20, 23, 41–2, 44, 51–2, 70, 78–9, 84–8, 95, 98, 100, 102, 107, 109, 111, 115, 119–25, 146, 165, 199, 242, 248, 251
Chilperic I 179
Christianbury Trust 69–70, 237
Christianity 38–41, 61, 63, 160, 162, 168–9
Cinead mac Alpin, king of Scots 170
Cirencester 178
Constantine II 172
Constantinople 179
Coppergate 161
Coquetdale 137
Corbridge 137, 212
Coupland henge 88, 91–2
Creswell Crags 89

cropmarks 9, 20, 25, 65, 67, 70–1, 75–7, 81–3, 151, 170–1, 192, 238, 244

Dere Street 70
Devil's Dyke, Cambridgeshire 206, 218, 220, 230
Discovering our Hillfort Heritage project 11, 14, 42, 62, 78, 99, 109, 121, 244
Doon Hill 163, 165–6, 186, 216, 219, 222, 246
Druids 27, 32–3, 101, 116,
Duke of Northumberland 56, 63, 101–2
Dunion, the 120
Dunnichan 171

Eastern ring-ditch 35, 37–9, 41, 96, 147, 150
Ecgfrith, king 168
Edinburgh 70, 135, 164, 215–6, 240
Edwin, king 24–5, 33, 38, 41, 51–4, 68, 139, 165–6, 168, 185, 191, 204, 237, 250
Eildon Hill North 44, 79, 115, 118–20, 125, 168, **6**
Etal 85
Ewart henge 88

Fawcett Shank 122
Featherwood East 70
Fenton Hill 76
Firth of Forth 135
Firth of Tay 135
Forteviot, Perthshire 143, 167, 169, 170–2

Galewood, Milfield 137
Gaul 75, 141, 178, 183–4
Geteryne, battle of 29, 33, 57
Glastonbury 102
Glead's Cleugh 121
Gleedscleugh 22
Glen, river 9, 18, 24, 33, 42, 47, 54, 71, 76, 84–5, 87, 95, 98, 186, 191–2, 197, 200, 230, **11**
goats 27–9, 34, 55, 57, 131, 135, 152, 156, 199, 205
Goatscrag 89–90, 92
Gododdin 186–7
Gosbecks Farm, Colchester 178
Great Enclosure 24, 38–9, 46–7, 50, 52–4, 66, 72, 75, 80–1, 90, 138, 145–52, 158, 164, 239, **12**
Great Hetha 113, 121, 238
Grey Stone (see Battle Stone)
Grimston Ware pottery 91–2
Grooved Ware pottery 94
Grubenhäuser 17, 82–3, 138, 238

Hadrian's Wall 11, 98–9, 101, 108, 203

Hallow Hill cemetery, Fife 142
Hambledon Hill, Dorset 115
Harehope, Peebleshire 151
Hayhope Knowe, Roxburghshire 151, 238
Hedgehope 42, 111
Hepple 137
High Knowes 76
High Rochester 70, 250
Historia Ecclesiastica 154, 160, 169, 191
Hope-Taylor, Dr Brian 9–11, 13–7, 19, 21, 24–9, 34–42, 44–7, 50–7, 59–60, 62–3, 65, 70–5, 87, 90–2, 94, 96–8, 107–8, 112, 115–9, 125–37, 139–43, 145–58, 161–5, 168–9, 174–80, 182, 185–8, 191–3, 195, 197, 201–36, **10, 16, 17, 18, 19**
Houseledge 20
Howick 88, 90, 136
Hownam
  Law 44, 120
  Rings, Roxburghshire 107, 151
  sequence 107, 117, 121

Ida, king 187
Ingleborough, Yorkshire 44
Ingram Hill 121, 125
ironworking 19, 31

Jobey, George 79, 103, 106–8, 111, 113–7, 121, 123–5, 212, 236

Kilverstone, Norfolk 141
Kirk Hill, Coldingham 152
Kirknewton 54, 56, 71, 75, 81–2, 86, 189–92

Lammermuirs 165
Lex Ribuaria 180–1, 183
Little Woodbury, Wiltshire 102
Lookout Plantation 20
Lowick 137

MacLaughlan, Henry 21, 32, 68, 76, 101–6, 111
Maelmin 25, 30, 41, 60, 138, 152, 185–6, 191–2, 197
Malcolm II, king of Scots 167
Mam Tor, Derbyshire 44
metalworking 29–31
Mid Hill 123–4
Milfield Basin 13–4, 19, 36, 84–6, 88, 90–2, 191, 194, **2**
Milfield North henge 29–30, 88, 94–5
Moncrieffe 169–73

Monday Cleugh 124
Moray Firth 166
Murton High Crags 76
Muschamp 189–90

New Bewick 82–3, 238
New Wintles, Oxfordshire 141
Norham Castle 120
Northumbria 24, 39, 139, 141, 143, 163–4, 166–8, 173, 187–8, 192–3, 209

Old Yeavering 25, 65, 67–8, 84, 237
Oppidum 46, 119, 125
Oswald, king 165

Paulinus 24, 33–4, 41, 54, 169, 185–6
Penda 25, 53, 148, 158, 239
Philiphaugh 144
Picts, Pictland 33, 141, 167, 169–72

RCHME survey 13, 42–4, 48, 100, 108–10, 1112
Red lady of Paviland 90
Rhineland 180, 182
Ring Chesters 121–3
Ring-ditches 20–1, 35–9, 41, 47, 95–6, 128–9, 135, 140, 147, 150, 239
Rome 44–5, 179, 182–3, 188, 203
Roos 189–90
Ros Castle 29, 32, 94–5
Roughting Linn 219
roundhouses 20, 22, 37, 54, 75, 78, 80, 98, 102–4, 114–6, 123–5

Samian Ware pottery 45, 78, 105, 108, 236
Sandy Knowe 21
Scone 69, 171–3
Sills Burn North 69
Sills Burn South 69
Sinkside Hill 120
Skateholm 90
Slonk Hill, Shoreham 141
Sprouston 139, 143, 152, 164
St Cuthbert 190
St Gregory's Hill 78, 124
St Joseph, J.K. 45, 65–2, 82, 107–8, 116, 223, 236–7
St Ninian's Point, Bute 142
Staw Hill 120, 123
Strathearn 170

string-graves 130–3, 138–40, 147, 239
Sutton Hoo 161, 230
Sweethope 137
Swint Law 20, 22–3, 49

Tate, George 1, 13–5, 17, 19–23, 24, 27, 29, 33, 42–3, 46–9, 54, 62–3, 79, 102–5, 108–9, 111–2, 116–7, 236
theatres 24, 65, 71, 143, 146, 154, 176–84, 188
Theodebert I, king of the Franks 179
Thirlings 82, 92, 141, 156
Thwing 140
Till, river 85, 90
Tom Tallon's Crag 20, 33
Toraja 156
Tosson 137
Totila, king of the Ostrogoths 179
Traprain Law 44, 120
Trohoughton, Dumfriesshire 142

Villa regia 75, 80, 83, 138, 145, 164, 168–9, 186, 189, 192
Votadini 53, 96

Wessex 108, 114, 119–20, 122–3
West Hill 78, 122, 124
Western ring-ditch 35–8, 47, 128–9, 135, 140, 129
Wether Hill 79, 117, 121
Whaleback 17, 19, 23–4, 34–5, 49, 68, 71, 75–6, 80, 82, 87, 193
Whitby 68
Whitehill 137
Whitton hill 95
Who were the British?, television series 202–4, 218, 229
Woden Law 120
Woodbridge farm 91
Woodhenge 94
Wooler 32, 69–70, 75, 81, 189, 192–3, 209, 213, 235
Wooler Water 85
Worm Law 20, 23, 49

Yeavering Bell 49, 51, 54–5, 59–60, 68, 74, 76, 78–9, 84, 87, 90, 95, 98–126, 168–70, 209, 235–6, **2, 4, 5, 6, 7, 11, 15**
Yetholm 190

If you are interested in purchasing other books published by The History Press,
or in case you have difficulty finding any of our books in your local bookshop,
you can also place orders directly through our website

www.thehistorypress.co.uk